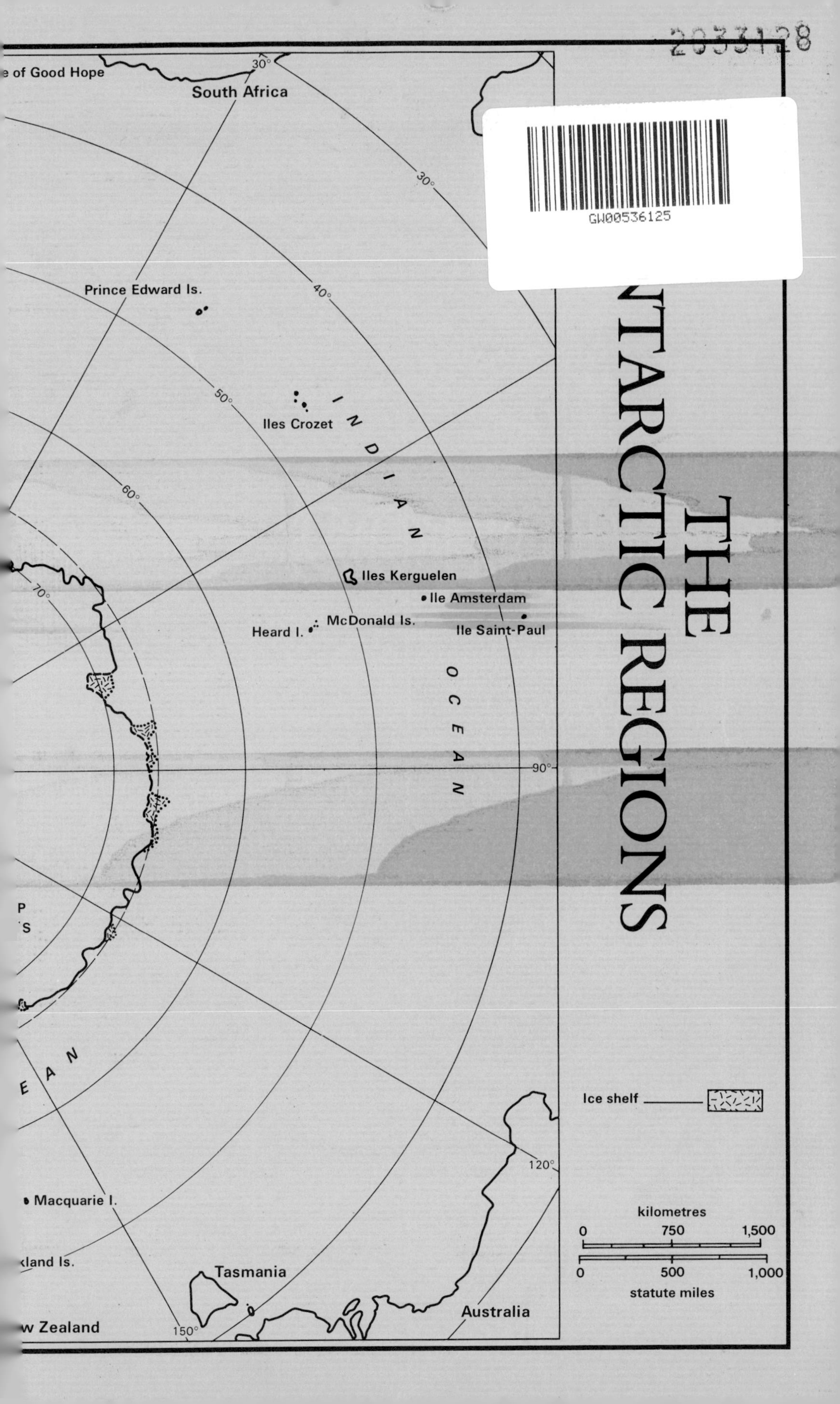

THE
NTARCTIC REGIONS
e of Good Hope
South Africa
Prince Edward Is.
Iles Crozet
I N D I A N
O C E A N
Iles Kerguelen
Ile Amsterdam
McDonald Is.
Heard I.
Ile Saint-Paul
E A N
Macquarie I.
kland Is.
Tasmania
w Zealand
Australia
30°
40°
50°
60°
70°
90°
120°
150°
Ice shelf
kilometres
0
750
1,500
0
500
1,000
statute miles

Captain Scott RN

Dr Wilson

Lieutenant Bowers RIM

Captain Oates, *Inniskilling Dragoons*

Petty Officer Edgar Evans RN

In Memoriam

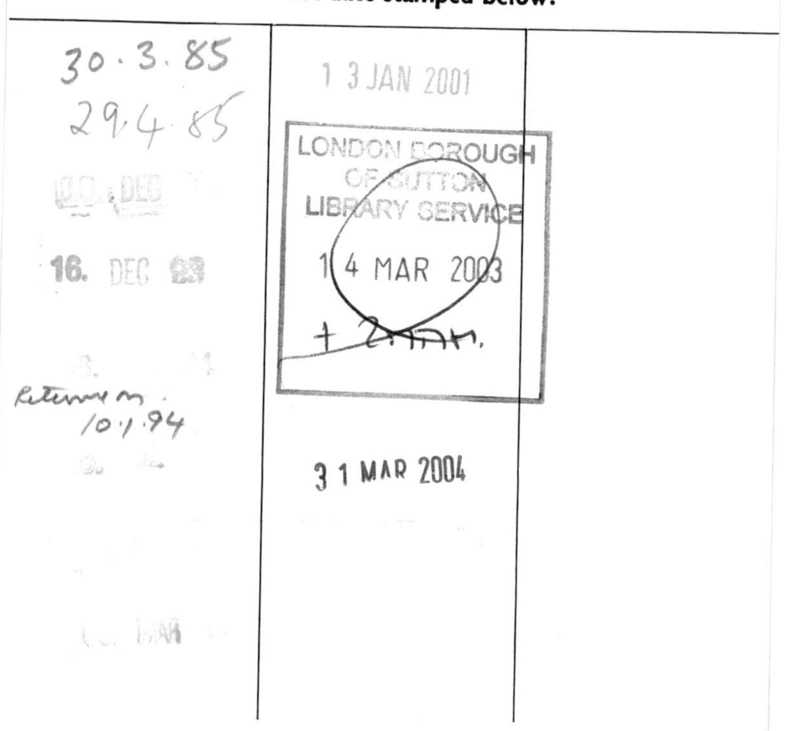

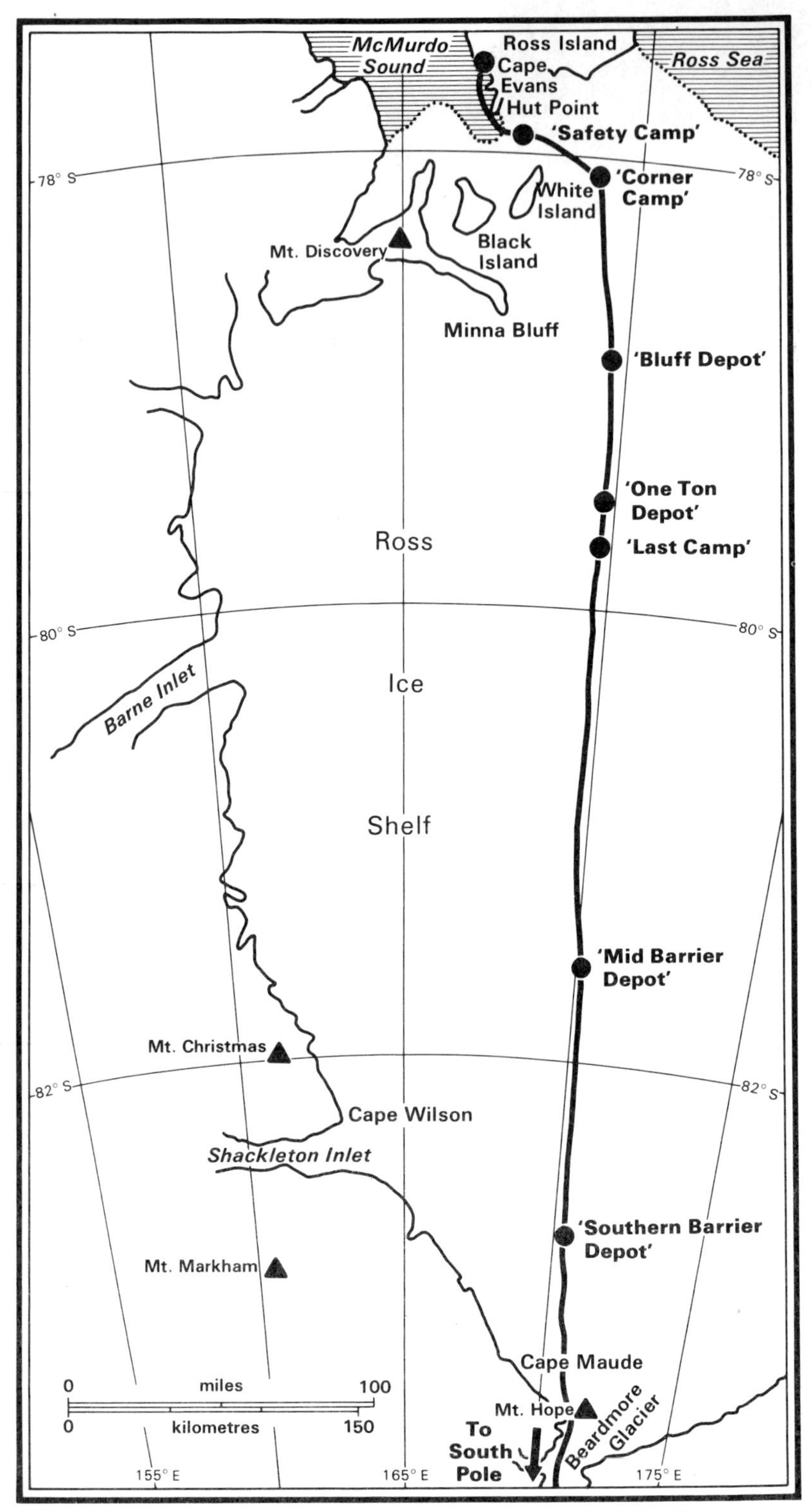

Route followed by polar party from Cape Evans to Beardmore Glacier. The last support party under Lieut. Evans turned back in latitude 87° 34′ S

Tryggve Gran's Antarctic Diary 1910-1913

The *Norwegian with* Scott

Edited by Geoffrey Hattersley-Smith

Translated by Ellen Johanne McGhie (*née* Gran)

Preface by Basil Greenhill

National Maritime Museum

HER MAJESTY'S STATIONERY OFFICE

First published by HMSO 1984

ISBN 0 11 290382 7

Contents

7 *Preface*
9 *Tryggve Gran*
21 *Foreword*
25 *List of ship's officers and shore party*
27 *Editorial note*
29 *Southward bound*
33 *In Antarctic waters*
41 *Cape Evans*
49 *Southward on the Great Depot Journey*
66 *Hut Point*
79 *In winter quarters*
98 *Winter nights in the* Discovery *hut*
101 *At Cape Evans*
124 *The spring journey on the Barrier, 1911*
131 *Survey and departures, spring 1911*
143 *The summer journey to Granite Harbour*
175 *Cape Evans again*
189 *To the land of the fallen*
194 *Back at Cape Evans*
212 *Southward bound in search of Scott*
223 *The ascent of the volcano Erebus*
228 *Cape Evans and relief*
238 *Retrospect*
243 *Place names*
245 *Biographical Notes*
250 *References*
251 *Index*

Plates

1 Terra Nova *and* Fram *in the Bay of Whales*
2 *Members of the expedition at Cape Evans before the start of the southern journey, October 1911*
3 Discovery *hut*
4 *Hut at Cape Evans*
5 *Western geological party, Granite Harbour*
6 *Mount Gran*
7 *Camp on sea ice, Granite Harbour*
9 *Forde cooking on western geological journey*
10 *T.Griffith Taylor*
11 *Frank Debenham*
12 *Tryggve Gran*
13 *Releasing a meteorological balloon*
14 *Mule at exercise*
15 *Mid-winter dinner at Cape Evans, 22 June 1912*
16 *Gran as clown*
17 *Some members of the search party, October 1912*
18 *Camp below summit of Mount Erebus*
19 *Mount Erebus in eruption*
20 *Approaching the summit of Mount Erebus*
21 *Pre-Christmas dinner at Shackleton's hut, Cape Royds*
22 *Outside Shackleton's hut, Cape Royds*
23 *The arrival of* Terra Nova *at Cape Evans*
24 *Norwegian 40 øre stamp commemorating Tryggve Gran's North Sea flight*

With the exception of plate 24, all the plates are reproduced from negatives in the Frank Debenham collection by permission of the Scott Polar Research Institute, Cambridge.

Maps

The Antarctic regions (inside front cover)
Cape Evans to Beardmore Glacier (frontispiece)
McMurdo Sound and Ross Island (inside back cover)

Preface

This is the first publication in English of the diary kept by the young Tryggve Gran[1], who as a Norwegian ski-ing expert assisted on Captain R.F.Scott's last Antarctic expedition. Several factors have encouraged the Museum and HMSO to go ahead with the project. First, a visit to the Museum by Major Gran in 1974, when amazingly alert for his age and as the last survivor of the shore party, he fascinated us all with his clear memories of the personalities and events of that heroic enterprise. Secondly, the interest of his family and particularly his daughter, Mrs Ellen McGhie, who translated the original with great skill and devotion, gave us considerable inspiration. Thirdly, the continuing lively interest of the public, both historians and lay people who are intrigued by the high drama and enigmas of the expedition, together with other recent publications, confirmed our feeling and a suggestion from Mrs Ann Shirley that publication of the first-hand account and views of a Norwegian, a compatriot of Scott's great rival Amundsen, would be timely and appropriate. Finally, and most significantly, Gran himself supported the idea of publication to the full.

The position of Gran on the British expedition might have been very awkward, and he admitted in conversation that had Amundsen announced his expedition six months earlier he would not have accepted Scott's invitation. The bargain made, however, Gran applied his skills, vigour, love of adventure and loyalty fully to the task. His diary reflects these qualities and the fact that despite all the stresses and problems of the expedition, when the relationship between leader and young expert was severely tested, he and Scott reached a mutual understanding. His loyalty and

[1] Gran, T. 1915. *Hvor sydliset flammer* [Where the southern lights blaze]. Kristiania og København, Gyldendalske Boghandel, Nordisk Forlag.

respect for Scott remained as a testament to the essential merit and integrity of both men until Gran's dying day.

The Museum is appreciative of Mrs McGhie's achievement in translating the text and of the fine editorship of Dr Geoffrey Hattersley Smith, and is grateful to Tryggve Gran's family in Norway, particularly Hermann Gran, for their support. We should also like to thank the Controller of HMSO and his staff, Mr David Joyce, Editor of Books, Mr Terry Walls, Assistant Director of Publishing, for agreeing to publish and, together with Mr H.G.R. King, Librarian of the Scott Polar Research Institute, Cambridge, for their ready collaboration with the Museum Publication Section over the production of this book. We are indebted to Miss Barbara Debenham for her co-operation in the use of photographs from her late father's collection as illustrations, many published for the first time. The copyright for Professor Frank Debenham's photographs is held by the Scott Polar Research Institute. Short excerpts from Apsley Cherry-Garrard's *The worst journey in the world* are included by kind permission of his widow Mrs Angela Mathias.

Among the National Maritime Museum staff Mrs Shirley (Ann Savours) and Mr David Proctor have been closely involved from the very beginning.

Basil Greenhill
Director, National Maritime Museum
October 1982

Tryggve Gran

by **Geoffrey Hattersley-Smith**

As an introduction to his diary it may be useful to consider the background against which Tryggve Gran joined Scott's last expedition, to comment on the content of the diary, on his role in the expedition, and his relations with other members, and finally to show that the traumatic events of the expedition did not damp his ardour for subsequent high endeavour. The main source is Major Gran's own *Fra Tjuagutt til Sydpolfarer*[TG][1], from which some passages are quoted *verbatim*, and reference is also made to the facsimile edition of Captain Scott's expedition journal.[2]

The original diary kept by Gran on the expedition is not available for scrutiny, nor is it known to the translator of this edition whether it still exists in its entirety. It is therefore impossible to say for certain that the text printed here is an exact translation of the diary kept by Gran in the field. Some items in *Fra Tjugatt* do not occur in the diary, possibly because they were edited out before publication in Norway in 1915. However, Gran was a prolific writer who, according to Griffith Taylor's half-jocular comment, was writing in 'six diaries' at the same time. It is quite likely that, while one of these was this diary, others recorded reflections and anecdotes not included in the day-to-day account.

Tryggve Gran was born in Bergen on 20 January 1889. His family lived in comfortable circumstances, his father being a shipyard owner who could afford to have his son partly educated in Switzerland. From school the young Gran went to sea for a spell before entering the Norwegian Naval Cadet College. He acquired an interest in polar exploration at the cadet college, while still in his teens, through the influence of Captain Viktor Baumann, a member of Otto Sverdrup's Second Norwegian Expedition in the *Fram* to Arctic Canada, 1898–1902. Gran possibly felt that, while sea training would be useful,

1 *See* References, page 250.
2 Scott, R.F. 1968. *The diaries of Captain Robert Scott.* Facsimile edition, Tylers Green, Bucks., University Microfilms Ltd.

the mould of a naval officer was at variance with an ambition to become a polar explorer. At any rate he left the college before taking his qualifying examinations, with a half-formed idea of organizing his own expedition to the Antarctic now that, as he put it, 'the Arctic region had lost its attraction', presumably with the conquest of the North Pole by Robert E. Peary in April 1909.

Soon his plans had advanced to the point where he was considering acquiring or building his own ship for an Antarctic venture, and his aspirations were given a great boost by the visit of Sir Ernest Shackleton to Kristiania (present-day Oslo) in October 1909. Earlier that year, on his great *Nimrod* expedition, Shackleton and his party had reached latitude 88°23′S on the polar plateau, and Shackleton was now to lecture before the Norwegian Geographical Society.

Gran and a friend decided that the best way to make contact with Shackleton was through the press, and they were duly commissioned by the newspaper *Verdens Gang* to prepare a special map of Sir Ernest's polar journey. The rest is best described in Gran's own words.

'When Ernest Shackleton's train halted at Frederikshald [Halden], I boarded the train bursting with eagerness and push, and it took me only a few minutes to get into conversation with the explorer and his lady. At first he took me for a journalist since I had produced the map in *Verdens Gang*, but when it quickly became clear to him that I was no reporter, but a young man with polar ambitions, he cast aside reserve and talked quite freely. That same evening Sir Ernest delivered his lecture in the old Loge Hall in Festningsplass which was filled to bursting point. The King was there and other personalities, including Carsten Borchgrevink, Otto Sverdrup, and Roald Amundsen . . . Shackleton proved a superb lecturer. He was a master of the art of involving his audience in the inner meaning of his topic. One could almost say that the splendid slides were superfluous. I drank in his every word. I fastened especially on his remarks about skis: "If we had had skis on the journey south and known how to use them like the Norwegians, we should probably have reached the Pole." '

Before Shackleton left Oslo, Gran found the opportunity to ask him 'whether he thought it was madness for a youth like me, without more than such experience as I had acquired at sea and on skis in the mountains, to go south in my own ship and with high-sounding ambitions.' Sir Ernest's reply was: 'I will neither encourage nor discourage you, my young friend, but if at least you see to it that you get hold of some experienced polar seamen for your ship, then your age is far from a handicap. And as a Norwegian you will certainly feel at home when you get ashore. My hut down there on Cape Royds is full of good things.' His last words were: 'Go ahead with your plan, my boy, and do it right away.' And Gran then decided to build his own ship.

He lost no time in going ahead with his plans since he had enough money to make the proposition viable. After he had approached the shipbuilder Skåluren, whose father had built Nansen's *Fram*, and the marine engineering firm of Bolinder, he decided on a ship a little larger than Amundsen's *Gjøa* (47 tons), 'constructed to accept an engine which produces about 10 knots. It must also be equipped for use as a sailing vessel, have sleeping bunks for 8 and be completed at the latest by the end of July 1910.'

He then sought meetings with three Norwegians who might best be able to advise him. The first of these was Roald Amundsen, at that time supposedly preparing for an assault on the North Pole, but Amundsen showed no interest in his plans and was unforthcoming to his questions – understandably in the light of later developments. He was received more cordially by Carsten Borchgrevink, Leader of the *Southern Cross* expedition, 1898–1900. But on Gran's proposal to winter at the Bay of Whales (where Amundsen later had his base) Borchgrevink was reluctant to comment, partly no doubt because he himself still had Antarctic ambitions. The third person approached – early in the New Year of 1910 and soon after Gran's Antarctic plans had been published in the press – was the great Fridtjof Nansen. By this time Gran was confident of the economic feasibility of the expedition, and Nansen was impressed to the extent of giving him moral support and allowing him to see his own, shelved plans for an Antarctic expedition. But, as it turned out, the most important result for Gran of this latter meeting was that he learned that Nansen had just received a letter from Captain Scott announcing his intention of visiting Norway in early March to test his experimental motor sledges. Nansen insisted that a meeting should be arranged with Scott, so that Gran could inform him of his own plans.

In due course, after he had started choosing men for his expedition, and selecting dogs and equipment, Gran was invited by Nansen to meet Captain and Mrs Scott at the premises of Hagen and Co., the Oslo equipment specialists and sports outfitters, who were supplying Scott with skis and sledges. It was now that Gran took the 'fateful step' of accepting Scott's invitation to attend the motor sledge trials at Fefor, the ski resort north of Oslo. The trials, which were a limited success, incidentally gave Scott the chance to observe Gran's mastery with skis, particularly since Gran was able to ski down to the nearest blacksmith with a broken axle for repair, and return within five hours, thus allowing the trials to continue the same day. Scott was also impressed by the two-stick technique demonstrated by Gran, which was new to Scott, and its potential for Antarctic work. Scott's reaction was such that, late that afternoon, he 'suddenly stopped and asked me whether I would consider the possibility of setting aside my own polar plans and instead accompany him to the south. I thought at first that I had heard wrong, and it wasn't until Scott explained that it was only now that he had gained a full understanding of what skis used in the right way would mean for him and his expedition that I became clear that my ears had not played me false. I had never been so astonished and it was some time before I gathered my wits. I recollect that I asked for time to consider and said that I never dreamed of being honoured by such an invitation.' The next day Gran accepted Scott's offer unconditionally, and Scott replied: 'I am very glad. I do not believe you will regret your decision.' No doubt the result of the meeting between Scott and Gran was as planned by Nansen. He saw that Gran would do well to serve an Antarctic apprenticeship before leading an expedition of his own, and the idea of a Norwegian skier on Scott's expedition appealed to him. Though Scott stubbornly refused to rely on dogs, he must not fail through lack of skiing expertise.

Before Scott left Norway, Gran arranged for him to meet Amundsen through an appointment made with the explorer's brother Gustav. Scott wished to make a proposal for co-operation in magnetic field measurements simultaneously in the north and south polar regions with similar sets of instruments. But Amundsen was not to be found at his home and he alone knew the reason for his reluctance to meet Scott. With Peary's conquest of the North Pole, Amundsen had by now secretly switched his sights from north to south. 'If Scott was deeply disappointed [Gran wrote], I was deeply embarrassed, and I can only add that the solution to the mystery emerged almost exactly a year later.'

Before leaving for England Gran made special arrangements to take his matriculation examination, which he passed successfully, and he also arranged for his own ship to be fitted out for use as a sealer while he was away. On 17 May 1910 he arrived in the Port of London, where *Terra Nova* also lay. Among *Terra Nova's* officers he was not an entire stranger, as he had already met Lieutenant Victor Campbell at a ski resort in Norway and he had a friend in common with Lieutenant Edward Evans, who had also visited Norway. He was duly signed on as a supernumerary ship's officer.

He had arrived in England shortly after the death of King Edward VII, and among foreign royalty staying at Buckingham Palace for the state funeral on 20 May were the King and Queen of Norway. King Haakon VII wished to meet the Norwegian participant in Scott's expedition, and Gran was received in audience at the palace by King Haakon, who presented him with Queen Maud's gift of a silk pennant, to be used as a sledge flag. 'The forepart consisted of a Royal Norwegian naval ensign and the back a red cross on a white background.'

Terra Nova sailed from London on 1 June under the command of Evans, for Scott was to sail a month later by mailship to Cape Town where he would take over the command. On the way down the channel towards Cardiff, the last port of call for coal, the ship put in at Portsmouth where the officers were entertained to dinner aboard HMS *Invincible*. As a Norwegian and a foreigner Gran was given the place of honour beside Captain Mark Kerr, and the Marines band played both British and Norwegian national anthems. From Cardiff *Terra Nova* sailed south on 15 June for Funchal, Madeira.

In reference to *Terra Nova*'s call at Funchal, where he took the opportunity to climb the second highest summit on the island, Gran later made the following note. 'Nearly three months later Funchal was to be honoured by another celebrated visitor. The polar vessel *Fram* with Roald Amundsen aboard arrived there on 10th September and anchored for three days. Just before the end of the stay, Amundsen announced to his men that his polar exploration plans had been widened. He was making for the North Pole *via* the South Pole.'

The next point of call was Trinidad Island[3], off the coast of Brazil, where Gran was a member of a party that had an adventurous time landing and getting off the island through breakers and running surf. He appears to have been the only member of the party to climb to the summit of the island; he later made it the setting for a novel, *Triumviraten* [The Triumvirate] (Oslo, 1923), about the crew of a wrecked Norwegian sailing ship who go ashore there and live like Robinson Crusoe. Of life aboard *Terra Nova* at this time Gran noted that 'we had got to know each other pretty well . . . and off duty everyone was on an equal footing from Teddy Evans to Gran, the youngest man on board. I do not know what an uninvited and respectable citizen would have made of us if he had glanced into the mess of an evening and seen how we scrimmaged and scrapped like idiots. The least he would have concluded was that somehow we had gone back to our happy schooldays.'

Terra Nova reached Simonstown on 16 August and left for Melbourne on 3 September with Scott in command. 'If the voyage from Cardiff to Simonstown had been characterized by splendid comradeship [Gran later wrote] the passage from South Africa to Australia was an even better proof that Scott had well understood how to choose men who get on well together. In Norway I had learned to know Scott as a cheerful and easy man, and this first impression was strengthened when

3 Ilha da Trindade (Brazil).

I again came close to him. He was short-tempered and not to be trifled with when angry, but if he had judged someone unfairly and discovered his mistake, he was quick to make amends.'

On arrival in Melbourne on 12 October Scott received an enigmatic telegram from Amundsen, composed at Madeira but actually sent from Oslo by his brother Leon on his return from Madeira, whither he had accompanied *Fram*. The telegram read: 'Beg leave to inform you *Fram* proceeding Antarctic. Amundsen.' After consulting Gran, Scott decided to seek clarification by cable from Nansen, who replied with one word: 'Unknown.' This reply could mean simply that Nansen did not know *Fram's* destination or, alternatively, that the ship was heading for then unknown Antarctic shores, such for example as lay south of the Weddell Sea. In a further communication with Nansen, by letter in early November, Scott expressed his disquiet about Amundsen's movements. On the one hand, it was inferred by people in Norway from a *Fram* news release, in which mention was made of oceanographic work in the region of Punta Arenas, that Amundsen would establish his base in the South American sector of Antarctica; on the other hand, Scott had received a telegram from London on 4 November surmising (correctly) that *Fram* was headed for the Ross Sea area, based on the fact that Amundsen had previously ordered special Admiralty charts of that area.

Gran travelled independently from Australia to New Zealand, and rejoined the expedition at Christchurch on 27 October. Some days later he was interviewed by a journalist on the subject of skis and skiing, at that time almost unknown in New Zealand. The journalist then [Gran wrote] 'put a question of a very different nature. He wished to know whether I considered my countryman Amundsen was a serious threat to Captain Scott. I paused quite a while before answering, then replied that I had all too scant knowledge of Amunden's plans to form an opinion. Furthermore, I had not heard anything to confirm that Amundsen's professed intention of sailing his ship south was with the object of making a thrust for the Pole. The journalist then immediately produced the interesting information that Amundsen himself had some months ago made it clear to the whole world that he had set course for the Antarctic in order to conquer the Pole. Captain Scott knew of this. A Wellington newspaper, the journalist went on, had through its editor made contact with Scott when he passed through the town, and asked for an interview. Scott had granted this but had remained silent when the questions turned to Amundsen. But the journalist would not give up. Then Scott had become angry and had put off the man by saying: "If the rumour is true that Amundsen hopes to reach the South Pole from a spot on the coast of West Antarctica, then I wish him good luck." It was now my turn to end the conversation, for it had pleased and re-assured me to hear how sensibly and sportily Scott had answered the journalist.' Thus, placed in a very awkward position, Gran did not fail in his loyalty to Scott.

During the last few days in New Zealand, members of the expedition were allowed to take a holiday, and Gran accepted an invitation to stay at a sheep station west of Christchurch. From there a splendid view of the snow-capped summit of Mount Cook, rising above the foothills, gave him the ambition to climb the highest peak in New Zealand. *Terra Nova* finally sailed from Lyttelton for the far south on 29 November 1910.

As the expedition's ski expert, Gran initially found favour with Scott both for his ability as a skier and as a ski instructor on the ice floes during delays in the pack ice on the voyage south. In his diary Scott referred to him at this time as 'strong, good-natured and willing', but also wondered whether 'he has heart enough for the final stage of this journey.' During the unloading of *Terra Nova* at Cape Evans Scott's attitude towards him changed, and he considered him 'a lazy posing fellow' who shirked his share of the work. 'He is only to the fore when he thinks he is being looked at and especially when a photograph is being taken.' Whether or not these accusations were just, it is clear that in the 'turn-to' by all hands Gran gave an impression of aloofness or unconcern which infuriated Scott. According to Griffith Taylor, Scott 'rather disliked Norwegian matters' at this time. From the telegram received in Melbourne Scott already had knowledge, though still limited, of Amundsen's intent on the Antarctic, and in the race to unload the ship this may well have exacerbated his feelings towards a Norwegian in his own camp. Gran's diary, however, shows an apparent unawareness of the feeling against him at this time.

On the depot journey that soon followed, south over the Ross Ice Shelf, Scott was glad of Gran's expertise on skis on several occasions as, for example, when he 'good-naturedly volunteered' to go back for the pony snow-shoes. On the other hand, Gran's unsuccessful efforts to lead a pony, while himself wearing skis, may well have accounted for him being 'much less patient than he should have been' with the animal.

But after the return of the depot party to Hut Point for an enforced stay of six weeks, until the sea ice formed between there and Cape Evans, Gran was again found seriously wanting in Scott's eyes. By this time Scott had received from *Terra Nova* news of Amundsen's landing in the Bay of Whales and of his plans for reaching the Pole. Gran was again accused of 'laziness' in his failure 'to learn the ropes', and 'he feels the cold more than anyone.' The climax of Scott's exasperation was reached in a two-page diary entry for 17 March 1911, when Gran was accused of malingering while on a short journey with a sledge. Scott would not accept his explanation that he had cramp in the legs, yet from his own diary this is what he undoubtedly had. Some are more prone to cramp than others but for no very clear physiological reasons, and it is not surprising that, when Drs Wilson and Atkinson examined Gran, 'they could find [in Scott's words] nothing wrong with him.' Possibly Gran overplayed the symptoms, although with really severe cramp it would be difficult to do so for disablement is complete, if temporary, as any sufferer can testify. It may be that an exceptionally muscular man (such as Gran was) is more susceptible to cramp than others. But it was this episode that provoked Scott into a 'bawling out' of Gran in full hearing of both officers and men, an incident that lived in the memory of Sir Charles Wright as most regrettable. Other members of the expedition were evidently of the same mind. In a letter home Bowers wrote that he 'could not help feeling a bit sorry for Trigger, as he always meant well and was the youngest of the party . . . he is in every respect a nice fellow', and Wilson was at pains to explain to Gran, according to the latter's account, that Scott had an almost pathological dislike of idleness or the appearance of idleness.

With the return of the party from Hut Point to Cape Evans in early April there was a gradual improvement in relations between Scott and Gran: on the one hand, the Post Captain RN, accustomed of late years to lonely command through subordinates and now, in close quarters with his officers and men, under continual strain from a variety of causes (the storm at sea in *Terra Nova*, the loss of ponies and a motor sledge, financial matters, and the activities of his rival Amundsen); and, on the other hand, the young Norwegian Sub-Lieutenant, literally his country's standard-bearer on this British expedition, full of ability and enthusiasm, if only these qualities could be brought out. References to Gran in Scott's diary became less harsh and finally sympathetic, quite possibly as a result of Dr Wilson's influence behind the scenes. In early May, Scott wrote of him that 'the boy has a certain amount of intelligence and a great fund of good nature under his thick crust of vanity. If the last can be thoroughly transpierced, we can find uses for the better qualities.'[4] In September, following the return of the depot-laying party to 'Corner Camp' under Lieutenant Evans, he was writing: 'Evans says that Gran has behaved very well indeed, took his share in all the work and was eager to do all aright. This is a great relief after my experience of last year [season] and confirms the idea that the first troubles were due to youth. With the winter he has found his feet and developed into a

4 *See* also the diary entry for 14 July 1911 when Gran was invited to stay an extra year.

thoroughly good boy ready to face hardship with the best.' There could be no handsomer admission by Scott that he had previously misjudged Gran.

It is likely that Gran's behaviour in the first months ashore justified some measure of annoyance to Scott, but not his intemperate outburst at Hut Point, which seemed to make Gran the scapegoat for all his frustrations at the time. It should also be borne in mind that disappointment, if not resentment, may have been felt by Gran, who had abandoned his own Antarctic plans to join the expedition, who had earlier enjoyed the confidence of Scott in connexion with Amundsen's intentions, and who now found himself no more than the unconsulted youngest member of a large party, his skiing expertise of no value when it came to marching with ponies. Scott's misguided decision not to rely on skis *and* dogs, and Amundsen's challenge practically ruling out Gran's participation in the polar journey, in competition against his countryman, had brought about a situation where Gran found his talents largely wasted.

In fact Gran showed remarkable resilience in the face of Scott's criticisms. He seems to have realized that Captains RN, are liable to 'sound off' from time to time – as indeed they are – and that later their displeasure is as often as not forgotten. It is pleasant therefore to record Scott's warm farewell to Gran who, by a strange chance, found himself the standard-bearer for Britain on the first stage of the polar journey. In the rush of departure, on 1 November 1911, Queen Alexandra's Union Jack for the South Pole was left behind at Cape Evans and Gran, as the fastest traveller on skis, took it forward to Hut Point. 'Scott smiled when I handed him the flag. . . . "The irony of fate, my dear Gran. Take good care of yourself over in the west. Good luck, my boy." This was followed by a handshake – the last ever as it turned out. . . .'

From the diary and from the overall impression given by his companions, Gran emerges as an attractive, well-balanced personality who got on well with his mess-mates. He may have been a little brash at times or inclined to show off, but such deviations were more than redeemed by his sense of humour, even against himself. Placed in a very difficult position because of Amundsen's expedition, none was more loyal to Captain Scott. Gran clearly recognized that Scott had to an exceptional degree the capacity to subordinate self towards a lofty purpose, which is the hall-mark of greatness. In Nansen's words he remained 'upright, and indomitable on the threshold to the long journey into the eternal stillness.' Had Scott been the unattractive and pig-headed leader portrayed in a recent biography,[5] it is beyond the

5 Huntford, R. 1979, *Scott and Amundsen*. London, Hodder and Stoughton.

bounds of possibility that his friends and companions should have held his memory so high. In the final analysis it is their testimony that counts, and in that company Gran might have had most cause to be resentful of the leader. Some of the reasons for irritation and misunderstanding have been given, and no doubt a part was also played by those trivial habits or mannersims that can become quite irrationally annoying among a group cooped up in ship, hut, or tent. In fact, Gran remained to the end of his long life one of Captain Scott's staunchest champions.

Readers of the diary will find the day-to-day descriptions of life at Cape Evans and Hut Point, and on sledge journeys, crisp, graphic and not overweighted with details of temperature, wind, and snow conditions. The account of the western geological journey, with its comparative picnic atmosphere amid fine scenery, is an excellent antidote to the brutal drudgery of the polar journey, mainly over the endless whiteness of barrier and plateau. The diary contains a number of interesting points not recorded or barely recorded elsewhere, such as: Scott's dialogue with Oates over the ponies near 'One Ton Camp' on the depot journey; his seeming to use Crean's cough as an excuse for sending him back from the plateau; the blow to Petty Officer Evans in particular in not being first at the Pole; the amount of useless material (geological specimens excepted) on the sledge at Scott's last camp; the accidental finding of Amundsen's letter to King Haakon; the way the depleted party tried to carry on normal life at Cape Evans after Scott's failure to return; the sad task of tidying up Scott's and Wilson's cubicles; the use by Gran of Scott's skis on the return journey from 'One Ton Depot' in November 1912, so that they would 'complete the 2,000 km trail'; and the ascent of Mount Erebus and Gran's near fatal adventure in the crater.

It is clear from the diary that Gran went out of his way not to embarrass Scott with regard to Amundsen. At the same time his assessment of Amundsen's chances of reaching the Pole were shrewd at the time and, as it turned out, correct. He even dreamed the date of Amundsen's arrival at the Pole. He was also right in expressing doubts, in the privacy of his diary, on Scott's complicated arrangements for the polar journey, involving four different forms of transport.

Gran himself had high ambitions to achieve something really notable on the expedition. After his exclusion from any part in the polar journey for understandable reasons. it was a sad blow to him that, as things turned out, he never had his chance to survey the mountains around the lower part of Beardmore Glacier, as promised by Atkinson when it appeared likely that the search journey would need to extend up that glacier. The desire to see what lay 'beyond that last blue mountain barred with snow' was felt more keenly by Gran than perhaps by any other member of the expedition. He had already given up plans for his own Antarctic expedition, but there are indications that he hoped to revive these plans at some future time.[6] Many years later he investigated the possibility of taking out *Fram* on a Greenland expedition, in collaboration with his countryman Willie Knutsen, who was later jointly to lead the Norwegian-French Arctic Expedition, 1938–39, with another ship. As far as is known, no other member of Scott's last expedition subsequently aspired to leadership of a polar expedition, yet from his first expedition emerged Sir Ernest Shackleton and Edward Evans (whose own Antarctic plans were merged in the last expedition and who later became Admiral Lord Mountevans), while from Shackleton's first expedition emerged Sir Douglas Mawson and from his second Sir James Wordie and Commander Frank Worsley.

On the return of *Terra Nova* to New Zealand, Gran set off within a few days on a successful ascent of Mount Cook, in the company of the well-known New Zealand mountaineers, Peter Graham and Charles Milne, while his shipmates were enjoying the green countryside and the fleshpots. That Gran should have done this was considered by Sir Charles Wright as a measure of his frustration in Antarctica. When Gran returned to Europe he looked for a challenge in the new field of aviation.

In Europe the French aviator, Louis Blériot, had flown the first full-sized, powered monoplane in 1907 and had made the first flight across the English Channel in July 1909. With his new-found fascination in flying, Gran went to France to meet Blériot who ran a flying school at Buc. Another pilot at that school in December 1913, Wing Commander Bentley Beauman, recalls Gran 'as being a quite outstanding character.' Gran soon learned to fly, persuaded Blériot to sell him one of his 80-horsepower monoplanes at half price, and set his sights on flying the North Sea. He set off from Cruden Bay near Aberdeen, Scotland, on 30 July 1914 and made the crossing to Jaeren, Norway, in four hours ten minutes. In atrocious weather, with his only navigational instrument a tiny compass, Gran used the size and direction of the waves as a guide. He was suitably feted in Norway on landing, but the flight received little outside publicity because of the outbreak of the First World War a few days later. His aircraft is preserved in the Norwegian Technical Museum, Oslo.

The outbreak of war brought Gran back to England, where he enlisted in the Royal Flying Corps in which he served with distinction on the western front, being credited with the destruction of 17 German planes,

6 *See*, for example, the diary entries for 14 and 26 November 1912.

and winning the Military Cross. He finished the war a Lieutenant Colonel in command of RAF units in north Russia, but wounds left him permanently deaf in one ear and with a badly scarred leg.

Gran received a permanent commission in the RAF in 1919, at a time when pilots were competing to fly the Atlantic. One competitor at this time was Admiral Mark Kerr, formerly of the *Invincible* and a distinguished naval airman, who had retired as Deputy Chief of the Air Staff and a Major-General RAF, in 1918. Gran's North Sea flight had remained for almost five years the longest out of sight of land, but his attempt as co-pilot to fly the Atlantic in the early summer of 1919 ended in a crash into the Bay of Fundy soon after take-off. The Atlantic was finally conquered by Alcock and Brown in June that summer.

Gran continued to serve in the RAF until May 1921, when he returned to Norway. He was later commissioned in the Royal Norwegian Air Force, and in 1928 played an active part in the search for Amundsen, lost flying during the search for surviving members of Nobile's ill-fated North Pole expedition in the airship *Italia*. Although Gran abandoned his own plans for a flight to the North Pole through lack of financial support, he took part in an expedition to Svalbard.

For the present purpose we leave Tryggve Gran's life in 1935, the year in which he retired from the Royal Norwegian Air Force with the rank of Major. For although he lived another 45 years, during which he lectured extensively on Scott's last expedition, his active work in polar exploration and in flying had come to an end. He will be remembered as the last survivor of the now legendary band of officers that sailed with Captain Scott, and he will be remembered in the annals of aviation and of war for his exploits in the air. He died at his home at Grimstad, near Oslo, on 8 January 1980 in his 91st year.

Foreword

Written by Tryggve Gran from his original diary

When evening shadows gently fall,
When stars awake and calm the night,
The myriad thoughts they stir and bind
The familiar mountain and the polar shore.

When my thoughts wander back to my boyhood days I always see before me the same picture. I see a small mountain lake beside which stands a small red hut. From the flagstaff flies the Norwegian flag, and in the heather nearby some friends are sunning themselves. In this hut I lived my boyhood's happiest hours. Here was no pressure or stress, nothing to restrict my freedom. All around was wild open country where I could wander in the peace of a summer night or in winter's storm. This life – a free man's life – became very dear to me.

The years ran out, boyhood days were gone, and I was suddenly grown up.

One day the news came to the world that a British naval officer had returned from the Antarctic. The story had a heroic cast and I was deeply moved by it. I pondered a few days and then suddenly my mind was made up: I would go South as well. I was just 21[1], had inherited a small amount of money, and immediately set about spending it by ordering a schooner of 115 tons, reinforced for Arctic ice. Of course I was very conscious of my youth and complete lack of experience. I understood that, if I were to stand the remotest chance of succeeding, I would need with me people experienced in the problems of Arctic living. Such people I managed to recruit, and while the ship's timbers were being prepared I set about collecting the necessary equipment. But fate was ready to play a hand. In April Captain Robert Falcon Scott arrived in Norway. He heard of my plans and invited me to dinner at the Victoria Hotel in Kristiania.[2] The conversation turned to skiing,

1 In fact 20.
2 The former name for Oslo.

and before the meal ended it was decided I should accompany Captain Scott to Fefor Sanitorium in Gudbrandsdalen.

We had a week of good snow and brilliant sunshine. Captain Scott and I became good friends, and one day he asked whether I would like to be a member of his team for the South. He would have use for my equipment. It was a tempting offer. 'Go with Scott', said Professor Fridtjof Nansen, and that made up my mind.

In May 1910 I joined the expedition in London. On June 1 the RY *Terra Nova*[3] was ready for sea and began her voyage to the distant polar land. The English nation had great expectations of Captain Scott, and it was an excited and admiring crowd that bade the expedition farewell.

From England *Terra Nova* sailed *via* Madeira to Cape Town, thence to Australia from where a course for New Zealand was laid. From New Zealand we pushed south for the Antarctic. On Ross Island, beneath the volcano Mount Erebus, Captain Scott landed. The spot was called Cape Evans. The ship then continued its voyage eastwards towards King Edward VII Land[4] where a party of six men under Lieutenant Campbell were to be landed. But ice conditions forced the ship to turn near Cape Colbeck and sail back westwards along the Barrier [Ross Ice Shelf]. In the Bay of Whales another ship was sighted – it was [Amunden's] *Fram*. After a few hours' stay *Terra Nova* continued her voyage back to Cape Evans to make a report. Thereafter, the vessel headed north and put Campbell ashore at Cape Adare, at the spot where Borchgrevink landed in 1900. Then it was 'goodbye' to the Antarctic for *Terra Nova*, for she was to winter in New Zealand.

During the summer Scott penetrated southwards to 79°30′ south and established a depot called 'One Ton Camp'. On his arrival back at the edge of the Barrier, Scott discovered that the ice in McMurdo Sound had broken up. Thus the depot party was prevented from reaching the winter quarters at Cape Evans. However, after great difficulties Scott reached a small hut built on his previous expedition[5]. In this hut the depot party lived many weeks until the formation of sea ice opened the way to Cape Evans. By May 1911 all were back at Cape Evans and the first wintering began. During the winter several short journeys were made. Dr Wilson with Bowers and Cherry-Garrard went to Cape Crozier in order to study the life-style and condition of the emperor penguin. This journey was among the most interesting of all those made in Antarctica. The experiences of these three men and what they went

3 Built in 1884 as a whaling ship, *Terra Nova* was a wooden three-masted barque of 749 tons and 187 feet long, equipped with auxiliary steam power.

4 Now Edward VII Peninsula.

5 The *Discovery* expedition, 1901–04.

through defies description. Towards spring, sledge journeys into the interior began, but the temperatures were so low that it was only possible to stay out in the open for a short time.

At the end of October the Polar party left Cape Evans with their ponies. At the foot of the Beardmore Glacier, the surviving ponies were killed, and 12 men pushed on towards the Pole. At latitude 85°S, Dr Atkinson and three men were dispatched home. They reached winter quarters in good condition. Eight men then continued southwards over the plateau until just after Christmas 1911, when Lieutenant Evans and Petty Officers Lashly and Crean were sent back. They had a tense journey home. Evans was stricken by scurvy and had to be dragged hundreds of kilometres on the sledge. Only just in time did he reach the coast where *Terra Nova* lay at anchor waiting, having returned from New Zealand.

Scott continues towards the Pole. He finds the Norwegian colours at the Pole and disappointed turns back north again. Petty Officer Evans dies at the foot of the Beardmore Glacier. The others continue. Frost-bite now begins to attack them. Oates weakens and begs to be allowed to stay behind. Finally, his wishes ignored, he leaves the tent in a storm. Thus died Captain Oates.

About 20 March Scott, Wilson and Bowers arrive at a point on the Barrier, only 21 km from 'One Ton Camp'. The snow-storm blocks their further progress and they are forced to lie in their tent, listening to the howling of the wind. They run out of food and, on 29 March, Scott perished. He died the death of a brave man.[6]

During the summer of 1912 a party under Griffith Taylor[7] struck north along the coast to a deep fjord named Granite Harbour. They spent several months there. They discovered new land and the geologists made important discoveries of coal and fossils. Finally, Taylor and his men were picked up again by *Terra Nova*. The vessel had called at Cape Adare on its way from New Zealand. Campbell came on board. He had found the area unsuitable as a working place and wished his party to be put ashore further south at a spot that earlier expeditions had named Evans Cove. This was done and the plan was for *Terra Nova* to collect him on its northward journey. But ice conditions prevented *Terra Nova* from approaching the coast, and Campbell was obliged to spend the winter there. *Terra Nova* left the winter quarters on 5 March. Scott had not yet returned, but there was fear that the ship would be imprisoned by new ice. About this time Cherry-Garrard, with Demetri [Gerof] went south with the dogs to meet Scott. He waited over a week at 'One

6 It was generally believed that Scott was the last of the three to die.
7 With Debenham, Gran and Forde.

Ton Camp'. Finally, he was obliged to turn back for home with his mission unaccomplished. He was very ill when he reached the old *Discovery* hut, where he was greeted by Dr Atkinson and Petty Officer Keohane who were there by pure chance. The ice had been blown out to sea, and there was nothing for this group to do but wait until they could again establish contact with winter quarters.

The ice formed again by April, and on the 9th Dr Atkinson reached Cape Evans, where there were nine men. To push south towards the Pole in search of Scott was at this stage pointless. If Scott were still on the Barrier, the worst must already have befallen. It was therefore decided to send a party north to the relief of Campbell. The party departed but encountered open water, and were forced to turn back. The second winter began.

In November 1912 eleven men left on a southward march to find Scott. After some weeks they found a snow-covered tent and inside were Scott, Wilson, and Bowers. It did not seem appropriate to move the dead and they were buried in the land where their life's work had been.

When the [search] party reached the sea again, they were greeted by the first good news for many a day. Campbell [and his party] had arrived safe and sound at Cape Evans. After surviving the winter, he had set off along the coast southwards to reach base safely.

This was in December 1912 and it was unlikely *Terra Nova* would arrive before January. During the waiting period the volcano Mount Erebus was climbed. It is an active volcano of 13,000 feet and the summit was conquered not without difficulties.[8]

At last on 18 January 1913, *Terra Nova* hove in sight. Embarkation proceeded at good speed, and then it was northward-bound to warmer climes and farewell to the land that had claimed so many splendid lives. The adventure was ended.

8 This was the second ascent, the first having been made on 10 March 1908 by members of Shackleton's *Nimrod* expedition, 1907–09.

List of ship's officers and shore party

Ship's officers

Robert Falcon Scott[1]	Captain RN
Edward R.G.R.Evans[1]	Lieutenant RN
Victor L.A.Campbell[1]	Lieutenant RN
Harry L.L.Pennell	Lieutenant RN
Henry E.de P.Rennick	Lieutenant RN
Henry R.Bowers[1]	Lieutenant RIM
Lawrence E.G.Oates[1]	Captain, 6th Inniskilling Dragoons
Wilfrid M.Bruce	Lieutenant RNR
G.Murray Levick[1]	Surgeon RN
Edward L.Atkinson[1]	Surgeon RN
Francis R.H.Drake	Assistant Paymaster RN
Tryggve Gran[1]	Sub-Lieutenant RNorwNR

Scientific staff (all members of shore party, except Lillie)

Edward Adrian Wilson	MD. Zoologist, Chief of Scientific Staff
George C.Simpson	Meteorologist
T.Griffith Taylor	Geologist
Dennis G.Lillie	Biologist (in *Terra Nova*)
Edward W.Nelson	Biologist
Frank Debenham	Geologist
Charles S.Wright	Physicist
Raymond E.Priestley	Geologist
Herbert G.Ponting	Photographer
Cecil H.Meares	In charge of dogs
Bernard C.Day	Motor Engineer
Apsley Cherry-Garrard	Assistant Zoologist

1 Member of shore party.

Petty officers and men of the shore party

W. Lashly	Chief Stoker RN
W. W. Archer	Chief Steward late RN
Thomas Clissold	Cook late RN
Edgar Evans	Petty Officer RN
Robert Forde	Petty Officer RN
Thomas Crean	Petty Officer RN
Thomas S. Williamson	Petty Officer RN
Patrick Keohane	Petty Officer RN
George P. Abbott	Petty Officer RN
Frank V. Browning	Petty Officer RN
Harry Dickason	Able Seaman RN
F. J. Hooper	Steward, late RN
Anton Omel'chenko	Groom
Demetri Gerof [2]	Dog Driver

The ranks are shown as they were at the time of the expedition. *Terra Nova*'s crew consisted of 25 officers, petty officers, and men.

2 As spelt on the expedition. The correct transliteration is Dmitriy Girev.

Editorial note

Few alterations have been needed in Mrs McGhie's excellent translation from the Norwegian of Tryggve Gran's diary of Scott's last expedition. But, in order to amplify or clarify certain points in the text, it has been necessary to include footnotes which are numbered consecutively within each section.

From the published accounts of the expedition by some of its other members, in particular Captain Scott himself, extensive use has been made of excerpts to illuminate Gran's diary and as insertions between square brackets within the text. This is a departure from the usual practice of relegating such supporting material to an appendix, where it is either not read or not seen fully in context. The arrangement adopted is believed to be easier and more rewarding for the reader. Excerpts are initialled in accordance with the list of references at the end of the book.

Southward bound

29 November 1910
All links with civilization are cut, and as night falls New Zealand sinks from sight. It is almost sad to think that years will pass before we shall once more see land with forests and green fields. We left Port Chalmers about 2 p.m. and sailed out into the fjord to the cheers of thousands of onlookers. We now lie off the New Zealand coast and are adjusting compass.

(*Midnight*) The Dunedin light is on the horizon. It is a wonderful night, starlit and mild. About 9 p.m. a breeze sprang up from land, and we are southward bound under full sail towards the unknown.

30 November
It was beautiful weather this morning, but this evening there is a fresh breeze from the west and the sky is dark and threatening. The ship is overloaded, so let's hope we don't run into bad weather. [Had it not been for the Royal Yacht Squadron ensign waving at the spanker gaff, the craft would never have received permission to sail out to sea – TG].

1 December
I am wet to the skin after standing watch. The weather has been foul, with high seas and decks awash for long periods. The wind blew up in the morning watch and the sea got up unbelievably fast. At about 5 p.m. we had a hell of a job with the sails; all but the staysail had to come down. With the shortening of sail *Terra Nova* lay almost dead in the wave troughs and great masses of water washed over the decks. The deck cargo had to be relashed, and we worked for hours almost like divers. The night watch has been no better. The coal sacks came adrift and had to be thrown overboard. And what a struggle it was to dump such a valuable cargo! This heaving and hauling needed great care. We had to wait for the ship to steady after each wave before getting a grip on the sacks. Last night, however, the waves often surprised us and

we had to be really quick. Between coal sacks deep under water, we were hurled from rail to rail. But now it is over for a while. The bunk awaits. That will be good.

2 December

What a state we're in! To keep the vessel afloat we have bailed with buckets since four this morning. The pumps have stopped, for the water has long since doused the boiler fires. I went down to the engine room this morning and to my astonishment found the crew down there working in water up to their necks. They were trying to get a hand pump working. In the heavy rolling, water slopped up between the boilers, and there was smoke and steam everywhere. It was not the most encouraging sight. Meanwhile the officers and men have done whatever they can to save the ship. Without let-up the crew have worked the hand pumps amidships, and we the 'after-guard'[1] have kept a chain of buckets going from the engine room. Now, at 5 p.m., our hard work has brought the water level down a few inches. Up on deck the deck hands are standing up to their waists in ice-cold water in constant danger of being swept overboard. Nevertheless, I can now hear their singing blended with the sound of wind and waves. In the engine room the water has swilled over the boilers for so long that it is almost boiling. We are therefore working more or less naked. Sadly, the sea and storm have taken their toll of both men and animals. This morning one of the ponies died, and another broke his leg and had to be shot. A dog was washed overboard, and we men lead a less than comfortable life. Most of the bunks are wet through, though mine is an exception. It was Cherry-Garrard's idea to have the ceiling covered with canvas; he had that done for all of us in the 'nursery'[2], but only I benefited from it and he himself is wading in water.

[3? December]

We were at it in the engine room until 4 a.m., so dog-tired we could hardly stand. Yesterday afternoon a wave swept away a section of the railing on the afterdeck, so now there is a great gaping hole and the water washes freely in and out. If we run into yet another storm, I don't know what will happen. This morning we managed to get the pumps going and the water is now down to a depth of one foot. We have lit the fires under the boilers and shall with luck be under steam by about 6 p.m. My Wellington boots are like eel-pots; the water gets in but not

1 The ship's officers and scientists.
2 The cabin shared by Cherry-Garrard, Day, Debenham, Gran, Priestley and Wright.

out, so I have to dry them time after time. Cherry has turned in, using my bunk; he hasn't had any real sleep for over 48 hours.

4 December
Our southward progress improves; the days lengthen and there are not many hours of night. We no longer keep watch for ships but for ice, which may heave into sight in the form of a drifting iceberg any time now. According to our observations we are now in the latitude of Cape Horn, in view of which the weather is excellent.

5 December
Southward bound. The sun came out around noon and it was really lovely to sunbathe after so many days of rough weather. This afternoon, when I was on the bridge, I saw clearly a greyish white apparition on the horizon on the starboard bow. I thought it was an iceberg and shouted. Up swarmed the whole stern watch, but [all] were most disappointed to see nothing. They thought I was pulling their legs, but I was quite convinced I had seen something on the horizon and climbed up to the crow's-nest. I saw nothing at first, but then suddenly I heard a swishing sound and at the same moment a large fin whale surfaced forwards on the starboard side. What I had seen was his 'blow', and not ice.

It is getting lighter; at 11 in the evening I could read the log without lighting the lamp.

6 December
Rainy weather and variable wind; the wind has swung round to the north and the temperature has risen again. Tonight we were in the same latitude as Kristiania, but all the same feel ourselves a vast distance from civilization. Of course there is a difference between south and north. Longing to get my skis on.

7 December
It can't be many hours now before we are in the ice. The temperature has fallen below freezing point and tonight the deck has iced up. There is a fresh breeze blowing and it is cold working in the rigging. But it is light the whole night and that's the main thing. Have passed part of the day in the crow's-nest looking for ice. It is just like sitting in the gondola of a balloon – to hear the wind singing and only see heaven and ocean; it is lonely and peaceful too, up there. During the day the weather has been changeable with intermittent sun and light snow showers.

8 December

This afternoon the first greeting from the south arrived in the form of two rather large icebergs. They were invisible from the deck and we had to climb up to the crow's-nest to see them. Towards the east lay the two ice mammoths, sun-lit and glistening white; it was as though the adventure in the south had begun. Tonight the temperature is 28 °F (–2 °C) and the deck is covered with frozen spray.

9 December

The venture has had a splendid start. At nine this morning we entered the pack, and since then have pushed on south through more or less open leads[3]. We have passed berg after berg – bluish and glistening, drifting past us towards the north. The albatross has now given way to the Arctic tern. It has been a heavenly evening, the ice floes lying as far as the eye can see, touched with a reddening sun. The still, shining leads have mirrored the purple of the sky, and some banks of clouds to the south flamed up in gold during the few hours that the sun was below the horizon. Now it is almost one in the morning and in a little while the sun will again shine over the ice. The temperature is several degrees below zero [C] and new ice has formed between the floes during the night. The farther we drive south the tighter the pack becomes, so we wonder how long we can keep going without a halt. If the ice permits, we shall cross the Antarctic Circle at four o'clock in the morning.

3 Navigable passages through the ice.

In Antarctic waters

10 December

Now we are in the land of the midnight sun; at 5 a.m. we crossed the Antarctic Circle. Hour after hour in the night I stood on the bridge and stared out over the leads where new ice spun its delicate web. In the distance the bergs sailed in their majestic might, sunlit and blue. It was as though we lived in a gigantic, wonderful fairy tale; as though we sailed over an ocean where thousands of white lilies lay rippling in the night air. And when the sun rose the white lilies took on a violet hue and the whole of fairyland lay in rosy light.

Towards morning the pack ice thickened, and at eight o'clock we made fast to a large floe to take on board ice for fresh water[1]. After several hours work cutting the ice, we resumed our laborious passage southwards. While we were working a penguin came near the vessel, the first I had seen. We tried to end its days with a shot, but no!, it just laughed at us and marched out of our range. Tonight, Wilson virtually washed himself in seal blood, and the deck is red – redder than the rays of the midnight sun. Yes, the midnight sun showed itself for the first time tonight. Our progress is slow – 10 km in an hour is about average. One officer is always in the crow's-nest and another on the bridge. Towards the south we begin to make out the contours of Scott Island[2]; until just before midnight we took it for a berg.

11 December

On skis for the first time today; on skis, that is, for every soul on board *Terra Nova*. It was a successful beginning and everyone is delighted with the sport. The surface was not of the best but luckily the snow was so wet that it did not stick to the skis. Captain Scott and Lieutenant

1 The salt drains out from the upper layers of years old sea ice, leaving it fresh – a fact known to polar mariners for centuries.

2 Discovered from the relief ship *Morning* in 1902, on Captain Scott's previous expedition, and named after him.

Evans acknowledged their satisfaction and Wilson declared that 'skiing of this type' was something quite new. [I'm much pleased with the ski and ski boots – both are very well adapted to our purpose – RFS]. At four o'clock this morning the pack halted us and thereby decided our fate for some time. How long this situation will last no one knows. Ski training will now be continued and, with the interest and aptitude possessed by the 'Terra Novians', a couple of days stay here will work wonders. This morning we were visited by four very lively penguins. They looked like human beings as they ran over the floes, diving head first into the leads and popping up like rubber balls on to the edge of the ice. They looked almost like creatures under military command. There is movement in the ice, and now and again the vessel grinds between the floes.

12 December

Since midday we have been breaking through the ice pack. It lies so thick and tight around us that it is really unbelievable that the vessel can force its way through. She goes very slowly, with bangs and crashes, and is sometimes stopped for longish periods. In the forenoon, Oates, Bowers, and I went on a trip to what we had thought was Scott Island, but it turned out to be an enormous iceberg. The going was better today, but there was heavy movement in the ice. On the way back we found ourselves several times drifting on ice floes, but after a few minutes they drifted into other floes, so that we could cross over. During one such manoeuvre, Oates fell through [the ice]. He took it quite calmly and lay there until I could give him a heave up. During our march we caught sight of a large seal lying asleep. We went over to it, woke it up, and generally irritated the beast. We were on board again at noon, after our trip of 13 km. They had set sail and begun to force the ice. After lunch all afterdeck hands[3] were issued with ski equipment.

13 December

This morning we were stopped again by pack ice and used the time to bring fresh ice on board. We tried to steam onwards, but the results were bad. As conditions seem unlikely to improve, we have let the fires under the boilers go out. Just before supper I managed to get a much needed and extremely beneficial steam bath in the engine room. This luxury was possible because of the emptying of the boilers.

14 December

Towards the southwest the leads are opening more and more. Although

3 The ship's officers and scientists.

we are still lying immovably fast between the ice floes, the situation seems to have improved a bit. During the morning I gave further ski lessons. Captain Scott and Lieutenant Evans are very good. But the same must be said of all aboard the ship. [. . . almost everyone proceeded to ski or in current parlance (*à la* Gran) to go 'mit dee shee op' . . . (TGT). Gran is wonderfully good and gives instruction well – RFS].

15 December

More ski instruction this morning and afternoon, but it has only been on a large ice floe and cannot have been much fun. Meares has also had the dogs out and they seem to work splendidly. Fat and out of condition they might be, but they took off at lightning speed and I was left behind on the shorter distances, even though the going was icy and fast. But, given the weight of the sledges, even if the terrain is flat, I believe it will be relatively easy to keep up with the dogs. Tonight skis were issued to those of the crew[4] who will accompany the landing party; without the right tools it was a tough job to get the irons [of the ski bindings] adjusted. [They are all very keen to learn (skiing) – RFS]. I had to use the engine room as a workshop and there wasn't really enough room to handle the length of a ski easily. The ice is loosening markedly round about us, and we can see miles of open water from the crow's-nest. Perhaps we will get going sometime tomorrow.

16 December

I stood on deck tonight and stared out over the ice. The scene reminded me of Finse[5]; it was like a bad spring day there, when the ice is melting on the lake and the fog lying heavy and thick.

The last few days of mild weather have loosened the ice considerably, and in the morning we set the foresails to have a go at pushing out into a lead that stretches away to the south. But hours elapsed, and we lay just as fast as before. Then suddenly, as we sat at lunch, the vessel began to creak and groan. I dashed on deck and saw to my joy that we had sailed through the pack ice and out into an open lead. But the rapture did not last long; an hour later we were gripped fast again. Fog and rain lie like a pall over the ice field and the west wind shrieks in the rigging; even the howls of the dogs are whisked away and cannot be heard aft. These are bad days for the dogs; they are wet through and crushed together so that they can hardly move, spending day and night under the open sky.

4 i.e. the ratings.
5 In Norway.

17 December
We've been bone idle today. The vessel has lain immovable. Two of the engine room crew made music down in the stokehold this evening. It was quite charming and I went down with Ponting. My astonishment grew in the half-darkness when I discovered that the tuneful notes came from a single, home-made, one-string fiddle. The sound box was a tin can, the arm a soldered rod. It is unbelievable what men can devise.

18 December
We have steam up again for another attempt to force the pack. At eight last night the ice eased considerably and we thought we were going to break out. But no!, now it is tighter than ever. I hear the ship's telegraph: 'stop engines' and then the sound of the grinding and scraping of the pack ice heaped around us. There's little doubt that the attempt was made too soon. [What an exasperating game this is – one cannot tell what is going to happen in the next half or even quarter of an hour. At one moment everything looks flourishing, the next one begins to doubt if it is possible to get through – RFS].

19 December
During the morning the ice slackened again and we made quite good headway. This evening it is rather overcast and the temperature has sunk to –3 °C. The pack ice is again massive and our voyage begins to resemble a passage down a frozen river. The engine is at full steam, the vessel shudders and a moment later rises up against great blocks of ice. Sometimes we make it, but sometimes the floes get the upper hand and we have to start the attack anew. Last night and today we have seen whales between the floes, but they were too far away for us to identify [them]. We often see penguins sitting on the floes, in groups of four, staring at us in wonderment as we push ahead. If we give them a song, they follow us; they seem to like music. We see seals surprisingly seldom.

20 December
The weather is brilliant, but the pack ice very extensive and so we have had to stop and let the fires go out.

21 December
We have lain fast in the ice the whole day. Although we tried a thrust in the morning, the ice was too strong for us and we gave up the attempt at once. Today Campbell and I have been tarring the skis.

22 December

Midsummer Evening! The sun, which has recently had a redder tinge, has now reached the most southerly point in the sky. We have not celebrated the event, for the situation is not really as promising as it should have been. Pack ice lies thick and tight, and we have had to let the fires die out. We are already beginning to discuss the possibility that we shall not be in a position to put the eastern party ashore.[6] This will be a hard blow for Campbell, for he must in this case be landed somewhere north of Cape Adare in order to investigate the coastline from there to Adélie Land. Pennell does not like it either; the coal stocks are falling, thereby reducing his means of carrying out a longish voyage in Antarctic waters. Of course Scott is also a little disappointed but does not show it.

In the past few days innumerable penguins have paid for their curiosity with their lives. The slaughter[7] continued today and the deck is more than flecked with blood. I tasted penguin steak the other day and found the meat excellent, almost like ptarmigan.

23 December

This morning the ice loosened and, as the wind was northerly, we set sail and pushed on for several hours. But at lunchtime we were stuck once more, and it was not until evening, when we got steam up, that we succeeded in advancing again. The prospects look quite bright now. Pennell is 28 today, and at supper there was a toast in his honour. Spirits rose and the evening passed in a very lively way. We hoisted Pennell up through the skylight, an honour hitherto reserved for two dead ponies. It is now decided that we shall make for Cape Crozier instead of McMurdo Sound.

24 December

It is strange to think it is Christmas Eve. The sun shines through light, roseate clouds over the ice and over the mirror-like leads. We have let the boilers down, for this morning the pack again defeated us by its impenetrability. Of course, it *would* loosen again some hours after the steam pressure dropped; so we set sail and made about 10 km headway. The evening passes quietly. The English do not celebrate Christmas Eve, only Christmas Day.[8]

6 In a footnote in the diary TG records: 'According to the plans, the eastern party was to have been put ashore on King Edward VII land' [Edward VII Peninsula].

7 Primarily to obtain biological specimens.

8 In Norway the main Christmas celebration is on Christmas Eve.

25 December
We celebrated Christmas this evening. The mess is decorated with our sledge flags; and my combined English-Norwegian effort has been given pride of place above the mirror. The weather today has brought us midway between laughter and tears. Tonight it's snowing and, in proper Christmas fashion, the deck is white and glittering. We lie with hoisted sails, but the ice is still too dense for us.

26 December
Thanks to a fresh northerly breeze we have pushed on several miles farther south. The weather has been horrid and raw cold, and during the night we had two hours of snow. Frank Debenham's birthday today; he is 27. He is an unusually nice chap, and we two get on particularly well together. None can complain about the 'nursery'. You would have to go far to find chaps like Wright, Cherry-Garrard, Day, Priestley and Debenham.

27 December
Weather sour and horrid today, but tonight the sun peeped through and lightened the heavy overcast. Today, under sail, we have forced our way some miles southwards; I am beginning to wish the voyage would end now.

A wonderful summer's day in the ice. The warmth has had an influence on the pack; the floes have become perceptibly smaller and are getting more or less porous. So we've got steam up again and since 8 p.m. have pushed on southwards. [Lieutenant Gran is a believer in a mild way in the powers of black magic. That evening he saw the discarded Bridge pack lying on the table and said, 'We'll see how many days before we finish with this ice. If I draw out a black card it will show us.' So he straightaway turned over a card, and it was the two of spades. . . . In forty-eight hours we were once more entering on open water – TGT].

It is going well – two miles in an hour. *Terra Nova* is an outstanding vessel for the ice. Her weight makes up for her slow speed. [The ship behaved splendidly – no other ship, not even the *Discovery*, would have come through so well. . . If only she had more economical engines, she would be suitable in all respects – RFS].

Seals and penguins are beginning to come on stage. The penguins come flocking to the ship to chat with us and even with the dogs. These birds are remarkable – perhaps they should not be called birds at all. It would be more fitting if they were classified 'human-ape-bird-porpoise'. They are musical and stand and listen when we sing; without a doubt they use a common language, and they are disciplined and more than a little curious. They are splendid underwater swimmers, and in this respect very similar to porpoises. When the dogs first saw a penguin they became quite wild, but they now taken them comparatively calmly.

29 December

When the watch changed, all we could see was open water – the ice had vanished. The southwesterly swell has given the ship a rolling motion. All sail is set and we are making good speed. During the night watch there was a snowfall; we could hardly see further than the ship's length.

30 December

Yesterday seemed to be the end of our days in the pack ice; now we are tossing about on the waves of the Ross Sea.

31 December

The last day of the year has come but unfortunately has brought back the pack ice with it. In some ways it's a blessing, for in the night the sea began to get the upper hand and the ponies suffered a great deal. A howling gale with snow showers has been blowing all day. We are keeping clear of the ice but are being driven north. We hope the wind will drop. The ice moves faster than we do, and the engine is started every hour to help us keep in the clear channels.

At 10 a.m. the weather eased and towards the southeast a sunlit mountainous landscape came into view. The jagged peaks and rounded tops, which reach towards the clouds, are like a secret Jotunheim massif [9] but much, much higher. I stood for ages, speechless, gazing through the telescope until my fingers were numb with cold. It was the most majestic sight I had ever seen. All hands came on deck, even those who had just turned in. [(Mounts) Sabine and Whewell (both of c. 3,000 m in the Admiralty Mountains) were most conspicuous. . . . Mount Sabine was about 110 miles away when we saw it. I believe we could have seen it 30 or 40 miles farther – such is the wonderful clearness of the atmosphere – RFS].

1 January 1911

The New Year has come and let us pray it will bring good fortune. At midnight we sounded the ship's siren and drank in the New Year with cocoa. All sleepers were aroused and I played a march on the pianola. Wind and sea have dropped and we are again making way southwards, the polar land mass shining in the distance.

9 In Norway.

The first day of the year was nice and sunny. It was quite like a summer's day in Norway long ago. The blue of the ocean leads the eye towards the sunlit mountains of Victoria Land. We have enjoyed ourselves, relaxing, lying on deck, and sunning ourselves the whole day. It is strange how strong the sun is, even in these high latitudes. At breastfast time it was as though the sea had been strewn with white ice lilies[10] after yesterday's storm; by dinner time they had melted away.

2 January

This evening we have Mount Erebus in sight, about 100 miles ahead. It is not quite clear yet and looks rather like a great, dark shadow on the horizon. I shall take a turn at stoking tonight to get some exercise, and therefore am not standing evening watch.

Mounts Erebus and Terror, the Great Ice Barrier[11], and the polar continent are close at hand, and so we have covered one great stage in our quest. We have passed the whole day off the Ross Sea coast.

I was a little tired after the night's stoking when I turned out at eight o'clock for breakfast. It was sunny and Erebus could be seen clearly, a huge mountain with smoke at the summit[12]. Far ahead of us lay the Great Ice Barrier. By 1 p.m. we were close under it. It lay like a great wall, stretching eastwards from the Ross Sea as far as the eye could see. We stood off westwards and sounded in a little bay, where Barrier and land came together. The sides were so steep it was impossible to get ashore. We pushed on to Cape Crozier, but it was impossible to land there either and we continued westwards to Cape Royds, where Shackleton wintered.[13] A good deal of pack ice lies in towards McMurdo Sound, but it is not so bad that we cannot steam through it easily. At Cape Crozier and along the Barrier there was a clear channel. The Society Mountains[14] came into sight to the west, sharp and jagged – quite different in shape from Erebus and Terror.

10 Pieces of new ice: pancake ice.
11 The Ross Ice Shelf.
12 Mount Erebus (3795 m) is the highest of the three active volcanoes in Antarctica.
13 On his expedition, 1907–09.
14 The Royal Society Range.

Cape Evans

4 January
We have reached 'port' and have stopped at Cape Evans in McMurdo Sound. We sailed past the site of Shackleton's old quarters, not stopping there because an expedition like ours needs to have a completely fresh site. Ours we have named 'Cape Teddy Evans'[1]; it is grand and new, lying under the precipices facing the mountains to the west. The ice is packed right into the inner McMurdo Sound, and [in that area] we cannot get closer to land than 2 km. [We could have gone . . . pretty well anywhere except Hut Point. My main wish was to choose a place that would not be easily cut off from the Barrier, and my eye fell on a cape which we used to call the Skuary. . . . It was separated from (Hut Point) by two bays on either side of the Glacier Tongue (Erebus Glacier Tongue) and I thought that these bays would remain frozen until late in the season, and that when they froze over again the ice would soon become firm – RFS]. At six this morning we anchored at the ice edge and have put ashore motor sledges,[2] dogs, and ponies. A swarm of penguins surrounds the ship. Flocks of them attack the dogs, which make a frightful row but stand with slack leashes just until the penguins are within reach. Then they pounce with deadly intent, nearly tearing the birds to pieces. Some of them escape but, infuriated by the dogs, fly back at once for revenge. This time death is certain.

5 January
I have driven a motor sledge this afternoon with Nelson. It works quite well, but of course at the moment the ice is perfect for it. We are building our hut on the slopes of Mount Erebus beside the beach of McMurdo Sound. The weather is calm with brilliant sunshine. We have been working 12 hours now, hauling a sledge over the ice hour

1 Or rather Cape Evans after Lieutenant Evans.
2 The expedition had three of these experimental vehicles.

after hour. The hut is taking shape and, if the weather holds, we shall start to cover it in a couple of days.

Today Ponting was nearly killed while he stood photographing some killer whales out on the ice. I don't know whether the whales spotted him, or whether they were hunting a flock of penguins who sat sunning themselves nearby, but whatever it was the ice beneath him suddenly broke under [the force of] their powerful blowing and their snouts rose up around him. It looked very dangerous, but he managed to jump from one block of ice to the next, and saved himself and his camera without, however, getting a picture. [Later that winter Ponting received the 'Jonah Medal' for this activity among whales, but he did not see the point of the joke and declined the honour – TG].

6 January

It is sunny and summery today too. I have been helping a good deal with the carpentry for the hut. The framework is now completed and we have begun the covering. Took an evening trip on skis and thus my first steps as a skier on the continent. It was a fine trip and all went well in spite of the ice-hard going. Today several people are snow-blind and will probably have to stay off work. So it's going to be tougher for those of us who can still see.

7 January

We're working at full steam from morning to night. I have been humping up hundreds of cases of provisions from 'tweendecks on to topdeck. This has gone on for 14 hours. The number of men suffering from snow-blindness is growing; several of the crew have had to fall out. All scientific instruments and provisions are now ashore. Only the coal remains to be unloaded.

8 January

Sunday has never been *Terra Nova*'s lucky day. Today our newest and best motor sledge sank in 120 fathoms. It happened early this morning while we were attempting to transfer it from the ship to safer ice. All went well for a time, and we thought we were home and dry, when suddenly one of the men, Williamson, went through the ice. We stopped heaving to give him a hand; at the same moment the ice under the sledge gave way and down it went. The rope we were hauling on was nearly 60 fathoms in length. We tried to keep a grip on it, but the tow cut through the ice and we couldn't hold it. The whole thing went to the bottom and was lost. Scott was not present, but was thought to have taken the accident calmly when he heard about it. [A day of disaster. I stupidly gave permission for the third motor to be got out this morning. . . . It's a big blow to know that one of the two best motors, on which so much time and trouble have been spent, now lies at the bottom of the sea – RFS].

One hour later Priestley went through the ice and was under water for several seconds. So the decision was taken to break contact with land. Everything that had been transferred to the ice was brought on board again, and thereafter work was suspended. We have begun to get up steam again. Tomorrow we shall attempt to force the ice lying farther north and closer to land.

9 January

Steam was raised by 6 a.m. and we began to break through the ice almost at once. At 8 a.m. we made fast to the ice edge a mile farther north. Here the ice is solid and should hold for a time. After breakfast we started unloading and continued right through till evening. I haven't been to the hut for the past two days, but I can see that rapid progress is being made. The weather has been fine today but tonight it is overcast with a nasty south wind blowing.

10 January

The horizon is dark. Erebus is shrouded in fog and there have been occasional heavy snow showers. Unloading has continued under great pressure. I have taken two trips to the hut this morning with loads. Bruce, Pennell, and I were in the traces and beat Campbell's team so throughly that he – holder of the sledge record – stopped us. Drake is sitting at the pianola [in the ship]. He has his own special job, which is to fetch ice from quite a distance by a regular route, now dubbed the 'ice-cream road'. Work on the hut proceeds under extreme pressure. Cape Evans reminds me of a great Indian camp. Horses, hounds, men and masses of birds swarm all around the big piles of provisions. The sounds of hammering and sea shanties are mixed. From time to time a transport pony that has got loose gets tangled between the tents, while the dogs whine and howl.

11 January

Blizzard this morning and into this afternoon, but by evening the weather is again splendid. Pennell had the boilers lit this morning, fearing that the ship might be crushed by the movement of the ice. But it was unnecessary, and the fires have been put out again.

12 January

All the provisions for our western party[3] were taken across to the hut

3 The party to be led by Griffith Taylor to the west coast of the Ross Sea.

today. True, the skis are still on board but I want to keep them here until the hut is nearly finished. To take them over now would involve a risk of their being buried under masses of snow. Tomorrow we are loading stones for ballast and I shall go ashore – thus ending my service aboard *Terra Nova*.[4]

13 January

The morning brought 11 degrees of frost and a raging wind from the south. We turned out late and breakfasted with shaking hands. At 9 a.m. we went ashore to collect stones for ballast near the hut. I went on skis, the others on foot. It is incredible how little one feels the cold in the open air. It must be because the air is so dry. Great progress has been made with the hut; there is already linoleum on the floor. [We are all LANDED eight days after our arrival – a very good record – RFS].

We have built a rope haulway from the snow displaced during building. Priestley and I did the steering while Campbell and Levick were station masters. It worked splendidly and we ferried 10 tons [of ballast] down to the ice. The horses look after the transport from the ice on to shipboard. It is blowing up tonight too, and clouds are beginning to form. The wind must be localized to the lower levels, for the smoke from Erebus rises straight up and only later begins to disperse, and in the opposite direction to that of the wind down here.

14 January

On account of the large stretches of open water, it has been decided that the motor sledges shall not go to the depot this year. This afternoon I had a longish conversation with Captain Scott who told me among other things that he had decided to take me on the sledge expedition [to lay depots]. [I have been making arrangements for the depôt journey, telling off people for ponies and dogs, etc. – RFS]. The party and the ship will start about the same time, but it is also possible that *Terra Nova* will put us ashore farther on along the [McMurdo] Sound. Departure and break-up [with the ship] will be between 20 and 25 January. Tomorrow Campbell and I are to go skiing. Priestley and Levick will come part of the way. The weather is promising.

15 January

Sunday has been a successful day. Campbell, Nelson and I have had a wonderful ski trip over untrodden ground. We started[5] soon after Sunday service and set course over the Barne Glacier towards

4 Gran apparently continued to sleep aboard *Terra Nova* until 24 January.

5 Accompanied at first by Scott.

Shackleton's old site.[6] Taylor and Wright had started earlier and we could see them as specks in the distance. Scott was angry because they had left without permission and ordered us to send them home again, if we came across them on our way. [Eventually I turned, leaving Campbell, Gran and Nelson . . . but not before I felt certain that the route to Cape Royds would be quite easy. As we topped the last rise we saw Taylor and Wright some way ahead on the slope; they had come up by a different route. Evidently they are bound for the same goal (RFS). Wright and myself received permission to go on the (Barne) Glacier – TGT]. But they kept to the lower slopes and we only came across their tracks once. We proceeded in single file, hitched together with a rope; we couldn't make any great speed for we had Nelson with us. He is excellent for a beginner, but even the best beginner has difficulties with crevasses and blue ice, and being roped up both fore and aft. Indeed, I think we didn't really need the rope, for all the crevasses were passable on ski. In some places the going was splendid and the skis slid along as on a frosty day at home with new snow. In other places it was ice-hard. High over us, to the northeast, Erebus loomed in all its might, with a smoke streamer at the summit; beneath us lay *Terra Nova* like a black spot against the shining ice fields; and far in the distance, beyond a bluish fjord where icebergs sailed with the tide, lay the polar continent with its peaks and summits, its glaciers and chasms. We rested near some small tarns, some kilometres from Shackleton's hut. We lay down and enjoyed our well-being, drank the clear ice water and smoked a pipe. Taylor and Wright went down to the hut which they found completely untouched by wind or weather. Everything was just as it was left by Shackleton's people.[7] The minimum thermometer in the hut showed an almost incredible –72 °F (–58 °C).

16 January

This morning we continued to collect ballast for the ship. At lunchtime we started getting ice on board from an iceberg which happened to drift alongside. However, this work came to a pretty quick end. During the work a block of ice of about 50 tons suddenly broke off and the iceberg began to lurch sickeningly; it was nip and tuck for the men working on it, but they scrambled aboard. The iceberg took with it some of their belongings.

Campbell, Priestley, and Levick went over to Shackleton's hut this afternoon to spend several days there in order to kill seals and climb the old crater on Erebus. Scott and Meares took a dog team to Hut Point

6 At Cape Royds.
7 In March 1909.

yesterday. They returned this evening after a successful trip. They found the hut all right but in a sad state. Shackleton had left one of the windows open and the result was that the hut was chock-a-block with icy, caked snow. There wasn't much point in digging it out. [There was something too depressing in finding the old hut in such a desolate condition – RFS].

17 January

A snow-storm when we awoke this morning and still snow-storm this evening. After lunch I trudged over to the hut.[8] Over one foot of snow had fallen and it was a tough job with a heavy load to struggle forwards against the wind and blinding snow. When I arrived at the camp, I found everything snowed in. In the hut they were hammering the bunks together, and during the afternoon I was glad of the opportunity to find a resting place. After supper I bade farewell to those in the hut and made my way through the snow towards the ship. I had the wind with me and went fast. But I received an unpleasant surprise when I arrived. The storm had forced them to take the ship out from the ice. They signalled me to turn back. The return journey was bleak and it was good to get my head inside the hut again at last. [We took up our abode in the hut to-day and are simply overwhelmed with its comforts – RFS].

18 January

Today when I turned out of my sleeping bag, it was 4 °F. That is about –15 °C and pretty cold. But it wasn't too bad; the hut was snug, unmoved by the clamour of the wind outside. However, the weather did improve and it was clear in between times. In the course of the night the ship had got up steam and was standing offshore. Shortly after I had turned back to the hut, the cables holding the ship to the ice edge parted and the great floe to which the ship had been anchored began to drift. By lunchtime *Terra Nova* had crept along the ice edge and now lies about a cable length[9] from the hut.

19 January

The day was passed greasing the sledge runners with 'Records' wax. Scott wanted the sledges for the depot in order. I was about half-finished before evening and Scott was very satisfied. I spent some hours in the hut tonight, listening to our first gramophone concert; it was a delight to hear Caruso, Melba, and Tetrazzini, among other famous stars. Ponting and I have now gone on board again. In order to enter my 23rd year clean and tidy, I have shaved my beard. The stove burns, Ponting has made cocoa, and I have stolen some tinned pears.

8 At Cape Evans.
9 i.e. 600 feet.

20 January

My birthday[10] passed in peace and quiet. I have finished the sledges and worked a bit on my bunk in the hut. This will be the last night for me on board *Terra Nova*; tomorrow I move everything over to the hut. After supper we played the gramophone and to celebrate my birthday some Norwegian melodies were included. It gave me a strange feeling.

The sledge [depot-laying] expedition has now been planned. We set out on Wednesday 25th – 12 men, [26] dogs, and 8 ponies. Wilson and Meares with the dogs.[11] The weather has been good; but a bitter east wind is blowing. Today some of the sledging equipment has been distributed among us, such as fur boots, mittens and *finnesko*.[12]

21 January

When I woke this morning we were rolling in the swell. The ice had loosened and we were drifting. During the morning we managed to get up steam, but with a moderate gale blowing from the north we kept under way some miles offshore. At lunchtime we made for land but we were over-eager, took it too fast, and ran aground. We set about immediately shifting the cargo fore to aft. Then we executed a rather unusual drill in which officers and men were paraded on the main hatch and on the word of command ran together from side to side.[13] In this way the ship was shaken loose, and with the help of the engines we were able to get off quite easily. We reached the ice edge quite safely and once again made fast. After supper Ponting and I went ashore to film some skiing. I climbed up a horribly steep ice slope [above the sea ice] and went as near the edge as possible. Then came the downhill run; at first all went fine with my Telemark turns and Kristiania swings. So much so that I deluded myself into thinking I should arrive at the bottom neatly, just in front of the camera. But when I swooped down on to the flat the ice gave away under me and I plunged forward involuntarily, ending up with my head just on the ice edge. For a time I lay half-conscious and could not speak when Ponting came to help. At last I came to and struggled back to the hut in a decidedly battered state.

22 January

I was to have fixed the bindings on the skis today, but as it was a rest day for all hands I put the job off until tomorrow. I am still pretty sore

10 His 22nd.

11 The party comprised Scott, Wilson, Lieutenant Evans, Bowers, Oates, Meares, Atkinson, Cherry-Garrard, Gran, Keohane, Crean, and Forde.

12 Fur boots of Lapp design.

13 An exercise known as sallying.

from yesterday. Today the weather has been all right, if rather bleak. It snowed this morning.

23 January

If I am aboard, the ice breaks up; if I am ashore and want to come aboard, it breaks up too! This morning I was awakened by the sound of the engines; we had been driven out from the ice and had got up steam. The ice in Cape Evans Bay[14] had been set adrift by a strong southeasterly wind and in the course of a few hours the bay was free of ice. The whole morning through we had to keep under way. We laid a trawl and made a fine catch of some new species of fish. Some huge sponges were also dragged up from the deep. We made for land at lunchtime. Our sledge expedition starts some time early tomorrow. All the equipment has been brought on board, and tomorrow all we have to do is to take the horses over to [Erebus] Glacier Tongue. [Bowers had been preparing lists of everything that had to be taken. 'How much have we forgotten then', asked Scott jokingly. 'Nothing – absolutely nothing', replied the little corpulent Birdie, who knew what he was talking about. Indeed, no omission occurred which could be set at his door. Bowers was really a tremendous man – TG]. The real journey begins tomorrow.

14 North Bay.

1
***Terra Nova* (left) and *Fram* in the Bay of Whales, January 1911**

2

Members of the expedition at Cape Evans before the start of the southern journey, October 1911.
Standing (left to right) Taylor, Cherry-Garrard, Day, Nelson, Lt. Evans, Oates, Atkinson, Scott, Wright, Keohane, Gran, Lashly, Hooper, Forde, Anton, Demitri. Sitting (left to right) Bowers, Meares, Debenham, Wilson, Simpson, PO Evans, Crean

3
Discovery hut after winter blizzards

4
Hut at Cape Evans after winter blizzards

Southward on the Great Depot Journey

24 January

The journey has begun and we are now lying in our sleeping bags, stiff and tired after the day's drudgery. At nine o'clock this morning we bade farewell to Cape Evans and set off with the horses down to Glacier Tongue where *Terra Nova* had tied up at the ice edge. We spent some hours aboard and then set a southward course. My horse is called 'Weary Willie.' He is strong but sadly slow on the march, and I had an awful time keeping him going. During the trans-shipment of the horses today Cherry-Garrard's horse fell through the ice and was within a hair's breadth of going under. [We got lashings round him and hauled him out. Poor 'Guts'! He was fated to drown, but in an hour he appeared to have forgotten all about his mishap, and was pulling his first load to Hut Point as gallantly as always – A CG].

25 January

The weather has been splendid with only a few degrees of frost. We turned out after a pleasant night and got going towards the ship after a simple breakfast. 'Willy' had recovered and took the lead several times. *Terra Nova* will sail north with the geologists tomorrow, towards the Western Mountains, and thereafter with Campbell to Edward VII land.

26 January

At last we have said goodbye to *Terra Nova*. We left the ship to the accompaniment of whinnies from the horses, hurrahs from the men, and the howling of the dogs. We reached our camp after some hours and now lie in the sleeping bags. Atkinson is snow-blind and has blisters on his feet. The weather has been excellent, but tonight it's blowing and the tent canvas is flapping.

27 January

We have moved camp about 7 km southwards. The establishment of these depots is a terribly tiring business, but it won't last all that long. The objective is to lay down a large mass of provisions right in on the Barrier, so that we are certain of the position [for next season] even if the sea ice[1] breaks up.

After supper we wandered over to the *Discovery* hut which is only a couple of kilometres from our camp. It wasn't many minutes before we stood on historic ground. It was in this area that Scott spent several years during the voyage of *Discovery*;[2] it was here that Sir Ernest Shackleton had spent the last night of his famous sledge expedition.[3] The hut was full of caked snow and our idea was to empty it. However, we had not been working long before the wind began to whip up the fallen snow into drifts and it began to look ominous; so we gave up the attempt. The weather is once more excellent.

28 January

Today for the first time we set foot on the Great Ice Barrier. The transition from the sea ice was little more than an even climb, and in spite of the deep snow the horses had no difficulty in scrambling up. We deposited our load about 3 km. in on the flat snow plain. Atkinson has been laid up today,[4] and 'Jimmy Pigg'[5] is also on the sick list.

29 January

Today is Sunday, but not a rest day, for we must push on. Divine service was held this morning – quite short as befitted the climate. It was really rather solemn to hear psalms here in the icy wastes.

After the service we set off south with our loads. For the second time we climbed the Barrier; for the second time we trudged homewards the same way. The going was heavy; we sank in and I decided to use skis on the next trip. After lunch I put on my skis, fastened a harness to 'Willy', and set off a little after the others. In the beginning all went well and I was in control of the situation. Just as everything was going splendidly, I lost one of my mittens and had to leave 'Willy' to himself for a second and go back a few dozen metres. Of course for once the beast got a move on and started hurrying after the others. I got up speed and pulled alongside. Whether he was frightened by the swishing of the skis, I know not, but suddenly he careered off. I tried to get hold of the bit, for by now he had reached the other sledges, which he passed at a wild gallop. Bowers thought the whole thing rather dangerous and

1 Between Cape Evans and Hut Point.

2 The *Discovery* was anchored offshore and used as living quarters, 1902–04. *See* 16 January.

3 To within 100 miles of the South Pole, 1908–09.

4 Atkinson had a bad heel.

5 'Jimmy Pig' was Keohane's pony.

made me take off my skis. [Gran tried going on ski with his pony. All went well while he was alongside, but when he came up from the back the swish of the ski frightened the beast, who fled faster than his pursuer – that is, the pony and load were going better than the Norwegian on ski. . . . Gran is doing very well. He has a lazy pony and a good deal of work to get him along, and does it very cheerfully – RFS]. The weather has been changeable. This morning and during the afternoon overcast, tonight clearing with intermittent sun. Tonight's temperature is –14 °C.

30 January

Today we have made camp on the Great Ice Barrier. A large depot will be established here and the place has been named 'Safety Camp'. Yesterday, during the sledging, we came upon two tents towards the northeast, and it turned out that they had belonged to Sir Ernest.[6] This afternoon we went down and dug them out. They had nearly disappeared. We found a primus with saucepans and other camping equipment. Otherwise, just a bit of rancid old cheese which no one could eat, so we can't be very hungry. [The cooker was there and a primus – Scott lighted it and cooked a meal; we often used it afterwards. And there were Rowntree's cocoa, Bovril, Brand's extract of beef, sheeps' tongues, cheese and biscuits – all open to the snow and all quite good – A CG]. It has been cold today, with brilliant sunshine, and windless.

31 January

The last day of the month will soon be gone. We kept to the camp and passed the day stacking away what we shan't need to take south. A cold, bitter wind is blowing with intermittent drift. Wilson and Meares left in the morning with the dogs for Cape Evans. The snow-shoes for the horses have proved excellent, but unfortunately we have only a couple with us. [We tried our one pair of snow-shoes on 'Weary Willie'. The effect was magical. . . . He strolled around as though walking on hard ground in places where he floundered woefully without them. Oates hasn't any faith in these shoes at all – RFS]. The aim now is to reach the hut[7] and fetch more snow-shoes, an enterprise which is unlikely to succeed since in my view the ice has broken up. I have said the weather is nothing to shout about today. In the morning it snowed in a light, windless fall, but tonight it is cold and blowing and the drift is hunting over the Barrier. The temperature tonight was the lowest so far, –15½ °C.

6 They were left by E. Joyce, of Shackleton's *Nimrod* expedition, on the 'Bluff Depot' journey of February 1909.

7 At Cape Evans.

1 February

It feels marvellous to turn in to the sleeping bag after hours of march in the icy-cold drift and windy blast. I quite enjoy the sensation of munching a biscuit while the storm roars and rages about the tent. I have just come back after a trip with the mail to Hut Point. I left camp after lunch and, with the wind at my back, went like greased lightning to begin with, but in the pass [The Gap] between Observation Point[8] and Crater Hill the ground was bare of snow and I had to plod on skis among stones for over 2 km. I did not want to take the skis off for I wanted to spare the *finnesko* as much as possible. I arrived shortly afterwards. I opened the door on the south side of the hut, which had come off its hinges, and crawled in.

Inside it was cold and bleak, and my hands were nearly numb by the time I had discharged my duty and hammered the mail bag to one of the walls. Meanwhile, the wind had risen, drift surrounded the hut and the weather looked anything but encouraging. I was not going to try for the pass again, but set a course over the sea ice round Cape Armitage. It was a longer way but better than plodding through the stones. The sea ice was appallingly bad, and I had to make large detours to avoid openings in the ice. There were places where the wind had driven all snow off the ice, and in the strong head-wind and driving snow it was only with the aid of my ski sticks that I managed to inch forward. I began to feel a little downcast. Erebus and Terror lay in a snow-storm and the Barrier was invisible in the drift. Occasionally a glimpse of the sun could be seen through the cloud layer and, thanks to this and the direction of the wind, I managed to keep my bearings. After about an hour, I was much relieved to catch sight of the first depot up on the Barrier. I took my bearings from this and pushed on. The drift was thicker here than on the sea ice, and after I had been going an hour without seeing any sign of the camp I knew I must have gone astray. I stood with my back to the wind and after a few minutes caught sight of the tents. [I sent Gran to the *Discovery* hut with our last mail. He went on ski and was nearly 4 hours away, making me rather anxious, as the wind had sprung up and there was a strong surface-drift; he narrowly missed the camp on returning and I am glad to get him back – RFS].

Wilson and Meares came back in the morning with unfinished business. They had met open water at Glacier Tongue. Atkinson is unwell. He will have to stay at the hut so as to catch the ship, if possible, when she arrives at Hut Point. Crean will stay with him. It isn't funny to be ill here. It's cold, –16 °C. Minimum tonight, –17 °C.

8 Observation Hill.

2 February
We are turning night into day inasmuch as our march will be by night. Scott is of the opinion that the going will probably be better in the lower temperatures. I don't believe it. [Travel by night . . . was a welfare question of the greatest importance, particularly for our ponies. It was clear that the only right thing was to rest during the warmest hours of the day – TG].

We broke camp today at 8 o'clock [p.m.] and at first all went well. But then the snow became soft, our horses sank in and it was only with the greatest exertion that our caravan put one little Norwegian mile (10 km) behind it. The only pair of snow-shoes we had with us on this trip was left by mistake at the depot this morning, and on arrival [in camp] I was given the task of getting them. The skis slid splendidly and the miles disappeared like smoke. [Gran has gone back for the snow-shoes – he volunteered good-naturedly – certainly his expertise on skis is useful – RFS]. It is 20+ degrees of frost.[9]

3 February
As I've said, night is turned into day. But there is not a great deal of difference. We broke camp at midnight; strangely the going was somewhat better, and the first kilometres were covered in a short time. We gave the horses a rest when we had gone 10 km. Towards morning the going got heavier and heavier, the horses sank in, and finally we came to a place where it became necessary to lead the horses several hundred metres without their loads and ourselves drag the sledges onto firmer ground. [The only set of snow-shoes was then put on to Bowers' big pony and he went back and drew the stranded sledges out (A CG). If we had more of these shoes we could certainly put them on seven out of eight of our ponies. . . . It is trying to feel that so great a help to our work has been left behind at the station – RFS]. We made camp after this manoeuvre. During the march tonight the temperature was –17 °C, but it was calm and clear and really pleasant to move about.

4 February
Onwards we go in brilliant midnight sunshine and –15 °C. Our little caravan – the world's most southerly – has covered 18 km today. The going is better and the horses no longer sink in up to their hocks.

5 February
For the first time we have been stopped by bad weather and have had to spend the night in our sleeping bags. The weather has not been so

9 i.e. below –20 °C.

bad that people could not venture out, but the difficulties of getting the dogs and horses going were so great that striking camp would not have paid.

Sunday morning – the primus roars so loudly that one can hardly hear the tent flapping. The temperature has risen sharply; just at this moment there are only a few degrees of frost and it feels like summer in the tent. Our horses and dogs seem to take the snow-storm quite calmly; the horses turn their backs to the weather and the dogs let themselves be snowed in. At the moment you can hardly see them.

We have adopted a certain routine. At nine in the evening comes a whistle from Scott's tent.[10] This means 'strike camp' and we crawl out of our sacks. Normally in the evening the temperature begins to drop and we shiver as we go about our respective jobs. Oates feeds the horses, Keohane cooks, and I tidy up the tent.[11] Our toilet does not worry us much, since dressing consists only of putting on our windcheaters. We shall soon begin to sleep in them too. We call breakfast 'the starting meal', so as not to mix up time, and in our tent it consists of pemmican,[12] biscuits, and tea. It tastes delicious. Then we pack up the sledges and set out at midnight for our next stop, 'lunch camp'.

On the march we cover about 3 km an hour and keep going about three hours before giving the horses a rest. Forde and Cherry, who have the lightest horses, lead when the snow is soft; Bowers when it is hard. I faithfully bring up the rear with 'Weary Willy' who keeps his own steady, funereal pace. When we fall too far behind, I use a ski stick as a whip and spur, and that helps a bit. The dogs are driven from camp an hour after us, and normally catch up after we have covered about 9 km. Then we bivouac and eat lunch (pemmican and biscuits) for one hour, and again set off for another 9 km march over this endless snow plain, which our predecessors honoured with the title Great Barrier. Early in the morning, Scott gives the signal to make camp. This takes place as a drill. We form up in two columns – in the first, Bowers and Evans to the left, and Cherry and Forde to the right; in the second column, Scott and Oates swing to the right, Keohane and I to the left. A line is stretched between our sledges to which the horses are made fast after they have rolled enough. Keohane and I erect the tent and start preparing the food, while Oates feeds the animals. Our 'supper' is a light meal. A sort of porridge, cocoa, and of course biscuits. The daily ration also includes a piece of chocolate.

The weather, which looked fairly bright this morning, deteriorated

10 Scott shared with Wilson, Meares, and Cherry-Garrard.

11 Oates, Keohane, and Gran shared another tent.

12 A ration of lean meat dried, pounded fine, mixed with melted fat and solidified in a cake.

considerably during the day, and now a howling snow-storm rages from the west. Have spent the day in the sleeping bags. Fed the horses at six this evening. It is bad for them but could well be worse.

6 February

The bad weather continues. The temperature has fallen, for the wind has backed to the south. The sleeping bag is our only refuge.

(*Later*) Oates and I have just been out to feed the horses – a job that took both the colour and feeling from our hands. Snow roars and rages over the icy waste. The poor horses are having a hard time and are so frozen they can hardly eat. I had a wonderful dream today. I was home, it was spring, and I was in a lovely garden; the cherry trees were in full bloom and I climbed one laden with blossoms. The white petals rained down and soon the meadow was white beneath me. I climbed higher – the mild spring breeze whirled the petals away over the green fields, over the silvery branches, out towards the fjord which lay glittering and blue. I reached the top, but the branch snapped and I tumbled down into the soft white bed of flowers. I wakened, the white flowers were snow. The tent door had blown open and we were exposed to the weather. Spring it was indeed!

7 February

During the night and morning the wind has blown itself out and the sun is shining with all its might over the snowy plateau. The blue of the Western Mountains [west of McMurdo Sound] can be seen in the distance beyond White Island, and sunlit clouds throw shadows over the steep, icy slopes. A large snow-drift has formed round the tents, and this morning we had a struggle to dig out the sledges. It's done now and we are ready to go.

(*A little later*) A storm of drift snow is on the rampage again. I wonder whether we shall get away tonight. It begins to look as though there will be good use for the sleeping bags.

(*9 p.m.*) At last it looks as if we are getting away. Weather fine again and we are preparing to strike camp. We have been here a long time – fully 84 hours.

8 February

After a night's march in sunshine and with excellent going, we have come 18 km farther south. True, it is not that far, but then our horses are really poor. [In my mind a firm conviction grew that the ponies would never manage to haul the heavy sledges after such a night. Fortunately my pessimism was put to shame (TG). Some of these ponies were very poor material. . . . Oates who was in charge of them started with a very great handicap – A CG]. The bearing from our last camp has been due south.

9 February

The southward trek is going well; tonight, in 19 °C of frost, midnight sun, and snow, 19 km were covered. It felt pretty chilly on the face at first, but after lunch it stopped snowing. Inside the tent it is almost like summer and, for once, possible to write sitting outside the sleeping bag. The horses also seem to enjoy the sun; even 'Blücher',[13] who looks like a question mark with a sack over his hind quarters and back, appears to look with more favour upon his surroundings.

(*11 at night*) The weather is threatening; overcast with a bitter wind. My sleep is disturbed by wild dreams – 'sleeping-bag delirium'.

10 February

It was bleak and horrid to begin with on the march tonight. Bad weather threatened and over Bluff Mountain,[14] with which we are now level, there were dark banks of cloud while Erebus and Terror lay wreathed in fog behind us. But after some hours the skies cleared. I have just been repairing my *finnesko* which were beginning to fall apart; let's hope it is only me who is unlucky with his footwear. Covered 21 km.

11 February

According to our reckoning, we have covered 20 km. tonight and should therefore be at latitude 78°45′ S. Just now the effect of the sun is wonderful, for at midnight it is beginning to throw its last rays. It is not many degrees over the horizon now. The sky has been overcast tonight everywhere but in the south, where there is a belt of clear, golden light a few degrees high. It is as if we have wandered into a world of pure gold. We don't get much variety here; good weather or bad weather, that is all the change we get.

12 February

We have not quite crossed the 79th parallel but are not much short of it. One thing is nevertheless certain, that I have now come farther south than Borchgrevink[15] and am therefore the Norwegian who has been nearest the Pole – provided, that is, Amundsen hasn't pushed farther south on the other side of the continent.[16] 'Blossom', 'Jimmy Pigg' and

13 'Blücher' was Forde's pony.

14 Minna Bluff.

15 Carsten Borchgrevink, Leader of the *Southern Cross* expedition, 1898–1900.

16 In a footnote in the diary TG comments: "Before we left New Zealand we had received information that Amundsen was also going to attempt to reach the South Pole, and it was our belief that Amundsen had stationed *Fram* for the winter in the Weddell Sea."

'Blücher' are worn out and are to be sent back with their respective drivers, Teddy Evans, Keohane, and Forde. We others will continue southwards. [We now had with us the two teams of dogs, driven by Meares and Wilson, and five ponies. Scott with 'Nobby'. Oates with 'Punch'. Bowers with 'Uncle Bill'. Gran with 'Weary Willie'. Cherry-Garrard with 'Guts' – A CG]. Just now Teddy sang out from the tent, 'You are the Norwegian who has been farthest south'.[17] I naturally responded with a patriotic hurrah. In an hour we shall strike camp. [This is to be called the 'Bluff Camp' (off Minna Bluff) and should play an important part in the future – RFS].

The weather is bitter and during the day there was a good deal of drift, but now it is clearing up. Oates and I have moved to Bowers' tent; Cherry-Garrard has moved to Scott's. During the day a new plan has been worked out. When our goal is reached, Scott, Wilson, Meares and Cherry will return with the dogs on foot, while Bowers, Oates and I will lead the horses back. That is the plan now.

13 February

We bade farewell to those who are travelling back, and bad weather has descended on us out of the blue. Scott and Cherry have taken refuge with us, for the dogs haven't yet reached us. So we are five in the tent. [Probably this was the time when Scott first thought of taking a five-man party to the Pole – A CG]. Tonight we have marched about nine miles south, so we should be at 79°05′S. It blew and at first it was difficult to prevent our hands freezing stiff. The snow has thickened so much that we can no longer maintain our course. We have built the horses a snow wall and they are standing behind it fairly snug.

(*11 at night*) The bad weather ended during the night and we are now ready to go, after an unexpectedly pleasant break. The dogs arrived at nine this evening.

14 February

We started as usual about midnight; the weather was splendid, but the going unspeakably heavy after the night's snow-fall. 'Willy' has the heaviest load and, heavy as he is himself, has completely worn himself out in the snow-drifts; in the end neither kick nor blow would shift him. It was painful to see him. His eyes had lost their sparkle and there were flecks of foam at the mouth. Then he fell and stayed down.

17 In fact, Amundsen had already been farther south on his first depot-laying journey from 'Framheim'.

Meanwhile Meares had come up with the dogs. He stopped 50 yards away. He hadn't seen that the horse had fallen but understood that something was wrong. But he soon knew what it was. The pack of dogs descended upon us like wild animals. I ran towards them but couldn't halt their attack. The whole thing happened so quickly, and before 'Willy' could catch his breath the beasts were on him. The horse fought desperately and so did we, but the snow was too deep for 'Willy' to lash out and our efforts seemed fruitless. It was a fearful fight – Meares, 'Willy', and I against the 13 wild dogs. I feared for a time that poor 'Willy' would be savaged. They went for his stomach, but after Meares had broken his iron-tipped brake pole and I my ski stick on the dogs, we managed to get the horse away from the pack. He was bloody and looked pretty bad, and I expected him to fall again at any moment. Scott had bivouacked half a mile to the south and I took the horse slowly over there. Scott took the incident calmly. [Gran did his best, breaking his ski stick. . . . The incident is deplorable and the blame widespread. I find W.W.'s load was much heavier than the others. I blame myself for not supervising these matters more effectively and for allowing W.W. to get so far behind – RFS].

After lunch Scott, Wilson, Bowers, Cherry and I went to fetch my sledge. Then we struck camp and I had a reduced load, for 'Willy' clearly needed rest, and after only one mile we made camp again. I built 'Willy' a big, tight snow wall. He has had a feed of warm, cooked oats and, in the circumstances, he seems to be feeling better. Sunshine, but cold. Minimum tonight, –21 °C.

15 February

The horses are beginning to tire and we have not advanced more than 12 km. The snow was soft. At the lunch bivouac we depoted [sic] a bale of fodder. The weather has been splendid all night – midnight sun and still. We also registered our lowest temperature, –26½ °C. I have just repaired my *finnesko*. They were covered with snow and ice, and it was a cold job.

16 February

The farthest point south I shall come this journey. 'Willy' can do no more and thus my fate is sealed. The others are continuing a half-day's march south to lay down a depot, and thereafter will return here tomorrow. Our march tonight was pretty chilly with headwind and 28 °C of frost. My fingers froze during the preparation of lunch, and the whole meal passed before I could bring them back to life again. During the march everybody's ears froze, even Bowers' and he therefore had to exchange his pride, the green hat, for a woollen cap. 'Willy' kept up with us until lunch and we managed 9 km, but afterwards he began to slow down. For that matter the other horses are not much to shout about. [Oates proposed to Scott that the animal ('Weary Willie') should be killed and that we should push on with the other ponies, but Scott rejected this suggestion. He had, as he himself put it, felt quite sick on account of the animal's sufferings. Even though Oates was of course a highly disciplined officer, he felt obliged on this occasion to press his views on his chief: 'Sir, I'm afraid you'll come to regret not taking my advice.' 'Regret it or not,' replied Scott, 'I have taken my decision, as a Christian gentleman.' As will become clear later from our story, it was only 21 km south of 'One Ton Depot' that Scott and his companions met death the following year, homeward bound from the South Pole – TG].

A fresh breeze is now blowing from the west, but the temperature has risen to –18 °C. It is sunny.

17 February

It was my farthest point south but the others haven't got farther either, for a snow-storm set in and ruled out a further march. Before supper we depoted out gear; it wasn't quite where we had planned it to be.[18] I am rather disappointed and foresee difficulties with the complicated transport arrangements. Of one thing I am certain, that we shall need luck if we are to reach the Pole next year.

It is –24 °C, cloudy and rather horrid. Tonight we head north again in two teams; Bowers, Oates, and I with the horses, Scott, Wilson, Meares, and Cherry with the dogs. Naturally we shall not be able to keep up; the dogs will outstrip us at once.

18 February

We bade farewell to our most southerly camp in 25 °C of frost, a fresh breeze, and a bad weather sun with a 'snow bow'. I had two horses, Scott's, a splendid animal,[19] and my own 'Willy'. 'Willy' was on the tow and took to it well. After half an hour's march the snow thickened so much that we could see only a few yards. Strangely enough the old horse tracks were still visible, and with their help we were able to keep going. The dog party left camp after us but overtook us in an hour, sweeping past to disappear into the fog. The drift worsened. We passed our 14th [outward] camp site and continued on, until we reached a fodder depot 6 km farther north. After we had trudged on another 5 km we suddenly saw something through the fog. It was the dog party's

18 It was known as 'One Ton Depot' (79°29′S) from the quantity of stores left.
19 Named 'Nobby'.

tent; they had bivouacked for lunch. Scott came to meet us; he was delighted with our progress in the thick snowfall. When we came up to the tent, they were ready to set off again and we parted a second time to the accompaniment of the baying of the hounds. We continued to this depot where we camped. It is cold and nasty.

(*9 p.m.*) We shall start an hour earlier today at 11 p.m. The weather is better. During the night[20] I had a frightful pain in my right foot. Hope it sorts itself out when I have been going a bit.

[Oates was a completely closed book to me until I shared camp life with him. . . . I (had) gained the impression that I did not find grace in his eyes. . . . On the return journey from 'One Ton Depot' Oates told me straight out that what he had against me was not personal; it was just that I was a foreigner. With all his heart he hated all foreigners, because all foreigners hated England. The rest of the world led by Germany were just waiting to attack his Motherland, and destroy it if they could. I was about to reply when Bowers quickly intervened: 'Could be something in what you say, Oates, but all the same I wager what you will that Gran would be with us if England is forced into war through no fault of her own.' 'Would you?', asked Oates. 'Of course,' I replied, and the next instant he grasped my hand. From this moment the closed book opened, and Oates and I became the best of friends – TG].

19 February

The night was fine, about 23 °C of frost but still. These days we have the wind at our backs, so if it blows we don't feel it much. It was clear and the midnight sun shed its last golden rays. I maintain station at the rear behind 'Willy' to make sure he is not being dragged[21] by the other horse. After we had covered 18 km, 'Willy' was tired. Blows could not move him and we had to make camp – a pity, for our old camp site, with shelter walls for the horses, was only 1 km away. This wall business takes us hours. We have only one spade and five walls to build.

(*Evening*) When we awoke this evening, we found that two of the horses had got loose and among other things had ransacked our store of biscuits. But they weren't at it long, so it hasn't caused too much of a problem. The weather is good, overcast but quite calm.

20 February

I have become an invalid. I can just move but that is all. It is not my instep as I thought, but my knee which is the trouble. I probably got

20 i.e. sleeping hours.
21 i.e. made to go too fast.

a bang during the attack by the dogs. Since that day it has just been uncomfortable, but today I really began to feel the pain. If this doesn't pass, it will be a tough return journey. I don't know whether it is water on the knee or just a swelling, but it's decidedly unpleasant. Tonight we covered 16 km and have bivouacked at our old camp site, where we parted from Teddy Evans.

21 February
The summer has gone; the midnight sun has left the scene and the air is heavy with tidings of bad weather. Autumn has arrived, and winter with hard weather and cold is just round the corner. We set off tonight in calm, snow-laden air, and soon the snow flakes began to fall gently, just as at home. In between times it cleared up and a pink blush of sunshine lay over the plain. Towards morning the bad weather arrived in earnest and dark banks of cloud piled up above us. The south wind came hunting over the plain, but it was behind us, thank God!, and the horses (including 'Willy') nearly trotted to keep warm. My leg was stiff but better, and I kept up well. We bivouacked at six this morning after covering 31 km. We passed several of our old camps which, with their wind-blown and snowed-down walls, looked for all the world like forgotten churchyards. It is my week as cook.

22 February
We overslept yesterday evening and it was well past midnight before we set off. The horses went well today too and by nine this morning we had covered 29 km. On our arrival at our 8th [outward] camp we caught sight of a snow cairn with a flag about a mile to the north. We went on and found a bale of fodder on the cairn with a note, signed 'T.E.'[22] containing the sad but easily divined tidings that one of the horses had died and was buried here on the 17th – that is five days ago. 'Blossom' had ended her South Polar venture. Oates and I had a bet a day or two ago that 'Blücher' would be dead by the 19th. If he dies, Oates will win a biscuit. We hadn't thought about 'Blossom', but we were certain about 'Blücher' and still are. No, our horses are nothing to boast about; Meares was badly taken in when he bought them in Siberia.

23 February
Our horses were pretty exhausted tonight after the preceding day's long march, and we therefore made camp at five this morning after covering 25 km. These past few days we have built the horses walls *before* breakfast – pleasant for the horses but not for us. When we have just finished

22 Teddy Evans.

building a couple of the walls and are beginning the third or fourth, it often happens that we hear a crash. A horse has knocked down one of the walls, either by tramping too near it or by chewing and banging at it. 'Weary Willy' is a real master at this. It is now almost certain that 'Blücher' is no more; anyhow it all points that way. I have therefore given Oates the biscuit. We presume 'Blücher' died on the 14th, after the snow-storm that kept Scott and Cherry imprisoned in our tent. A new bet has been laid – that 'Jimmy Pigg' has also gone. Oates is the pessimist this time as well. [The soldier takes a gloomy view of everything, but I've come to see that this is a characteristic of him. In spite of it he pays every attention to the weaker horses – RFS].

It was a marvellously calm night with wonderful colour changes in the evening, night and morning. Towards morning it clouded over and now looks like snow.

24th February

With the exception of the first few hours, the march tonight took place in thick fog – by 4 a.m. it became so dense that we could not see and therefore had to bivouac after covering 20 km. It was heavy going for us and the horses. By 7 a.m. it cleared up and now the sun streams warm into the tent where we lie in our sleeping bags. The fodder is nearly all used up.

25 February

We have made camp about 18 km from 'Safety Camp' after covering 20 km. At first it was heavy going for the horses, but towards the end it improved considerably. It has been hazy all night and only now can we see our surroundings. Towards Cape Crozier we can make out a camp with two tents. At this very moment they are striking camp. We don't know which of our people they are, nor yet where they are making for – but perhaps to 'Corner Camp'.

(*'Safety Camp', 12 midnight*) Arrived here, great surprise: *Amundsen has landed 400* [23] *geographical miles east of us with 8 men and 119 dogs.* More of this tomorrow – I am too astonished to write now.

26 February

Yes, it was as I say a great surprise to hear that Amundsen had landed 400 miles east of us in the Bay of Whales. I had only a brief account of the event yesterday evening from Meares. He came out of his tent in his pants, and when he caught sight of me shouted: 'Good news for you, Gran! Amundsen landed 400 miles east of us with 8 men and 119 dogs.'

23 Actually 350 geographical miles

I felt as if the glacier had opened under me and a thousand thoughts rushed into my head. Was I to compete with my own compatriots, with my own flag? No, it was not pleasant to contemplate.

Terra Nova had sailed along the barrier towards Edward VII Land and had arrived at a point somewhat east of Cape Colbeck. But they found no place to land, and the vessel therefore had to set course back towards the Bay of Whales. It was thus that the historic meeting between *Fram* and *Terra Nova* occurred. Amundsen invited Campbell to remain,[24] but Campbell would not and decided to head northwards to Robertson Bay, near Cape Adare. Amundsen had built his hut 2 km in on the ice shelf, and was going to spend the winter there and strike for the Pole at the same time as us. I believe, from what I have seen, that Amundsen's chances are better than ours. First, he is one degree [of latitude] further south than we are and, secondly, his speed is far superior to ours, since our horses are not first class. *If we reach the Pole, then Amundsen will reach the Pole and weeks earlier.* Our prospects are thus not exactly promising. The only thing that can save Scott is if an accident happens to Amundsen.

Terra Nova could not get farther than [Erebus] Glacier Tongue. From there a ski party had gone up to the *Discovery* hut, deposited the mail, and brought mine back. I hear Scott took calmly the news about Amundsen, but sees clearly the big danger. [The proper as well as the wiser course for us is to proceed exactly as though this had not happened. . . . There is no doubt that Amundsen's plan is a very serious menace to ours. . . . I never thought he could have got so many dogs safely to the ice. His plan for running them seems excellent. But above and beyond all he can start his journey early in the season – an impossible condition with ponies – RFS]. When we arrived at 'Safety Camp' last night, we found just a tent and some dogs snowed-in. Wilson and Meares were the only ones left in camp; the others had set course for 'Corner Camp'. So that was the camp we had seen! Evans' party, as we more or less knew, had a fearful return journey. 'Blücher' died first, then 'Blossom', but 'Jimmy Pigg' had survived and was now with Scott on the way to 'Corner Camp'.

27 February

Thick snow-storm today; we can hardly find the way to the horses, although they are just a few steps from the tent. I have just been down there with them; the snow lies upon them like a sheet of ice. Poor animals, they do have a rough time. But luckily we got here before the bad weather broke upon us. We came with empty sledges without

24 i.e. to make his base there.

any provisions for the horses. What on earth would have happened if we had been held up some days? We have spent the greater part of the day in the sleeping bags. In other words, time to let our thoughts go free. They have changeable weather at home and in the east, where Amundsen is. Today at home they are probably holding the *langlauf*[25] competition, but at Holmenkollen this year Bjaaland[26] and Gran are not appearing; no, these two are training for a longer *lauf* [run], the most southerly and not the most northerly in the world.

28 February

Poor 'Willy' lies fighting death outside the tent. We cannot help him; we have only been able to build a snow wall for protection against the wind, which hunts icily over the Barrier. Scott, Cherry and Crean arrived at lunchtime at 'Safety Camp', and orders were given for a general break-up and a move to the *Discovery* hut. The dogs[27] started at 4 p.m. and we an hour later with the horses. Poor animals, the storm has played havoc with them. We could hardly recognize them, they were so thin and under-nourished. We had only gone 5 km when 'Willy' fell, and it was absolutely impossible to get him to his feet again. We made camp and built a massive wall round 'Willy'. At supper we spoke about Amundsen. Scott is clearly very ambitious; this is natural, but he tries to hide it.

At this very moment I can hear 'Willy' make a vain attempt to get up. Poor animal, he is fighting hard for his life.

1 March

Luck does not seem to be with Scott in his plans; everything seems to be going against us. 'Willy' died this morning; we knew it had to happen but had no inkling what the rest of the day was to bring us.

Our party is split up and we seemed like a defeated army – dispirited and inconsolable. I am now in the 'gap' in the dog-party's tent. [Cherry-Garrard and Crean went on whilst Oates and Gran stayed with me – RFS]. Wilson and Meares are in the *Discovery* hut. When we turned out at six this morning, 'Willy' was dead. Scott, Oates, and I harnessed ourselves to the sledge and took off towards the sea. We followed the horse and dog parties' tracks, and were dismayed to find these led to the edge of a cliff straight down into the sea. The sea ice had moved off seawards and large chunks of the Barrier had broken off. It was not at all nice. Did our people reach safety before the ice broke off?

25 German: cross-country skiing.
26 Olav Bjaaland, a member of Amundsen's party and an expert skier.
27 Driven by Wilson and Meares.

5

Western geological party, Granite Harbour, Christmas Day 1911, (left to right) Forde, Debenham, Gran, Taylor

6
Mount Gran (2235m) to the west of Granite Harbour, December 1911

7
Camp on sea ice, Granite Harbour, December 1911

8
Stone hut at Granite Harbour, December 1911

9
Forde cooking on western geological journey, December 1911

10
T.Griffith Taylor on western geological journey, December 1911

11
Frank Debenham

We followed the coastline eastwards one mile in from the Barrier, but within a short time we were forced to move farther inwards, for wherever we went the ice began to crack. When we reached the slopes up towards Castle Rock, Scott and Oates bivouacked while I pushed on up to 'Safety Camp' on skis with a note to Evans,[28] who was not yet back from 'Corner Camp'. On the way back to the tent I saw two dots up on the mountain side at Pram Point [north-east of Cape Armitage]. They were moving in the direction of the tent, and I understood they must be some of our people. At last I recognized them – they were Meares and Wilson.

These two had just reached land the previous night, when the ice had broken up. From the heights round The Gap they had been able through a telescope to make out a party with horses in wild flight from floe to floe. Scott was very worried and rushed out of the tent to scan the horizon with a telescope. Suddenly he caught sight of something in the direction of 'Fodder Camp' [near the ice front]. It moved and in an instant I got my skis on. This 'something' turned out to be Crean. He was tired and looked done in, and I was nearly afraid to ask about the party's fate. I ask carefully and am answered robustly, 'All right, Sir'. This answer was encouraging in a way, but unfortunately it was clear, after some probing, that the situation was not quite all right. They[29] had camped in the evening on solid sea ice, and the horses were quite exhausted after the storm. After a few hours' sleep they discovered by accident that Cherry's pony had gone through the ice and that they themselves were drifting. There then began a desperate flight westwards from floe to floe towards White Island. As I said, they managed to reach firm ice. Then Crean had made off in the direction of the spot where I had found him.

We struggled on towards the tent beneath the slopes of Castle Rock. After our arrival it was decided that Scott, Oates, and Crean should go to the help of the horse party, while Wilson, Meares, and I should go to the hut. Crean has been given my sleeping bag, and Wilson and I will change about.

28 Warning him about the ice.
29 i.e. Bowers, Cherry-Garrard, and Crean.

Hut Point

2 March

Turned out in the twilight at one tonight and skied down the slopes to the hut. My aim was simply to make time pass without completely freezing up from the cold, and I trudged up and down between the walls. There were plenty of biscuits in the hut, and while I continued my parade up and down I tried to eat but without much progress because my teeth were chattering so much. I also tried to sing myself warm; the notes sounded good in this ice-ridden hut. I even dared to try grand opera. When the performance was over, I managed to get a fire going in an iron box, and got a sardine tin warmed up and my frozen hands moving again. In short, it was not a particularly agreeable night, and involuntarily my mind went back to Sir Ernest's description of his night in this hut about two years ago.[1] When I heard Shackleton's lecture at the Geographical Society at home, I had no idea I was to go through the same experience so soon.

At 7 a.m. I went up to the camp again and routed them out for breakfast. Then we went back down to the hut. We partitioned an area off as a sort of room and built a fireplace of loose bricks. Then back to fetch the dogs and the tent.

We have now had supper. It was cooked on our home-made fireplace, and the hut is full of smoke.

3 March

I am sitting writing in the glow from our fireplace. It is midnight and soon my turn in the sleeping bag. It will soon be 24 hours since I slept, and it is difficult to keep awake. It is no use trying to rest outside the sleeping bag – you freeze at once. I tried with the tent cover, but it just made my teeth chatter.

1 28 February 1909.

4 March
After breakfast we went up to The Gap to fetch two dogs each. Half a gale was blowing, and it was a heavy job to get the animals down to the hut. It was worst for Wilson for he was dragged along like the wind. We had just returned to the hut, when we caught sight of two people struggling down from Crater Hill. It turned out to be Teddy Evans and Atkinson. They had bivouacked beneath Castle Rock and all was well with them; 'Jimmy Pigg' was in the best of health. They knew nothing of the fate of the other party. They moved on again after lunch. Dr Wilson accompanied them part of the way. Tonight a storm with drift and snow. According to Evans' story, the Barrier must be in a dreadful state with stretches of open water right up to 'Willy's' grave. The 'Fodder Depot'[2] has presumably vanished; let's hope the same won't happen to 'Safety Camp'.

5 March
After breakfast, at ten o'clock, we left the hut and went up to the dogs, and then left to meet Teddy Evans' party. According to the plan they were meant to bivouac on the heights between Crater Hill and Castle Rock, but no tent was visible up there. A fierce wind was blowing and it was really foul. Suddenly we saw a black dot far away on the snow slope which turned out to be Atkinson. He told us the party had been deflected from its course but was alright, although only Scott's horse was alive. When Scott came to the rescue of the horse party he gave orders to leave the horses, which were on drift ice. This was done and the party bivouacked a good step in on the Barrier. The next morning they found that the horses had drifted in a short distance to the west, and they tried to get them over to firm ice. This had nearly succeeded when two of the animals jumped the wrong way and fell in. Atkinson added that Scott and Evans were resting beneath Castle Rock and would be very grateful for 'help with the tow'. I accompanied Atkinson, while Meares and Wilson returned. I took lunch in Scott's tent, and then skied to 'Safety Camp' for provisions. The going was heavy, and I did not return until midnight. Scott had gone over to the hut and only Teddy, Oates and Keohane were back.

6 March
For the first time for ages the depot party is reassembled; all 12 are now in the *Discovery* hut. We broke camp at Castle Rock at nine this morning. All four pulled the sledges to the top, and then Oates and Keohane went down to fetch the horses. Teddy and I continued with

2 Close to the old ice front.

a light sledge which had been hauled up the day before. We had not gone far before the people from the hut came to meet us. There was a snow-storm up on the plateau, but Dr Wilson knew the ground and led the way. It was like a hurricane on the slopes above the hut, and slippery too. After some delay we arrived at the hut, frozen and hungry. Inside it is dark and unpleasant; the fireplace smokes almost unbearably. Well, this is a real 'retreat from Moscow'.

This afternoon Oates and Meares constructed a blubber stove which was demonstrated tonight with great success. Dr Wilson fried seal liver for supper and, thanks to his culinary skill, it tasted excellent. [Luck had not been with us on this depot journey – that's for sure – and the spirits of the men inside the four bare walls were not of the highest. Naturally enough, of us all Scott was the one with the greatest cause to be discouraged, but in fact he tried in every way to cheer us up. . . . All things considered, it was the loss of the ponies that worried him most. His thoughts and feelings about Amundsen he kept to himself, at any rate in my hearing. . . . Neither Scott nor Wilson could have any decided view on whether our stay at *Discovery* hut would be long or short, even with their extensive knowledge of (ice) conditions at Hut Point and McMurdo Sound. But everything pointed to the likelihood that many weeks would pass before the sea ice would be strong enough for the homeward trek to Cape Evans (TG). One way and another we shall manage to be very comfortable during our stay here, and already we can regard it as a temporary home – RFS].

7 March

After breakfast Wilson, Cherry, Crean, Forde, Keohane, and I went off hunting seals. We went over the plain and down the slopes to Pram Point. The seals are swarming about in the pack ice, and the slaughter began immediately. After a couple of hours we were bathed in blood and reeked. The weather was excellent but cold, and our fingers froze when we pulled them out of the innards of our bloody victims. As we made our way back by the same route, we were really heavily laden and arrived famished at the hut at 6 p.m. Evans, Bowers, Meares, Atkinson, Keohane, and I leave in the morning on a three-day sledge and ski trip to fetch Bowers' tent which was left behind.

8 March

We started at eight this morning from the hut, and by the time we had reached the abandoned tent the shades of night had spread over the ice field, while Erebus and the Western Mountains still lay bathed in the snow's pinkish hue.

9 March
Arrived beneath the slopes of Castle Rock after trudging heavily laden all day on skis. The weather has been splendid but cold. Some of the party began to tire towards the end, and it was decided for a change to cover the last few kilometres on foot. The consequence for me was that some of my toes froze. Now I am lying in the sleeping bag, my teeth chattering, biting back the pain. It is overcast and looks like snow. Lunch bivouac at the 'Fodder Depot' – so it wasn't swallowed up by the sea.

10 March
We are sitting round the fire in the hut once more, and it feels good, for the day has been pretty rough. It was a long time before I slept in the night; the pain in my feet took hours to disappear. But when I once got off I slept very well, indifferent to the temperature which was down to 25 °C below. We struck camp at one this morning. A savage wind sprang up during the march, and when we got to the top of Ski Hill[3] it nearly froze the marrow in our bones. We unloaded [and left] our sledges at this point, since we were only taking essentials downhill. We had to bind 12 pairs of skis to the sledges, using bare hands! God knows, there will be nail biting after this job. In the inhabited part of the hut some striking improvements have been made. The stove has been rebuilt and moved out into the middle of the floor, and other parts of the hut have been tidied up. [(The sledge party) had thoroughly enjoyed their trip and the pulling on ski – RFS].

11 March
We have had to dry our clothes and gear at the fire today. Outside there is a foul wind blowing and driving snow. The minimum night temperature was 20 °C of frost. We are all lying in our sleeping bags and I am close to the stove, which decided to have a smoking fit this afternoon. Oates and I have tried to construct acetylene lamps. Titus has not yet tried his. I have; mine blew up and nearly killed Meares, covered me with carbide, and created alarm and despondency in the hut. Perhaps Titus will lose courage. If his blows up, the hut goes with it.

12 March
Foul weather! Our daily fare consists of seal; in the morning in the form of stew, in the evening fried in butter. Both taste splendid. In addition we have cocoa and biscuits from the old *Discovery* days. We have tea for

3 Ski Slope, between Arrival Heights and Hut Point.

lunch and plasmon biscuits from Shackleton's left-over stores. Other old provisions include some tins of Danish butter, peas, and salt meat. The *Terra Nova* people brought up dozens of sardine tins, milk, and some marmalade. It appears these are only for special occasions. Lunch tastes marvellous; the mouth positively waters at the warmed-up plasmon biscuits and a little butter. The wind is howling even louder today in this already windy corner. We find some ten-year-old reading matter and bury our noses in it.

13 March

The foul weather continued throughout the night, and the day has passed with hurricane-force squalls from the southeast. The sea has been blown all the way here to Hut Bay,[4] and the spray is drifting well beyond [Hut] point. [Our animals were sheltered and cozy on a sort of verandah on the south side of the hut – TG]. Spent the day eating, reading, and eating again. Oates and Dr Wilson have continued their work with the 'wonder lamp'; I have offered my assistance but they merely look at each other and laugh. That's all the thanks you get when you want to give good advice.

14 March

The western party[5] have arrived; they came in this afternoon clean and white compared with us. However, their purity won't last long here in the hut. They have had an excellent trip, with fine weather, and they were only halted by the storm in the last few days. They came along the Barrier past the Dailey Islands. They looked pretty good but their boots were in a pitiful condiiton. They had hardly used their *finnesko*. I have a spot of leg cramp.

15 March

I can only hope that 15 March 1912 will be more encouraging than this day has been. My leg cramp was so bad this morning that, after hauling a sledge up to the plateau, I simply fell and couldn't get up. The team consisting of Taylor, T. Evans, Wright, and Debenham halted and tried massage. It did not help much, but after a while I struggled to my feet and with much toil and effort dragged myself here and turned into my sleeping bag feeling downcast both in body and in spirit. After lunch I washed up pots and pans, a measure that had become really necessary. In

4 i.e. the small cove below the hut was ice-free.

5 Comprising Griffith Taylor, Debenham, Wright, and PO Evans.

the early evening the other hut dwellers returned; they had been on a seal-hunting trip to Pram Point and slain 11. I have had a medical examination but there was nothing to see, and my symptoms were attributed to ordinary cramp caused by too little exercise![6]

16 March

Eight men[7] went off to 'Corner Camp' [with supplies] today, and at the same time I made for Pram Point. But I couldn't keep up – I had to go at a snail's pace and was several times on the point of giving up. Luckily the weather was splendid, so I could take it easy. The journey back was better, although I had a heavier load – the skis I had left there on 1 March and two strips of blubber. When I got to the top and it was all downhill to Ski Hill, I laid the blubber on the skis and myself flat on my stomach on top. I careered off at full speed on the sheer ice and down I went like a streak of lightning. I was back at the hut by 5 p.m. having used six hours for 40 km. What a speed! The sledge party reached Pram Point this morning, using the route taken by Wilson, Meares, and me. I saw them bivouac on the Barrier, strike camp, and continue on skis in the direction of 'Safety Camp'.

17 March

The wind that got up from the north in the evening kept up in the night and towards dawn backed to the west. But the weather was good enough to go out and fetch blubber. My legs are much better and I took only three hours to make the whole trip. True, I shortened the distance somewhat by cutting along the ridge down towards The Gap, but on the return journey I carried about 10 lb.

18 March

The weather has changed from a light, fine snow shower to a hurricane-force snow-storm. What devil's weather it is!

19 March

Sunday and vile weather. The wind god seems to love this hut, despite the cross on its cornerstone.[8] How grateful we are to be here! The people out on the Barrier must be having a terribly rough time. Tonight 24 °C of frost and stormy. We are sitting round the stove philosophizing.

6 *See* p.16.

7 Lieutenant Evans, Bowers, Oates, Atkinson, Wright, Cherry-Garrard, Crean, and Forde.

8 In memory of Able Seaman G.T. Vince RN, of the *Discovery* expedition, who died accidentally, 11 March 1902.

This blubber stove is made up of two oil cans in which bricks are placed. It burns splendidly and warms the proximity pretty well.

20 March
Today started with a shift to fine weather, and I made a trip over to Pram Point. While I was away, the others had caught two seals close to the hut; they had been driven in on a floe on the north side of the point. PO Evans and Keohane have put together a new cubicle in the main part of the hut. The good weather didn't last long; now it's overcast and a real storm from the south is blowing up. The waves are white and break far into the ice. In these conditions there is not much chance of new ice forming.

21 March
I am lying writing in the glimmer of a blubber lamp I have patented myself. It is ridiculously simple and consists merely of a cube of blubber with a piece of wax stuck into it. It functions well and has achieved general recognition. Again a terrific storm tonight. The sea came in over the ice, and the hut and the poor dogs simply froze fast where they lay. Towards the morning hours we went out and decided that to save their lives they must be allowed to run loose, and we therefore let them slip. After breakfast I built a snow wall for the dogs and took over housekeeping. Deb[enham] and I have long thought it would be nice to join forces and travel west next summer. I shall talk to Scott about it – such a plan would obviate competition with my own flag.[9] During the night the storm swept one of the dogs away.

22 March
My discovery yesterday has prompted me to carry on my experiments in the service of light; I have made a 'luxury lamp'. The container is a metal matchbox with a double burner and reflector. It functions splendidly. The main thing is to get the flame close to the oil. Dr Wilson accompanied me to The Gap today. He is a splendid fellow.[10]

23 March
The Barrier party have come back safe but frozen. It had been – 41 °C and they were very proud [of themselves]. [It seems that we might have grasped that these temperatures were lower than might have been expected in the middle of March quite near the open sea – A CG]. I met them when I went over to Pram Point this morning, and helped them

9 i.e. with Amundsen's expedition.
10 Gran evidently sought advice from Dr Wilson on this occasion. *See* p. 16.

the rest of the way down to the hut. As regards wind and weather, it had been better for them than for us in the hut and the going had also been good. They had used skis the whole time. They dried themselves at the fire this afternoon.

24 March

In a thick snow-fall Wilson and I went over to Pram Point this morning to fetch blubber. It was a pleasant trip, except that the lumps of blubber became slippery in the high temperature and difficult to manage. When we got back to the hut, it was snowing terrifically heavily with thick flakes, just like at home. The high temperature has caused everything to melt in the hut; it is dripping *über alles*[11], and nasty and wet on the floors. The temperature was +18 °F.

25 March

The 'melt' in the hut continues today too. When I shut my eyes and listen to the drops, my thoughts are carried involuntarily and with melancholy pleasure to a rainy day at home. It will be marvellous after such a long, long time once again to feel the rain in one's face.

26 March

Kept to the hut all day. The weather has been good, but even so most of us have spent Sunday reading indoors. Incidentally, apart from reading some years-old magazines, our thoughts mainly turn on food, food, food! Tonight we have had stew made from ten-year-old peas and seal liver. I have eaten about a litre of the stuff, and I can't say I feel really satisfied yet. Everyone tries to introduce variations, that is to say using the same ingredients in different ways. Wilson made a cheese-flour-butter pie for lunch; I made the coffee and, in honour of the day [Sunday], we had condensed milk. I have been deep in a wild adventure story all day, and now I am going to bed to read with an 'electric' lamp on the 'bedside table'. Our stove is my 'bedside table'. This life is quite interesting despite its monotony. Time goes unbelievably fast and that is the main thing really.

27 March

New ice is beginning to thicken in by the Barrier. Today I went to Pram Point to try it.

28 March

I wanted to make something ingenious today. As ingredients I had

11 German: everywhere.

pemmican, peas, flour, butter, and coffee, so its success or failure depended on my culinary skill. It was only a partial success and I was myself disappointed. Deb is making flapjacks for lunch. He is a splendid baker. At this moment I am in a rather unwashed state. So much so that I am dirtying the paper I am writing on. My clothing is soiled, sooty and a bit tattered. My beard and hair are rather long, and I don't believe anyone at home would recognize me. We all look pretty villainous.

29 March

On my way to Pram Point I accompanied [Lieutenant] Evans to the top of Observation Hill. A splendid view. This afternoon I went with Deb up to Castle Rock. I climbed to the summit – it was quite easy. It was an unusually nice trip; the weather good, calm, and mild, and from the top of Castle Rock an excellent view. Unfortunately, there didn't appear to be much ice to the north but open water more or less everywhere.

30 March

Storm this morning and I had to postpone my trip to Pram Point. Incidentally, there is only meat left now[12], and this is so deep-frozen that it has to be chopped up bit by bit with an axe. It is beginning to get dark early and even on a fine day we have to light up at 7 p.m.

31 March

I have spent the morning helping [Lieutenant] Evans to chop out a path in the lumpy ice down to the sea for our two horses. This is a sign of departure. Even though the wind was horribly cold, it was a job after my taste. It is a good thing there is plenty of food in the hut, for our imprisonment begins to seem long drawn out.

1 April

Keohane and I went over to Castle Rock this evening. Towards the north the ice now seems to be solid. Marvellous weather and 18 °C of frost.

2 April

There was a wonderful display tonight of Southern Lights. The sky to the southeast seemed full of organ pipes. I stood outside the hut for a long time and stared up towards the tongues of flame, and my thoughts flew home to days gone by. [Splendid aurora in the night; a bright band of light from SSW to ENE passing within 10° of the zenith with two waving spirals at the summit – RFS].

12 The pemmican was finished.

3 April

It has been a bitter cold day. [Lieutenant] Evans, some of the others, and I spent the whole day chopping away at the ice to make this path to the sea. I wonder whether Evans would not get on better by dividing the work out more evenly. It is blowing tonight and it looks like bad weather.

4 April

As forecast, the weather today was horrible, with drifting snow and gale-force winds, so we have spent the whole day in the hut. Seaman [PO] Evans is a jovial lad who improves on acquaintance. Wright, Teddy Evans, Atkinson, and I spent the afternoon yarning about everything under the sun. A surprise dish was served up tonight. Seal is splendid fried in butter, but fried in penguin fat, as it was tonight, it is dreadful. It was funny to see the different grimaces on the faces of those who had dipped their spoon in this 'pemmican'. Most of them gave the meal a miss – even Wilson, the founder of the feast. [It had a flavour like cod-liver oil and was not much appreciated – RFS].

5 April

Calm and clear tonight and the Southern Lights flicker; the temperature is down to –25 °C. The day's weather was splendid, and the sea is freezing over. We finished the path to the sea this morning. My diary was spattered with blubber oil today, and the first pages are scarcely legible.

6 April

Our stay here draws to a close, or so it seems. Scott declared this morning that he would try his luck the day after tomorrow. He, the western party, Bowers, Crean, Evans and I will proceed on foot; the day after, the dogs with Atkinson, Cherry and Meares; and on the third [day], the horses with Oates, Keohane and Forde. That is the plan, but the Lord alone knows whether it will come off.

7 April

The weather looks very threatening, so I doubt if we shall get away tomorrow. The temperature has risen to –12 °C, there is heavy overcast, and the wind is blowing hard from the southeast. It is already snowing a little. In the morning went over to Pram Point to fetch a spade. I went over the ice and on the way back found a fish frozen in with another little fish in its mouth. [It looks as though both small and large are caught (by the ice) when one is chasing the other – RFS].

8 April
Yes, just as I guessed, the plans fell through; bad weather has set in, the ice has broken up, and we are pretty crestfallen.

9 April
With luck this will be the last Sunday we spend in the hut. Tomorrow we shall make an attempt to reach Cape Evans.

10 April
Ill luck pursues us; a thick snow-fall put a stopper on our march this morning. This afternoon it cleared up a bit and Bosun [PO] Evans, Crean, and I went up to Castle Rock. A thick blanket of snow lies on the plateau. Tonight it is hazy but I believe tomorrow will bring fine weather and with it a step forward. Life is beginning to get rather monotonous; our provisions are dwindling and the high temperature has again brought a thaw to the hut. It is dripping and wet everywhere.

11 April
[Started from Hut Point 9 a.m. . . . Party consisted of self, Bowers, PO Evans, Taylor, one tent; (Lieut.) Evans, Gran, Crean, Debenham, and Wright, second tent. Left Wilson in charge at Hut Point with Meares, Forde, Keohane, Oates, Atkinson, and Cherry-Garrard – RFS]. Now ten o'clock. We have had to bivouac because we couldn't see in the thick snow. It is dark. Little Razorback [Island] is just behind us to the north.

12 April
Soon [will have] spent 24 hours here and they have been truly awful. I don't dare to take my boots off for fear I shall not get them back on when they stiffen. The sleeping bag is wet through and my teeth chatter as I lie writing this.

13 April
At last! Back at the hut. We arrived here at ten in the morning. It was like entering fairyland. Everything is in abundance here, the gas lights shine, the dynamo purrs, the bell rings, and the table groans under victuals calculated to make an explorer's mouth water. All is well and we have only lost one horse and one dog [at the station].

Our journey from Hut Point to Cape Evans was not exactly a pleasure trip. On the contrary, it has been the worst of the whole depot expedition. We bade farewell to the *Discovery* hut [on 11 April] in air heavy with snow. Scott, Taylor, Bowers, and Seaman [PO] Evans hauled a ten-foot sledge while T. Evans, Debenham, Wright, Crean, and I took a 12-footer. Those remaining at the hut accompanied us to Castle Rock. Here we said our farewells and continued, the going heavy, along the ridge of the peninsula. But when we had come some miles northeast of Castle Rock, on the slopes down to the sea, the fog became so thick that we had to bivouac. We made lunch and meanwhile the weather improved a little, so after one hour of rest we were able to continue. We kept going one hour and then were halted at the top of a 30-foot drop. We roped up and let the men and sledges down. Scott, who came last, was winched down by us from below with the rope running over a piton we had driven into the ice wall. All went well, even though we were so enveloped in drift snow that we could hardly see more than a few feet ahead of us. But we soon set course over the bay towards Glacier Tongue. I began at last to believe we should reach Cape Evans during the night.

After some hours march we reached Glacier Tongue, and managed with much effort to get our sledges up on the glacier at its lowest point. The surface was broken by fissures and crevasses. Some of us fell into one and dangled, hanging in our harness until pulled up by the others. We got over the Tongue without injury, bivouacked at the foot of the ice down by the sea, and made a meal to keep up our spirits. Darkness had fallen on the ice and dark clouds fled across the sky, but the stars shone and glittered through the dark blue gaps. We packed up the tents, for the last time on this journey, as we hoped, and set off into the night towards the point we could still make out against the sky to the north. But we had not gone many miles before the snow-fall intensified and, when we had reached Little Razorback, Scott was uncertain how far the ice was safe and did not dare continue. We therefore made camp near the island, although I believe we all wanted to press on.

The tents were set up, the sleeping bags unrolled, and we turned in, sweaty and wet after the march and rather disappointed at not having reached the hut. But the night would soon pass, and so to breakfast in the hut. Our mouths watered at the prospect. But alas, when daylight [on 12 April] began to filter through the canvas, and we stuck our heads out of our wet, icy bags, a storm was raging so savagely that the tents looked like blowing away, and the ice desert was a turmoil of snow and wind. There was nothing for it but to contain ourselves patiently and sit it out. Dry cold is not intolerable, even when the temperatures go down to the [minus] 50s and 60s, but wet cold pushes man to the limits of endurance. We lay on the sea ice, and the warmth from our bodies quickly created a slushy underlay which saturated our sleeping bags. During the morning it went on snowing and at three in the afternoon, orders came to move camp up on to Razorback icefoot. It was a rotten job but at any rate a change for the better. All the same I shall never forget the hours I spent there. Above us rose the steep mountain wall and beneath us lay a precipice, the bottom of which we could not see in the drifting, whirling snow-storm; there was just room on the ice ledge for the tent. Then night fell, and it was dark and cramped in the tent with hardly room to turn over. The storm raged and plucked at the tent, and beneath us in the void the wind roared and howled as if the devils from the wilderness were after us. It sounded as though we were at the bottom of a huge waterfall. There wasn't much sleep for any of us, and God knows there was a sigh of relief in the tent when a pale glint of dawn crept in. During the night it had cleared up but the wind was still blowing strongly. Our provisions were at an end and we made a very meagre breakfast. But what did that matter for in a few kilometres, perhaps an hour, we should be home and dry in the hut. [I roused the party at 7 a.m. (on April 13) and we were soon under weigh, with a desperately cold and stiff breeze and frozen clothes – RFS].

We struck camp and pushed on northwards towards Cape Evans. We got nearer and nearer but still the ice seemed to stretch as [far as] eye could see. What was that? A black thread stretching out towards Cape Evans – that must be Simpson's apparatus.[13] Just a bit more and we saw a flag; it *was* Simpson's observatory on the heights above the hut. We reached some stranded icebergs, passed them round the point, and before us was the hut, peaceful and untouched by the elements. Someone standing outside saw us, disappeared, and soon the people from the hut poured out to meet us. It was 80 days since we had seen each other and we greeted one another with warmth.

How wonderful to set foot inside the palace! It was as if we couldn't grasp or believe what we saw. Was all this possible here in the wilderness? Well! The table is laid and it is really strange to see cutlery again. Soon a bath – and then to bed!

13 For his balloon experiments. *See below* 5 May 1911.

In winter quarters

14 April

It was heavenly to sleep in a bed last night; I felt as though I were floating – it was so soft with its spring mattress. Breakfast was outstanding; we could not live better in civilization. Clissold is a splendid cook and a first-class baker. It is evening, the acetylene lights are flaring, the gramophone playing and our thoughts wander. You can almost weep at the sound of Melba's voice. At home it is Easter; the ski huts are full and the mountains thronged. The heights are swarming with people whose voices echo from the sunlit peaks. I spent the day preparing a map of the surroundings, a job assigned to Teddy Evans and me. The air has been snow-laden and threatening, and it won't be long before we have bad weather again. Yesterday evening we sent up rocket signals which were answered from Hut Point.

[When we had turned our backs on Cape Evans in January we had left our winter quarters in a very primitive condition. It had hardly been finished or fitted out at all. When we returned after an absence of 80 days, we found the hut completed and indeed almost unrecognizable. Of course it was not luxurious but it really was quite comfortable, and good and warm. Nor did we have to move around in half darkness: acetylene lights had totally banished the shadows. Bernard Day, who had fixed the lighting, was someone who mastered everything he turned his hand to.

The floor area at Cape Evans measured 125 square metres. Since we were 25 men with 5 square metres each, we had plenty of room to move without treading on our neighbour's toes. A wall consisting of cases of groceries divided the hut in the ratio of 2:3. The smaller part, near to the entrance, consisted of crew's quarters and galley. The larger part housed us officers, who with the exception of Scott and Ponting had grouped themselves in sections [of] 2–3 and 5. Ponting slept in his own dark room. The expedition was based as much on scientific as on geographical exploration, and a visit to our Antarctic home at Cape

Evans, first and foremost to the part occupied by Simpson and Wright, would prove this statement to everybody's satisfaction. In the innermost corner of the hut, on the right side, you could from time to time hear the sound of dynamo and motor, and you would see the most wonderful instruments measuring air temperature, electricity in the atmosphere, the magnetism of the earth, and the wind's strength and direction. The Simpson-Wright corner reminded me of nothing so much as Captain Nemo's laboratory, courtesy of Jules Verne.

To the left and in front of their domain, Dr Atkinson conducted his parasitological studies, an activity that, because of its limited attractions, was for the most part carried on in solitary state. A few steps to the left took you to Ponting and his rectangular dark room in the centre of the east wall of the hut. In it you could hear many a strange tale. Ponting was not only a distinguished photographer but also an unusually gifted interpreter of all the remarkable things that had happened to him. An hour with 'Ponko' was like an evening at the cinema – and he always made people welcome to his den. At the rear of this wall, and in the second back-corner, Wilson and Teddy Evans made their camp. A large rectangular table covered with gorgeous water colours, sketch maps, and finished and half-finished drawings was the outstanding and characteristic feature of this section of the hut. And you were welcome there too, even though both Teddy and 'Uncle Bill' were usually busy with something or other. You didn't drop in on Bill and Teddy just to pass the time of day but rather to get advice. If you were feeling low and went to see Wilson, you'd be certain to feel better when you left him. Not without cause was he called 'Uncle Bill'.

The next enclosure on the north wall was Scott's, and there he lived his private life in Spartan simplicity. His writing table consisted of a renovated packing case, the bed [was] his chair, while a naval greatcoat with brass buttons and badges of rank served as his quilt. At the end of the north wall in the officers' quarters was an open-ended enclosure of the most modest architectural merit. This, in great simplicity, housed Cavalry Captain Oates, Lieutenant Bowers, Dr Atkinson, the zoologist Garrard and the dog expert Meares. The arrangement of the bunks resembled five-horse stalls rising from one base.

If you turn your back on this strange five-man lair and jump over the long mess table, you land at the entrance to the Day-Nelson abode. These two had spent the summer at Cape Evans and had fashioned a splendid place out of the alloted 6–7 square metres. Day was clever with his hands and 'Marie' Nelson was full of ideas. Day's and Nelson's closest neighbours were Taylor, Debenham, and I. Though I say it myself, we three had also made a good show out of almost nothing and made ourselves cosy and comfortable. I had the top bunk, with Griff beneath, and it was up against the wall connecting with the crew's quarters. [. . . the legs of his wire bedstead hung over my head and feet, and caused many bruises at first – TGT]. Debenham had rigged up his bunk opposite mine on the same level, so we had room on the floor level below for a small writing-table and some chairs. Taylor, Debenham, and I went under the name the 'Ubdugs' and our den was called the 'Ubduggery'. And the Ubdug motto was, 'The pen is mightier than the sword, but the tongue is greater than either.'

Our common ground 'the mess' was Spartanly furnished, the most luxurious item being the pianola. On the wall in Scott's quarters hung a large portrait of King George [V]. A huge, round stove, which would warm up the hut however cold it was outside, dominated the scene like a lighthouse.

After this visit indoors let us now take a look at the immediate surroundings of our Antarctic home. It was through an alcove-like outhouse called the 'gasworks' that we emerged into the open air. A couple more strides between high snow walls and we are in the stable, which stretched along the northern wall of the hut. Coal bricks and bales of pressed fodder provided the building material for this strange zoo. It was sheltered if dark in 'Château Oates', but the dogs strutted around full of health and well-being. Oates simply loved this stable and we could find him there, and Anton the Russian groom, at any hour of the day or night. In the glare of the glowing blubber stove or by the light of a candle you could see these two men – so completely different in background, character and life-style – united and indeed inseparable in their work. Little Anton, cradled in the Caucasus Mountains, soon came to worship his master. 'Captain Oates very very good with ponies and me', was the reply to almost any enquiry. He spoke or understood almost no English.

From the stables the tour continued to Windmill Heights, a partially glacial ridge just south of the hut. On the way there we went past the 'magnetic ice cave' but, as there was nothing to see save ice-bound instruments, we continued on to the top with its meteorological windmills. We reached our goal in a few moments, and beneath us there opened up a panorama of strange beauty. Towards the north lay the sea, in the summer shining like a mirror and dotted with drift ice and, in the winter moonlight, frozen and white as silver; towards the west and southwest a mountainous country whose peaks seemed to touch the very heavens; towards the south barren islands wreathed in ice; and towards the east high, high over our heads stood the volcano Erebus.

And while we paused up there atop Windmill Heights in deep wonderment at the savage beauty of the polar wilderness, we might hear the bay of the hounds along the northern ridge. Then we would take a last lingering look round the horizon and make our way down towards the dog camp. If our visit were on a sunny day the dogs radiated a feeling of well-being and satisfaction, but in foul weather we would soon be overtaken by an uneasy feeling of sympathy. 'Poor miserable brutes' was our involuntary reaction as we hastened back to the hut. We might not have seen all the camp could offer but at any rate we had covered the most essential features – TG].

15 April

[Young Gran was handed over to me to help with the survey work and astronomical observations which had to be taken from time to time. He was a most entertaining assistant. Without complaint, he stood patiently shivering in that cutting winter wind, whilst I swung around the theodolite telescope and took angles for him to write down from time to time – ERGRE]. During the morning Teddy and I went out to establish a survey line for our triangulation. Demetri accompanied us; he is a nice, clever chap. It turned nasty in the morning, and we therefore postponed our work and I have been working on my own things. The bunk will soon be ready. Teddy Evans told me today that in a letter Rennick had expressed his conviction that Amundsen would reach the Pole first. I have seen some photographs Campbell has sent Scott, including a group picture of the Amundsen expedition. They are nine. Of these I have so far only identified Amundsen, Bjaaland, and Johansen. I am not sure whether Gjertsen is among them but I believe so, for according to Nelson a 'young lieutenant'[1] had asked Campbell a lot about me. Campbell had eaten in Amundsen's hut. The hut looks pretty small from the photograph; the Norwegian flag flies from the gable. As to whether this is their winter quarters or not, opinions are divided; some believe they went to sea during the autumn storms, others that the cold on the Barrier will kill the dogs; I and some others believe his choice of site is in conformity with the whole plan. Everything depends on luck; if it is with them, there are great advantages in that site for they are a whole degree nearer the Pole than we are here; if luck is against them, it will be disaster. 'All or nothing' is Amundsen's motto, they say, and I agree with him. It is beginning to get colder now, the temperature in the night dropped to –23 °C.

16 April

Easter Sunday and we had a service in the hut this morning. All the

1 Lieutenant H.F. Gjertsen, R.Norw.N., Second Officer in *Fram*.

same, Teddy Evans and I have been at work on our triangulation; we must make use of the daylight while we have it. It was an unpleasant experience.

17 April

Scott, Bowers, Day and Nelson[2] left this morning for Hut Point. The weather was quite good, although a cold wind from the northeast was blowing. The whole morning and a good deal of the afternoon I passed with Teddy. We nearly surveyed ourselves to death for there was more than 20 °C of frost.

18 April

At breakfast we discussed Amundsen. Most of those here consider he will reach the Pole first, if he is not driven out to sea. Their hut is built on the sea ice right under the Barrier.[3] According to the people in *Terra Nova*, there were cracks between it and the hut. But I am convinced that experienced people like Amundsen and Johansen would not build on unsafe ground, if there were better to be found. It seems my compatriots were not about to be pumped. There was absolutely nothing about their plans in the letter to Scott. I have made up my own mind on how Amundsen will strike out for the Pole. This year he has made a depot journey south; he will have judged that we have been on Beardmore [Glacier]. It is difficult to say how far his journey has taken him, but I should imagine it is between latitude 80° and 81°.[4] He is therefore ahead of us. It was clear this morning with wind and 25 °C of frost. Teddy Evans and I went on with our work and spent the whole day on triangulation.

19 April

The night was cold, calm, starlit and the Southern Lights flared over Erebus. After breakfast Teddy and I went out to our survey line and completed it. After lunch we went over to another station, but a sudden storm blew up from the south with drift snow and we had to take to our heels immediately. We spent the rest of the day indoors. This evening Ponting related anecdotes from his journeys in Japan, and we laughed loud and long. It is really rather nice in the hut now that there are so few of us. I wish this situation could continue but tomorrow it will be swarming with people. Today, again, we are discussing Amundsen; I

2 Also Lashly, Crean, Hooper and Demetri.

3 In fact, the hut was built on a low part of the ice shelf, which Amundsen rightly believed would not break away.

4 Actually latitude 82°S.

wonder if the world is too? Our theme at the moment is Amundsen/ Scott.

20 April

Snow-storm and foul weather the whole day. Teddy and I have buried ourselves in cartography. It is impossible to stay outside. Storm and –25 °C.

21 April

'Hark the herald angels sing' [on the gramophone]. It sounds like home; [the] voice is wonderful and has great warmth. This morning Teddy and I went out surveying. As usual it was cold and nasty work; I hope we have finished with this part [of the job]. In the afternoon we made preparations for the map drawing.

(*Later, at 10 o'clock*) Scott, Wilson, Oates, Atkinson, Bowers, and Cherry-Garrard[5] have just come through the door having started at 10 a.m.[6] They had a pretty rough passage which took two days. Day had a frost-bitten toe and has been laid up in the *Discovery* hut. They are still discussing Amundsen. I can say nothing. God knows I am in a difficult position, and I hope to avoid the worst predicament by going with the party to the Western Mountains. I really don't want to compete with my compatriots.

22 April

Calm, good weather for a change. The sledge party has dried out its gear, and Teddy and I have kept on with our cartography.

23 April

For the last time in many long months the sun could be seen over the ice tongue to the north. Daylight will soon be gone and the Antarctic night will rule the scene. It's Sunday, but we have busied ourselves anyhow in our map drawing. This afternoon and this evening I worked on at my cubicle, and it is nearly finished now. The wall is decorated with my sledge flag and some photographs, and the cook has installed an electric light to read by. We have begun night watches now that winter has arrived [. . . mainly for the purpose of observing the aurora – RFS]. Scott is on duty tonight. My first turn will come on 3 May.

24 April

The first day of winter was beautiful – mild, calm, and clear. Have spent

5 Also Crean and Hooper.

6 They travelled from Hut Point, leaving Meares in charge, with Nelson, Day, Lashly, Forde, Keohane, and Demetri.

the whole day surveying along the coast. In this calm weather it was a real pleasure. Although we did not see the sun today, the mountains were covered with a pinkish light. In a short time this too will disappear.[7]

25 April

A beautiful day again. Teddy and I have been surveying along the coast to the west. This was most interesting, for all the land hereabouts was virgin and untrodden. We discovered under the ice what seemed to be an island and deep bays carved out of the ice mass. I am also taken with the idea that the hut too is on an island, quite separate from Ross Island; our geologists do not entirely agree with me. Time will tell.

26 April

I climbed up to the heights[8] this afternoon and re-erected a flag that had fallen down. I thought I saw a sledge party down on the ice. I signalled down to the hut, and in an instant all stood to. But then I found that what I had taken for people were only some stones that had taken on strange shapes in the foggy weather. There was nothing for me to do but to correct my mistake. I ran down over the stones in a shower of ice chips, and got down in time to stop Scott before he had got more than a couple of hundred yards from the hut. However, he took it quite calmly.

Later, I went out hunting for a likely ski jump and found one quite suitable for beginners. As yet there is not a trace of snow on the hill, but this situation can quickly be remedied by building a wall towards the south. I built up the jump and wall with sand from down the hill. I baptized the place 'Finse'.[9] [I had been clear that my first task was to root out that opposition and ill-will towards skiing which had characterized previous English South Polar expeditions. There was no doubt that the best way to set about it would be to demonstrate personally what a colossal advantage a man with skis had over one without them in a snow country like Antarctica. I had been lucky enough during the summer depot expedition to have several opportunities of showing how useful the 'wooden planks' could be. On our return to . . . Cape Evans it became quite a natural thing to get out the skis when the weather permitted. Most of them managed very well – TG].

Our 'den'[10] in the hut is now very cosy. It is quite private; we have

7 On this date TGT gives figures from a routine medical check, showing that Gran's measurements were: height 5′11″, waist 31½″, chest 40″, weight 13st 3¾lb.

8 An unnamed hill east–north–east of the hut.

9 A ski resort in Norway

10 Shared by Gran, Taylor and Debenham.

hung curtains to shut out the world. [Gran fixed red linen borders on the shelves made from photographic 'window' material, while I draped my bunk with a deep blue hanging, which had originally formed part of the Sunday tablecloth – TGT]. Our neighbours have made an awful mess of their area, are very envious, and call our place 'an opium den'. They may be right, for Ponting says it does bear a close resemblance to one.

27 April
I took Ponting and Taylor over to Lands End to show them a wonderful ice grotto I had discovered during our survey work round the coast. [We found that the caves were really the exposed ends of crevasses – TGT]. The air was heavy with snow but calm. I spent the afternoon round the hut, and kicked a football about with Ponting down on the sea ice.

28 April
Calm and clear this morning; the survey work could therefore proceed. We left after breakfast and did not return until 4 p.m. By dinner it clouded over and the wind sprang up. It was cold work, and both Teddy Evans and I had slight frostbite. The stretch we did today was the coast of Inaccessible Island.

29 April
Aurora yesterday evening, but only for a few hours. By 11 p.m. it had gone. According to Wilson it was the best he had seen here in Antarctica. After breakfast Teddy and I went out to our work. The cold was so savage that after a couple of hours we doubled back to the hut. Later in the afternoon I went up to 'Finse' with some cases which I set up as a snow-screen on the hill; hope it will do the trick.[11]

30 April
The last day of the month has arrived, calm and clear, and in a few hours will be gone, and we shall be in May, with summer and sunshine home in the north. I wonder how our people are, and what they are thinking and saying now that they know the situation between Scott and Amundsen. Of course I hope Amundsen will beat us – that is just straightforward patriotism. I would have given a great deal to have been a fly on the wall in the 'thousands of Norwegian homes'[12] when the sensational news was published in the newspapers.

11 The cases would provide a lee where snow could accumulate.
12 A quotation from the Norwegian national anthem.

1 May

This afternoon I shall lay out a 'football pitch' on the ice. Oates and I have chosen teams and we aim to have the match tomorrow morning.

(*Later, 10 p.m.*) Wilson introduced the winter's lectures this evening with a very interesting description of the birds of the South Polar region; it was followed by a discussion. [The discussion lasted till nearly ten, each man being called on by Scott in the order in which he happened to sit at the table (TGT). Three lectures a week were too many in the opinion of the majority (A CG). All officers took it in turn to 'face the firing squad' – TG]. This afternoon I have continued work on the football pitch; I only hope the weather will hold. It is perfect tonight with intermittent aurora.

2 May

Deb, Taylor, and I are sitting round the table in our cosy little corner. We had the match today and my team lost. We were fearfully unlucky because in the last half a gale blew up. [. . . a harassing southerly wind sprang up, which helped my side to the extent of three goals (RFS). . . . curious was the composition of the teams. There was little five-foot Anton, our Russian groom, who knew no English and had probably never seen a football. Somewhat of a contrast were Crean and (PO) Taff Evans, about six feet tall, and two of the biggest men in the navy. Wright's knowledge was based on ice hockey. I had played rugger in 1905, and now found that the rules differed considerably. Atkinson was our star player, though Gran had played football for Norway – TGT]. The return match will take place as soon as possible. It was really cold to play football today; the biting, frozen air took our breath away. We played 20 minutes each way.

3 May

I am on night duty. It is blowing up with drift; for once I wish the aurora would stay away, but no, it appears – cold, ghostly and mysterious.

4 May

The hours of night creep on, and it won't be long before I can flop in my bunk. Surprisingly I am not as sleepy as I thought I would be, and time has gone remarkably quickly. Around about four I had a splendid Norwegian meal of grilled ptarmigan.[13] How delicious it tasted! Just for a moment it was as though I were at home. I've been really lucky. It is overcast and calm. The aurora cannot penetrate the fog belt.

(*4 p.m.*) Not unreasonably, I spent most of the day in my bunk. I

13 Purloined from Shackleton's hut at Cape Royds.

turned out at noon to play football. It was the return match but, alas, we lost this time too, although we played much better. The result was 5–4. [We had an excellent game of football again today – the exercise is delightful and we get very warm. Atkinson is by far the best player, but Hooper, PO Evans, and Crean are also quite good – RFS]. Tonight I have been chatting to Ponting in his quarters. He is a very nice chap and has seen a great deal of the world.

5 May

One day passes very much like another. Now and again Simpson sends up a balloon with self-recording instruments. Up to now he has mostly lost the line and the instruments. Cherry-Garrard is building a stone hut for the seal flensing. Oates looks after the horses. Atkinson is being the scientist and searching in vain for bacteria, etc.[14] Bowers helps with the balloon experiments. Wright studies, and looks after the light.[15] Wilson paints, Ponting develops his pictures, and Scott reads and writes; he seems relaxed. Taylor and Deb keep diaries and write half the day. [Gran kept his diary mostly in Norwegian, but there were many words coined in our Expedition which had no Scandinavian equivalent, and Gran failed to translate them, in spite of his having more imagination than any one amongst us (ERGRE). Gran and myself were probably the most voluminous writers – TGT]. Simpson slaves away, living in a separate world of science. The weather has been calm and clear today.

6 May

We were to play [ice] hockey today, but our home-made puck broke to pieces at bully-off, and we played football instead. My team won. Conditions were better today; it snowed a bit, but the weather was calm and not particularly cold. It's Saturday evening and only four o'clock, but the shades of night have already reached the hut. Atkinson had a good catch of fish today. He caught 40 big and small in a wire net shaped like an eel-pot.

7 May

Sunday and rest day. Ponting, Teddy and I went for a walk over to the Barne Glacier. At the point [of Cape Evans] the ice was thin and we nearly went through. The weather has been good, calm, fairly clear, and quite mild.

8 May

Tonight Captain Scott outlined his plans for discussion and

14 Atkinson's main interest was in parasitology.

15 The acetylene lighting arrangements for the hut.

consideration. His attack on the Pole will be wholly based on Shackleton's model, as regards march distances and provisioning. [. . . the problem of reaching the Pole can best be solved by relying on ponies and man haulage – RFS]. The number of men is still undecided. He doesn't wish to rely on the dogs or the motor sledges. He has grounds for the latter view, but I personally doubt whether the dogs are as useless as he says. [Everyone seems to distrust the dogs when it comes to glacier and summit – RFS]. I wonder whether there isn't an element of complacency in his attitude, when we compare Amundsen's plan with his 100 dogs? We shall see. He will use skis as far as Beardmore [Glacier] in any case. Moreover the whole journey will be undertaken as if Amundsen did not exist. But the most important fact to emerge from his talk was that, in order to fulfil his plans, it will clearly be necessary to spend one more year down here. He does not intend to start before 1 November 1911 and will be equipped for 144 days. The polar party will spend 84 days on the plateau. [He (Scott) said the great difficulty would be on the plateau – TGT]. A long discussion followed.[16]

9 May

There is rather little work for me. I am supposed to be T.Evans' assistant, but he can't be surveying all day. My real job is ski instructor, but I can't undertake any for the time being. There is no snow ashore, and on the [sea] ice only the worst sort of mixture of snow and salt. On this the skis won't slide; it is like trying to move in thick porridge. But things will doubtless improve as time goes on. Before lunch I gave Cherry a hand carting stones over to his hut – number 2; the first has had to be pulled down because of its proximity to Simpson's sensitive instruments. Simpson and Wilson are helping too.

10 May

Our cosy den has become a place where people drop in for a chat or to tell stories. Tonight Ponting got the conversation going with his experiences in trains. This evening he showed a number of slides from Burma accompanied by a talk. The projector didn't quite work, and old 'Ponters' got frightfully irritated. Finally the whole thing fell over and burned him, so now he has a huge bandage on his head. But at this moment, as I said, he is sitting here and telling stories in his good-humoured, easy-going way. [His descriptive language is florid, but shows the artistic temperament. . . Our lectures are a real success (RFS). No officer nor seaman . . . could have had too many of Ponting's lectures – A CG].

16 On the possibility of getting ponies up the Beardmore Glacier.

11 May
We played football today. 26 °C of frost, but even so the game was very lively; the team-work was better than before. Moonshine tonight, but otherwise it has been very hazy. There was aurora the whole night.

12 May
'My last night in Norway has come, it is strange to think. When shall I see again the hills darkening against the night sky?' This is what had passed through my mind on 12 May 1910. So a year has passed since I said goodbye to the friendly shores of Norway and home. It was spring then; now it is winter, half-dark and stormy. When I awoke this morning the wind screeched and howled around the hut, and it's been the same the whole day. Last night we saw a remarkable ring of vapour round the moon. It was quite clearly a harbinger of storm. With the arrival in the hut of Meares, Keohane, Forde, Nelson, Day and Demetri we are now all assembled. They were all in good shape.[17] Teddy Evans and I went out in the forenoon on survey to the Barne Glacier. It was fine moonshine when we left the hut, but with a forecast of snow [judging] from the ring around the moon. This turned out to be quite accurate for a gentle fall had set in before lunch.

14 May
Sunday has passed in peace and quiet. Taylor finished a world map today showing the lands and islands visited by the present members of the expedition. According to this, Captain Scott is the most travelled among us, though I come a close second. Evans comes third and Meares fourth. I am clear winner in Europe. In America Scott and I are level pegging. I am pretty weak in Asia, Africa, and Australasia. [It was soon evident that the contest lay between Captain Scott, the oldest, and Gran the youngest of the party! – TGT].[18]

15 May
Debenham wakened me in the night. He had made cocoa. About midnight it is good to get a night-cap like that. In the morning Teddy and I went out to Barne Glacier to measure distances. The cold seemed unusually savage because of the fresh northerly wind. This afternoon I worked out a table for the forthcoming ping-pong tournament. It is quite a tricky job to get it right. Tonight Wilson is giving a talk on penguins.

17 This group had been at Hut Point since the end of the depot journey and now returned with the dog team and two ponies.

18 Scott had visited 59 countries and Gran, 53.

16 May

It was sour and threatening this morning, but I went out anyhow at 11 to take in some of our [survey] station flags. When I came back to the hut, the wind had dropped and the others were just going to play football. The match was a success with full teams and good teamwork. Atkinson and I were on the same side and we won 4 – 1. [. . . we had a capital game of football. The light is good enough, but not much more than good enough, for this game – RFS].

The weather was truly awful tonight; a howling gale is blowing. Today is 16 May and at home they are preparing for tomorrow.[19] Towards morning a striking aurora shone. The ping-pong tournament began tonight.

17 May

Greet this great day,
These sun-drenched hours.
Greet each our flag
That waves on towers.
I cannot reach Thee with voice or eye
But heart is willing as ye shall spy.

Our day of freedom has arrived. The Norwegian flag over my bunk indicates my sentiments. I was surely among the first to celebrate the day. At midnight I went out in the storm, gave a cheer for Norway and sang: 'Ja, vi elsker'[20] to the echo over the icy wasteland. I hoisted the flag over my bunk and the representative of Australia [Taylor] paid it honour. Then, in the night hours, my thoughts were homeward bound. It was vile weather; there were snow-drifts round the hut and the wind howled and shrieked. But inside the hut it was calm and quiet, and I sat by the fire reading and dreaming.

In lonely dream
Thoughts fly to home,
For that is where life's lived.

We lost a dog during the night. God knows what he died of; the scientists have no idea. It whimpered and groaned all night, and I woke up Meares who went out several times. It is eight in the evening here, and nine in the morning at home. In my mind's eye I can see thousands of people marching through the streets, waving banners and flags; I can hear the thunder of the cheering and the bands playing. There is a carnival spirit in Norway at this hour. Oates gave a talk tonight on horses; he is

19 Norwegian National Day, 17 May.
20 The Norwegian National Anthem.

not exactly ready with words, but even so it was quite entertaining. [. . . Oates's horsy yarns were particularly popular. (He) seemed very reserved in daily life, but revealed a singular sense of humour during these sessions; he ended up by producing a punch line which had his hearers in stitches – TG]. In the evening I played 'Ja, vi elsker' on the gramophone.

18 May
The days are getting darker; even at midday it is nearly twilight. Football again today. There has been a snow-laden sky and wind the whole day.

19 May
Today was the football match. However hard we try, we don't seem to be able to win, though we are clearly superior both as a team and individually. We shall try again tomorrow. Before the match I went out with Nelson and helped him with some depth soundings. Spent the afternoon in the hut; we had a discussion on the important off-side question [in soccer], something that creates arguments all over the world. Tonight Wright is to give a talk on ice crystals and, were it not for Charles' sake, I should undoubtedly have gone to bed.

20 May
We have completed the second round of the ping-pong tournament. Tonight the weather is bitter, with wind and 31 °C of frost. [Wilson and Bowers went to the top of the Ramp and found the wind there force 6 to 7, temperature –24 °(F); as a consequence they got frostbitten – RFS].

21 May
Time passes. Today is Sunday and rest day again. I have helped Teddy Evans to make his observations. While we were doing that, the aurora flared up, first as a shining bow over the horizon in the south and then as golden drapery from the zenith above Erebus right down to the mountains in the west. It was a splendid sight. Ponting has taken some photographs but without success. He is very disappointed about this because he believes his camera better than the one used by Professor Carl Störmer [of Norway]. In this connexion there has been a long and heated discussion between him and Simpson.

22 May
Scott, Wilson, Bowers, Atkinson, Petty Officer Evans, and Clissold went to Cape Royds this morning [. . . with a 'go cart' carrying our sleeping-bags, a cooker, and a small quantity of provisions. The 'go cart' consists of a framework of steel tubing supported on four bicycle

wheels – RFS]. Teddy and I went surveying before lunch. The stars are now visible night and day. The sky looks menacing and the air is laden with snow.

23 May
The Cape Royds party is back; they arrived at five in the afternoon. Bowers is now himself again.[21] He brought with him some of Shackleton's tinned stuff for general use. I haven't yet tried it. It had incidentally been a very good trip and shorter than expected. The distance to Cape Royds is not more than five geographical miles – not seven as shown on the map. The weather has been clear but rather sharp.

24 May
Today I have been on skis for the first time since our return from the depot journey. I wanted to try the snow, and left at 11 o'clock on my cross-country skis in the direction of Turks Head. I took off along the coast over untrodden ground, and after passing Turks Head found myself in a large bay. It had already begun to get rather dark, and I set course for home. There was a fresh breeze from the north, and it was savagely cold the last five miles with the temperature at –20°. This evening Atkinson gave a talk on parasites and bacteria. It was very easy to understand and interesting. Overcast tonight, the temperature has risen and it looks like snow.

25 May
A heavy snow-storm has raged the whole day from the south and without exception everyone has stayed indoors. [Gran is writing one of his six diaries with Deb's nib, which he blunts. He has a patent plasticine pen rack, which doesn't improve the handle. I told him to learn Russian, or write an Antarctic novel in Norwegian, for he will be at a loose end until ski-ing is possible – TGT].

Yesterday I heard that Taylor will go with the western party during the coming summer and not southwards, as originally planned. It seems the reason is that Scott is in a hurry and will not have time to stop for scientific observations during the journey. Debenham will go with Taylor. Naturally this is a disappointment for him[22], but he has decided to remain one more year so as to take over the leadership [in geology] next summer. Taylor had a longish discussion with Scott yesterday about summer plans; he asked whether he could have me in his team, but Scott would not make a decision about this, since so much could happen in the

21 Bowers had suffered mild frost-bite.
22 For Debenham, as he would not now take charge of the field geology in the west.

course of the winter. But I hope and trust that I shall go with the western party in the summer. This evening the snow-storm is worse than I have seen before in these parts. The wind is blowing with a speed of 130 km.p.h.

26 May

The storm blew itself out in the night, and the forenoon was calm and clear with stars visible. This morning Debenham and I had a long and friendly discussion about my English. He gave me some examples he had noted. One from Dunedin showed that I had said 'there was a wire for him'. I had pronounced this so that he had understood me to say 'there was a surveyor for him'. The result was that he went up on deck to meet the gentleman. After lunch I went out to see to the skis and fixed the bindings for Scott, who took a trip out over the sea ice. [The surface is quite good since the recent snowfall and wind. This is satisfactory, as sledging can now be conducted on ordinary lines, and if convenient our parties can pull on ski – RFS].

27 May

The weather has been bitter and foul, and we have for the most part kept indoors. However, in the morning I went out and dug the skis out and assembled them in one place. Tonight Bowers gave a lecture on sledge equipment through the ages.[23] It was an excellent talk, and even though I had adopted a horizontal position in my bunk I managed to stay awake.

28 May

Sunday today and peace in the hut. I helped Ponting take some magnesium [flash] pictures down on the ice, and afterwards shaved. So I managed to pass the morning.

29 May

Ponting gave a successful illustrated lecture on Japan tonight. More and more I want to visit this 'land of the lotus'. The weather has been good but rather cold. Tonight it is overcast.

30 May

Today I have spent mainly writing. In the morning I fixed Oates' bindings, and went out on skis for one hour in the afternoon. The weather has been splendid and not really cold. At midnight the temperature is only –21 °C.

23 In fact, the subject was the evolution of sledge rations.

31 May

The sky has been threatening all day with an unusually high temperature. Bowers, Simpson, and I went out at 6 p.m. to The Ramp – they to take some temperature readings, I to fetch the flag from 'Dreadnought'.[24] It was fine snow, just the same as at home, and a real pleasure to glide through the patches of snow between the stones. But the oddest thing happened. We had barely got inside the hut before a storm blew up from the south, with so much drift snow you could hardly see your feet. It is almost midnight, and still howling and moaning out there. [I have never known a storm come on so suddenly, and it shows what possibility there is of individuals becoming lost even if they only go a short way from the hut – RFS].

1 June

We left London a year ago today, and to celebrate we drank a toast at dinnertime. Yesterday's storm continued with undiminished force throughout the night,[25] and today too it has been blowing hard from the south.

2 June

The nights are getting longer; it is 3 a.m.[26]

[*Later*] During the night it cleared up and at four o'clock the aurora began. The wind is holding steady, and it is rather cold to go out to take readings. The temperature is high; at midnight it was –14 °C, but by 4 p.m. it had risen to +12 °C. Last night I found a family photo of Mother, Margit, Lilla, and myself. It is a good picture and nice to have with me now. I wonder how they all are? Lilla will be nearly grown up when I get home. It will be lovely now at home with everything in bloom. Sunshine, summer, and warmth at home in Norway. I am warming up a ptarmigan on the cooker. I shall eat it when I come in at five o'clock after the readings.

3 June

I have spent the day writing; the weather has not tempted anyone out of doors. But for a bit of fresh air before supper I walked up The Ramp with Wilson and Bowers. On our return I came upon a dog fight. 'Peary' had attacked 'Cook'. The racket attracted the other loose dogs, and it was turning nasty. Oates was there but was bare-headed and in slippers. As I had mitts and boots on, I went in and separated the devils.

24 A knoll behind the hut.
25 RFS reported that gusts reached 72 mph.
26 Gran is on the night watch.

They snarled and limped away bloody into the dark. 'Cook' and 'Peary' went for each other again later. Simpson gave a talk on meteorological and magnetic instruments. Then Nelson, Meares, and I tried to work out an arrangement of new automatic instruments. A cold wind tonight but clear, with a display of aurora.

4 June

It has been a splendid day, clear enough to see the stars, calm, and not particularly cold. Daylight has not completely disappeared yet, for at midday a golden afterglow can be seen over the horizon to the north, like sunset on a winter's day at home. Teddy Evans and I went out on skis in the morning. We went round Inaccessible Island; the surface was excellent, and it turned out to be a fine trip. A beautiful evening. The aurora is shining along the ridge of [Barne] Glacier to the north and takes on the strangest forms. We all went out and watched it for a long time.

5 June

We have passed most of the day discussing Antarctic problems. I borrowed from Scott the photographs of Amundsen's camp which the *Terra Nova* people had collected. Taylor, Debenham, Nelson and I scanned them to see whether we could find any clues as to the ice conditions in Whale Bay,[27] but I fear without significant results. This led us farther into the topic 'The Antarctic Continent', on which all had their opinions and theories so that there was no positive consensus about this either. My own view is that the coastline of Antarctica is congruous with South America. The Dominion Mountains[28] are a continuation of the Andes, which run on southeast [thence beyond the South Pole] towards Graham Land, etc. King Edward's Land is just an island [in fact a peninsula]. After dinner we continued our discussion following Taylor's lecture on the Beardmore Glacier. My own and the general opinion is that this glacier is not as formidable as people think.

6 June

It is Captain Scott's birthday, and we celebrated it suitably this evening. [It is my birthday, a fact I might easily have forgotten, but my kind people did not. . . . I discovered that great preparations were in progress for a special dinner, and when the hour for that meal arrived we sat down to a sumptuous spread with our sledge banners hung around us – RFS].

I had a couple of hours discussion with Debenham this morning about Amundsen's ethical position.[29] This afternoon I helped Teddy Evans

27 The Bay of Whales.

28 The Dominion Range, on the west side of the upper Beardmore Glacier.

29 In 'stealing a march' on Scott.

prepare for some of the nightly readings. We took some survey measurements after dinner, and we are now carrying out some calculations on the moon's position. Deb has been in the firing line. We have been discussing in Ponting's den the question of votes for women. The Australian [Debenham] upholds the right of women to the franchise and also to political equality with men, and is prepared to stake all on it. It has been bitterly cold but fine weather. Tonight both moon and aurora are on show.

7 June

The seventh of June[30] and therefore 'God Save the King'. But, as we are inside the hut and it is night, I must suppress my patriotic fervour. I could have gone out as I did on 17 May but a harsh, cold wind was blowing and I decided to wait until tomorrow. The reason I am still up is that Teddy's energetic observations of the moon have continued well into the night. Luckily the wind has now put a stop to further observations. It is Day's watch; he is sitting drawing.

(*Later*) Captain Scott gave a talk on the Great Barrier tonight. [I have strung together a good many new points and the interest taken in the discussion was very genuine – RFS]. He contends it is floating and as proof points to the speed of the Barrier's northward movement. My belief that King Edward's Land is an island was contradicted by Deb who showed that granite had been found there, something that hardly ever occurs on small islands. To this I replied that the rocks could have been carried there from the continent by the ice. I gave as an example the rock that had been transported from Norway to south Germany during the Ice Age. But in the end this talk was too much for me and I took a walk with Ponting to the icebergs. It was a marvellous night, and fabulous to wander between these icy giants lying bathed in moonlight, throwing their huge angular shadows over the sea ice.

30 Marking the accession of King Haakon VII of Norway, 1905.

Winter nights in the *Discovery* hut

8 June

I am under way again after two months at anchor, so to speak. Debenham and I arrived here at Hut Point at five in the afternoon, after four hours' march from Cape Evans. The reason for this midwinter journey is Debenham's wish to transport his fossil collection[1] to our winter quarters at Cape Evans. When we turned out this morning there was a terrific storm and we gave up hope of starting today. But towards noon it calmed down, and by 1 p.m. when we were ready to start the weather was perfect in all respects. We set off with one nine-foot sledge, sleeping bags, and some provisions. When we were clear of Cape Evans, the moon shone large and golden on Glacier Tongue and the whole of McMurdo Sound lay bathed in light. Our skis ran well and we soon left Razorback and Tent islands behind; after one and a half hours Glacier Tongue lay across our course.

Deb had not had much practice with skis, and somehow or other the friction scraped the skin off his toes so that he had to remove his skis and continue on foot. It was a tough journey for him; for my every step he took at least two. Meanwhile the sky to the south began to look threatening; dark clouds began to bank up over Castle Rock and soon the cloud mass covered the whole sky. No longer was McMurdo Sound bathed in golden light; no longer did Castle Rock cast its long shadow over the ice. But at 7 km an hour we were making progress, and we soon reached Arrival Bay.[2] Before us lay Hut Point, its cross[3] emerging sad and silent from the murk. It was not long before we were at the hut, which had been covered by drift snow since my last visit. There seemed nothing to distinguish 'land and sea' but, as on our first visit, we were able to make our way to the door without difficulty. A surprise awaited us when we had dug our way into the entrance.

1 Acquired on the western journey.
2 Below Arrival Heights.
3 *See* 19 March above, footnote 8.

Before we departed in the morning Meares told us that on his homeward journey he had lost one of his dogs[4] and we might possibly come across its tracks at Hut Point. Yes, indeed, but we found more than tracks – we found the dog himself at the door, in surprisingly good shape given the circumstances. He growled and barked at us when we approached. His jowls were bloody, which gave us a clue as to how he had kept alive. There is no doubt he had caught a seal on his lonely wanderings. Indoors the hut was just as I had left it, but naturally rather colder at –17 °C. The blubber oven was in order, and it was not long before we had it aflame. At 9 p.m. we signalled [by flare] to Cape Evans, but got no answer.

9 June

Deb and I have passed a day in our sleeping bags. It was pretty cold in the night, but how cold I do not know for the minimum thermometer was not functioning properly and showed 80° of frost. Deb suffered the cold more than I did, and he got up at six to get the fire going and, while I slept on, prepared our breakfast of fried seal liver and cocoa. He has, incidentally, continued as cook. This evening he fried pancakes '*á la* Hut Point'.

10 June

The weather precluded a move this morning, so we remained faithful to our sleeping bags. We have slept, eaten, and slept again – the only things we can find to do. I have taken over cooking and served up seal liver, etc. The blubber stove is outstanding – it burns with a great heat. It really is quite strange to do as we have today – lie in our sacks for hours on end and gaze into the spluttering oil flame. Our thoughts float involuntarily to far distant places.

11 June

When we awakened this morning, the weather looked promising and we therefore decided to set course for Cape Evans. With the dog, which I had fixed up with a sealskin cover, we set out around two o'clock but had not gone far before the wind got up, with drift. Deb proposed that we should turn back and, as I had nothing particularly against the idea of staying a day or so longer at Hut Point, we left the sledge, humped our sleeping bags on our backs, and trudged back against wind and weather. When we got in we put the stove at full burn, drank tea, and spent quite a pleasant Sunday afternoon. I sat at the fire and talked and talked, while Deb lay in his sleeping bag listening.

4 Named 'Mukáka'.

Strange how time flew; it was nearly midnight when we looked at the clock. I went out to find mountain and wilderness bathed in the fairytale light of a full moon. It was a truly wonderful night, starlit and clear. The temperature is clearly very low but, alas, we have left the thermometer on the sledge.

12 June

The day has not upheld the promise of the night; when we got up this morning, the strong wind and drift were really very unpleasant. Without hesitation we crept into our sleeping bags again and slept the day through with the greatest of ease. After more or less 24 hours' sleep, we did not feel particularly sleepy again in the evening, so we had a song recital. I fear Deb has no voice at all, but manfully he put his best foot forward and thus somehow we passed the hours until midnight [. . . they seemed to have had stronger winds than we – RFS].

13 June

God knows what the time is. Debenham's clock has stopped and mine, I hope, is in New Zealand. It is not particularly easy to tell the time by the moon. When we were at lower latitudes it was a much easier matter, but now that the moon swings round the horizon day after day it is a very different thing. We must have slept long for the dog, which I had spoiled with a huge meal before turning in, once more indicated symptoms of a terrific appetite. We turned out early, hoping to bid farewell to the hut and reach Cape Evans for breakfast. The weather was promising, but when we were ready to march the wind started again with drifting snow. We tried our sleeping bags again, but this time it soon became obvious that we were saturated with sleep and it failed to come. The weather at this point is superb, cold but calm with moonlight. We are ready to start for Cape Evans. I hope that our luck will hold this time. I have made a harness for 'Mukáka'.

(*Cape Evans, nine in the evening*) After seven hours march we arrived at 5 p.m. here at Cape Evans. It was a splendid trip though rather cold. On our arrival the thermometer showed –30 °F and, as the temperature at Hut Point is 4–5° lower, we have thus experienced an average temperature of around –30 °F. 'Mukáka' hauled like a hero; he seemed to understand that we were making for better things. We covered the distance without skis for, as I mentioned, Debenham had blisters on one foot. Our load weighed only about 150 kg but felt heavy in the salt-ridden snow.

In our absence life in the hut had gone on normally in peace and quiet. Bowers and Cherry Garrard returned this evening from Cape Royds where they had spent the night. The gramophone is playing and it is very pleasant to hear music again.

At Cape Evans

14 June
Bowers brought back from Cape Royds a collection of illustrated magazines, and I spent this morning reading them. It is strange how one devours pictures in this desolate landscape. We were lucky to get back yesterday because in the course of the day and this evening a terrible snow-storm gradually built up. It is now moaning and howling like a devil in torment. This afternoon I helped Cherry with his hut. We managed to lay the roof so that when the storm broke, we had some shelter from the stone walls. [The Cape Crozier party were now busily engaged with their preparations for the midwinter journey to the haunt of the Emperor penguins. For some weeks Cherry had been practising hut-building near Skua Lake (a pond near Cape Evans). He used the kenyte boulders, which lay scattered around the hut. It was roofed with sealskin – TGT]. Tonight Nelson gave a talk on marine biological research.

15 June
Nelson has built a sort of Eskimo igloo southwest of Cape Evans, and in it is conducting his marine observations. I helped him today; it was a cold job.

16 June
I again spent the day helping Cherry with his hut. We completed the roof, and thus 'Seal Hall' is finished. This evening Deb gave a lecture on volcanoes. It was followed by rather a vigorous argument which sounded like the Stock Exchange in Bergen. Nelson and I made a wager as to who had seen the finest eruption. A strange outcome; we had both seen Stromboli on the same date, the end of May 1907! Today it has been overcast, but mild and calm.

17 June
During the night I sat up for a long time writing. Cherry, who was on duty, served me with cocoa and cakes. I started after breakfast to try to construct a Finne binding using it in combination with a Huitfeldt patent [binding]. I hope I can turn this idea to practical use. I kept at it until lunchtime.

18 June
Night watch and all safe. Ponting and Nelson are asleep. I have just finished a novel, the end of which was so terribly sad that I really feel quite depressed. Everything had seemed so perfect and so promising, and then came death to shatter it all.

La vie, c'est une rêve, douce d'amour.
La nuit lui prête son mystère.
Il doit finir – il doit finir avec le jour.

There is indeed more than words in these lines!

This morning we had our body measurements taken. I weigh 85 kg (the same as last month), 30″ round the waist, 40″ round the chest.[1]

19 June
I have busied myself the whole day with the ski-binding combination. Only time will tell whether it will prove a success. Otherwise, the scientists excepted, we are all preparing for the journey to Cape Crozier. Day is working on a blubber stove. This evening he gave a talk on motor sledges. I feel almost sorry for Day; he is so optimistic, almost too optimistic about the future of his sledge, and I fear he will be disappointed. A pity, he is such a nice chap. [He seems very hopeful of success, but I fear is rather more sanguine in temperament than his sledge is reliable in action – RFS].

20 June
Moonshine and excellent weather but a fresh breeze. Tonight sat in the galley with Ponting – a first-class cook – and ate toast '*à la* Ponting'.

21 June
Cold weather seems to be setting in; today the temperature was down to –37 °C. During the night it will probably drop into the forties. In the morning I went on with my ski-binding experiment and in the afternoon went out to South Bay to take readings of the various instruments set up there. This is because I have taken over Bowers' turn

1 *Compare* 24 April, footnote 7 (1 kg = 2.2 lb).

while he is at Crozier.[2] However, it was pitch black and a frost smoke covered the ice, so that it was impossible for me to find the thermometer box although I searched for over an hour. Tomorrow Bowers will come with me for I have not been there before. This evening Ponting saw a flame from Mount Erebus, and describes this as an eruption.

22 June

Today was midwinter day and the hut has been lively all day long. It has been a day of celebration and champagne.

The day began with the gramophone playing: we kept this up till after lunch. Then we had the day's biggest event – the publication of the 'South Polar Times'. Cherry is the editor. He has put a tremendous effort into the job as he does with everything. He has also had splendid help with the illustrations and also with the binding, which has been carried out by Day with sealskin and wood. On the front cover the [initial letters of the] name [were] engraved: S.P.T. Its contents are a mixture of prose and poetry. All the contributions are anonymous, but we could pretty well guess the authors' identities. Wilson, Bowers, Deb, Atkinson, Ponting, Taylor, Nelson, and of course Cherry are assumed to be the writers. 'S.P.T.' was read out by Scott and was a tremendous success.

We had a large [Buszard] Christmas cake at lunchtime which had been brought by Cherry. While the table was being set, Cherry and I went out to the temperature station. It was a superb night with 35° of frost but quite still, and the stars shone with magical light. Indeed the millions of stars provided such a strong light that the night was not really dark. Erebus appeared as though it were in a shadowy dawn. On our return to the hut, everything was ready for the feast. [. . . the table had been set so elegantly that it might have been done by the headwaiter in a celebrated restaurant. As at Christmas, the dinner was sumptuous – TG]. I had to climb over about 50 bottles of Heidseck 1904 stacked up in the crew's quarters. This was a sight that promised well for the evening. Captain Scott opened the official speeches with a reminder that the celebration was a stage in the expedition's history. According to the original plans we had now reached halfway. On the achievements of the first half we could build the basis of what was to come.

Then the speeches continued clockwise round the table, and it wasn't long before it was my turn. As Scott had said, 'we don't need proper speeches',[3] I thought the same and started in carefully and, I hope,

2 The Cape Crozier party did not in fact leave until 27 June.

3 RFS wrote: '. . . one seemed to know so well the style of utterance to which each would commit himself.'

diplomatically. It is not easy to make such a speech in the competitor's camp,[4] but I think I struck the right note. Anyhow the applause that followed was hearty. As I say, the situation is very complicated. However, after the speeches were over, spirits were high and the atmosphere jubilant. Then Ponting showed lantern slides consisting entirely of pictures from the expedition. It was splendid. Then Bowers appeared with his Christmas tree and little presents for all of us, laying aside the distinction between officers and men. The Christmas tree consisted of a ski-stick for the trunk and feathers for branches, the decorations of presents, candles, and sweets. Ponting took photographs, and then came the gift giving. I received a bottle of eau-de-Cologne and a badminton racket. Oates got a wooden gun and a flute, presents which he valued very highly. [Ponting and Taylor – the most talkative – received muzzles, Atkinson and Debenham chocolate paper (for reasons unknown); the youngest man, Tryggve Gran, was given a milk bottle and bib, and Captain Oates a paper cannon, a sword and a wooden horse – TG]. After this revelry we amused ourselves with the presents just like children. We danced, made speeches, and talked about everything between heaven and earth. It really was a lovely party.

23 June

The morning after the night before, as they say at home! But anyhow such a party once a year is worth every bit of it.

24 June

A year ago I climbed the highest mountain in Madeira and was nearly choked by the heat; today I am not particularly plagued by the heat. I have mostly kept indoors and busied myself quietly with my ski work. After lunch I went on skis to South Bay to take the temperatures. The weather has been superb – no wind and only 20 odd degrees of frost.

25 June

At home today it will be the ski races at Finse. I wonder who will win my cup this year?[5] Sunday has passed quietly. I slept a good part of the day, for I had been out early to South Bay. It was bitterly cold and rather misty, so much so that on the homeward journey it took me a while to find the hut. This afternoon I have been writing. Taylor and I have had a competition to name the respective authors in 'S.P.T.' Teddy Evans and Cherry were the umpires and the victory went to Taylor who won by one point, having himself been author of three of the pieces. [The

4 Referring to the rivalry with Amundsen.
5 One that Gran had previously received.

guessing at authors was very funny. Gran was rabidly curious – TGT].
It will soon be midnight and time to turn in.

26 June
Taylor gave a talk tonight on the Western Mountains. To judge from the slides the region seems a lot like Norway. I hope I shall get an opportunity to judge a bit more accurately than by pictures alone. Tomorrow the Crozier party will leave – Dr Wilson, Bowers, and Cherry. If possible, I shall see them on their way as far as Hut Point. This morning I took a trip and logged the temperatures. The weather was superb, if rather cold. Nelson and I usually go out together nowadays. He goes to the igloo to fish. We part there and I make for the thermometer station. After half an hour I return to the igloo and then we head for home. This afternoon I helped Wright to place some scientific instruments – 30° of frost and blowing! The Crozier party decided at first that they would go on skis, but have now changed their minds and will march on foot. It is very dark now on the Barrier, and as they are inexperienced the skis would cause them too much trouble.

27 June
The Crozier party departed this morning and are now, it is hoped, already at Hut Point. They left at 11 a.m. and were led by Meares, Simpson, Nelson, Taylor and me. To begin with the weather was fine, but when we reached Razorback a nasty blow began. At this point Taylor and Nelson left us, while we others continued. The wind really set in and after another hour's march over *sastrugi* and drifts, when we were 9 km from Cape Evans, Simpson and Meares decided to turn back. The weather looked threatening and, as Dr Wilson would not take the risk of letting me continue, I had to bid them farewell too and turned home on my skis. The wind was in the right direction and I covered the distance in about 50 minutes – 40 minutes less than the other two.[6] [This winter travel is a new and bold venture, but the right men have gone to attempt it – RFS]. This afternoon I had a conversation with Scott about skis and ski boots. [On the depot journey I had used ordinary ski boots, but these had proved chilly and even risky. Scott had used some felt boots. They were far better than the leather boots, but Scott and I agreed that the only solution for the trek to the Pole would be *finnesko* in a sort of galosh with a stiff sole. The idea was to affix the galosh to the ski permanently, so that all you had to do was to stick your foot in it – TG].[7]

6 Simpson and Meares.
7 The bindings were made up by PO Evans.

28 June
The aurora has flickered the whole day. Towards the north it is as though dawn was already beginning to show a faint glimmer.

29 June
It is difficult to keep a diary. This life is of little interest; one day is just as monotonous as the next. Under such conditions weak nerves will either get stronger or crack. There is little happening.

30 June
We have been following the thermometer with interest today, for it has been on the point of dropping into the [minus] forties, something which has not yet happened. At about midday I went with Day to South Bay to help him take some theodolite and tide measurements. My hands went dead, and the only way of reviving them was to put them on my stomach. I also helped Teddy Evans before dinner with observations, which was a cold task too. It is wonderfully clear.

1 July
Tonight we played poker for cigarettes. I had no idea how to play and lost heavily at first. In the morning we were out in South Bay. It is beginning to get light, and at one o'clock I could just read the maximum thermometer without a light.

2 July
One more Sunday has gone in peace and quiet. In the morning a trip southwards and a longer walk this afternoon. Splendid weather, 40° of frost.

3 July
I'm on night duty. Aurora above Erebus and a deep rumbling sound from the glacier. It is cold.

4 July
Snow-storm today and huge masses have piled up around the hut. We defied the elements by going down to South Bay to log temperatures.

5 July
Atkinson was the cause of some excitement today.[8] Because of the storm and thick snow-fall, common sense dictated that no one should venture

8 Both RFS and TGT give 4 July as the date for the following incident.

too far from the hut. Nevertheless among those who tempted providence were Atkinson, Taylor, and not least yours truly. At four o'clock we headed out [entirely without my knowledge – RFS], Atkinson and Taylor towards The Ramp [behind the hut] and I to South Bay – all to log temperatures. It was vile weather, and I had not gone many steps before I lost any sense of direction. There was only the wind to steer by, and even that was highly unreliable. I turned windwards so as to head towards land, but this did not work; I trudged on and on, but still did not hit a landmark. I half-turned, tripped, and fell in a snow-drift. I had begun to feel a little uneasy when suddenly I saw some black stakes a few steps ahead of me. They were Day's tide markers. Well, I was not far from home and I set off again. Even so it took me half an hour to find the hut, which was really only a couple of hundred yards away.

Atkinson and Taylor were not in the hut when I got there, but Taylor arrived a few moments later. It was then five o'clock. Taylor told us that after repeated attempts they had at last found the thermometer screen, but that Atkinson on their return had got the bit between his teeth and, ignoring advice, had gone on out again to find 'Archibald'.[9] This really was tempting providence. He was completely lost – even when he got near Tent Island, which he wrongly identified as Inaccessible Island. [Atkinson's continued absence passed unnoticed until dinner was nearly over at 7.15. . . . Although I felt somewhat annoyed, I had no serious anxiety at this time – RFS].

While he was thus wandering wildly about we for our part tried to attract his attention by lighting a bonfire and sending up rockets. At first we went out in small groups over the sea ice, armed with lanterns to maintain contact with land and each other. But all these efforts were in vain. Taylor, Deb, and I later went out across the peninsula to South Bay. At ten it began to clear; the wind, which had been blowing at between 60 and 100 km.p.h., dropped and the moon gradually but steadily emerged. This at least should have put Atkinson on the right track. But no, 11 o'clock came and the situation was unchanged – no Dr Atkinson.

At this juncture three parties were sent out: one south and one north along the coast, both equipped with sledges, sleeping bags, etc.; the third, consisting of Wright, Lashly, and me, went west between the bergs and around Inaccessible Island. The weather was fine, and we simply could not understand why he was still missing. Perhaps he had met with an accident, twisted or broken his ankle. Perhaps he had fallen into a tide crack in the ice, or simply frozen stiff. We pressed on

9 The North Bay and South Bay thermometers were known respectively as 'Archibald' and 'Clarence.'

so fast that we sweated profusely, hermetically sealed, as we were, in our windproofs. But we saw nothing. The moon shone with uncanny brightness, the icebergs cast their jagged shadows, and from Cape Evans the bonfire flamed and flickered. On our way back towards the hut a green, shimmering flare rose over an iceberg that lay in our path. We all cried out as one, 'Alright', and hurried on towards the hut. Taylor came out to meet us. Yes, Atkinson had arrived, his right hand frost-bitten but otherwise alright. He himself could not really say where he had been, although he thought it was near Inaccessible Island. He was understandably extremely embarrassed, and went round saying 'sorry' to everyone as they came in from the search. The northern party returned at one, the southern at two [a.m.]. While all this was going on, Scott seemed rather put out, but appeared very pleased when Atkinson finally returned. [. . . we must have no more of these unnecessary escapades. Yet it is impossible not to realise that this bit of experience has done more than all the talking I could ever have accomplished to bring home to our people the dangers of a blizzard – RFS].

6 July
The temperature is falling, the mercury[10] is getting viscous and is dropping towards –50 °C. The weather is superb.

7 July
A dubious pleasure to be outside today, – 40 °C and a stiff southerly breeze. It is good to stay inside the hut.

8 July
After breakfast the night's fine weather turned really vile. It began with drift of moderate strength, but this was followed by conditions the like of which we had never seen before. The wind reached 35 m.p.h. and the temperature –35 °C. If you stuck your nose out of the door, it took your breath away. Ten minutes outside in this weather without windproof clothing would probably have finished anyone off. Most of us have spent the time reading or playing chess; in such weather we really prize the fact that we have a roof over our heads. I wonder how Wilson, Bowers and Cherry are faring. They should have reached their destination[11] by now.

9 July
Scott kept watch last night. He fell asleep and woke up at 5 a.m.; the

10 Mercury freezes at – 39 °C.
11 Cape Crozier.

fire went out and he had to wake Clissold to get it alight again. He couldn't find the [lighting] wood. The weather has kept us in today too, though it is a lot better than yesterday. I spent the morning in my bunk, not asleep but dreaming of Norway. It's quite nice just lying and thinking and reliving old memories, while the wind blows and howls.

10 July

The bad weather continues and it is still inadvisable to move out of doors. We therefore passed the time going round chatting with each other in our respective cubicles. Ours seems to be visited the most despite the fact that Taylor greets everyone by saying, 'Goodbye, Nelson, goodbye whoever-you-are.' Before lunch I went out to see to the skis, for if they had blown over they would have been lost without trace. Poor dogs, they have an appalling time. Those on the loose seek shelter behind the hut and in the outbuildings. Those on the leash seek protection against the wind by huddling down covered by snow. Taylor and I played dominoes this evening. Of course I lost.

11 July

It is still heavy with snow and stormy but a bit better, and tonight the moon shone through the cloud cover. I spent part of the forenoon in Ponting's cubicle. I really succeeded in scaring him with my tales.

12 July

This bad weather is getting a bit much; it kept us indoors again today. I slept through the morning, something which I have not done until now, except after night duty. After lunch, despite the weather, I took a little trip to the high ground around the hut. It wasn't so bad when I first went out, and the sky was nearly clear, but after a bit the hills and small lakes seemed to become the eye of a whirlwind of snow. The wind howled dreadfully and was so strong you simply could not walk into it. It was a good job the hut was not far away. In spite of the last week's bad weather we are becoming aware of the sun's approach; the sky in the north reddens at midday. I have been sitting in Ponting's armchair this evening, listening to the gramophone. Ponting himself was sleeping like a log.

It is really peaceful in the hut tonight; the gramophone is silent, for outside in the stable one of the horses is dying. I feel really sorry for Scott; he really doesn't deserve all these setbacks. [We have had a horrible fright and are not even yet out of the wood. At noon yesterday one of the best ponies, 'Bones', suddenly went off his feed . . . – RFS].

13 July
The weather has at last improved, and we have been able to go out.

14 July
When I woke up this morning, there had been two changes in the night – one good and one bad. The horse was better, but the weather was lowering and thick. The horse had had an infected intestine. The big news for me tonight is that I am to go as navigator with the western party. [For my reckoning it could hardly be otherwise. I was a Norwegian and so was Roald Amundsen – there is no need to say more. A disappointing arrangement for me, but inevitable – TG]. Captain Scott wishes me to stay here an extra year, but has given me a free choice.

15 July
Simpson accompanied me to South Bay today.[12] The weather had improved during the morning, and the moon shone over the ice floes. But one day passes very much like the next. After breakfast Evans goes to his cartography, Scott to his diary, Day to his 'make and mend' [with the motor sledges], Meares to his harness-making [for the dogs], Oates (at 12) to his horses, Ponting to his photographic plates, Deb to his rock specimens, Taylor and I to our geographical studies or to our diaries. At noon Atkinson with Taylor or Ponting go up to The Ramp. Then comes lunch with cocoa, coffee, cheese, marmalade and honey.

The afternoon is like the morning, except that after five o'clock the pianola starts up. Day, Ponting, and Atkinson are the main players, supplemented occasionally by Deb and Meares. Then comes supper. Taylor waits impatiently for the pudding. Finally it comes and the meal ends with the lighting-up of cigars and pipes. Atkinson or I put the gramophone on. Then we play dominoes or chess until ten. Nelson is the chess champion. About ten we begin to turn in; we read in bed, some till nearly midnight, and Deb, Nelson, and Ponting often later. Deb is the worst. Out go the lights at 11 and on goes the night watchkeeper's lamp. At midnight and at 4 a.m. readings of the barometer and thermometer are taken. Naturally the watcher is on the look-out every hour for signs of the aurora. At 7 a.m. Clissold is wakened. Hooper, Teddy Evans, Simpson, and the night watchkeeper turn in until lunchtime.

16 July
I was on night watch last night and slept out the morning. Charles

12 In a footnote in the diary TG explains: 'Simpson, as the expedition's meteorologist, came out with us from time to time to inspect our temperature stations.'

Wright and I went on skis over to South Bay in the afternoon. Despite the wind and drift we found the thermometer bank at first go. With the wind at our backs the return journey went like greased lightning.

17 July
I intend to turn in early to read Ibsen's *The Lady from the Sea*, which Captain Scott has lent me. Scott is an admirer of Ibsen. Weather is threatening and foul.

18 July
Weather still uncertain. The red reflection from the sun is getting larger, and by midday the icebergs cast shadows. Atkinson and I have been to South Bay on skis. It has now turned out fine.

19 July
Seaman [PO] Evans spends his days preparing sort of outer casings for the *finnesko* to use with the Huitfeldt binding. They're made of sealskin and work perfectly. The idea is to use them on the polar journey. As it was yesterday, the weather has been splendid but rather cold. Venus has appeared like a sun in the northern sky. The red light of the sun increases from day to day, and at midday we can now read out of doors.

20 July
It's blowing with drift tonight. I went out in my indoor clothes a while ago, for a quick look round. It was as much as I could do to withstand the whirling mass of wind and snow, and I could hardly find the door to the hut. In the morning it was lovely, and I went out to the thermometer after first having accompanied Nelson to a gigantic tide crack, where he is taking soundings.

21 July
A noteworthy event today – Day has cut his hair. I also washed myself and changed into clean, new underwear. In other words, a very eventful day. The weather is beautiful and calm.

22 July
Bad weather and snow-storm. At home there is summer and warmth. It will be long before I get home – not next, but perhaps the following, summer.

23 July
Today has been proper *Terra Nova* weather, and even in the hut it has seemed nasty and raw. I have therefore stayed in my bunk most of the

day, reading, writing, and dozing. At supper I had quite a long discussion with Scott about Norwegian conditions, including the political situation in the 1905 period. Scott is very interested in such matters. The temperature has risen sharply, and the wind gusted intermittently up to 82 m.p.h. The gramophone and pianola have been going all day long.

24 July
Wind and weather improved in the night and Nelson and I have spent the day taking soundings through cracks in the ice. We came across two of our dogs during our trip; they had mercilessly attacked a lonely seal. The battlefield was red with blood; the fight must have taken hours.

25 July
Nelson's igloo has been buried by the snow-storm and drift. His ropes and measuring instruments are lying under metres of snow; it will be a terrific job to get them out. We made rather a feeble attempt today. Stormy, ugly weather the whole day.

26 July
The Western Mountains are visible for the first time in months, bathed in a red glow from the coming sun.

27 July
Changeable weather these days. If one day is good, you can be pretty sure the next will be rotten. Went out before lunch, a short trip on skis with Atkinson and Day, but it blew hard and our noses suffered accordingly. No, the hut is the best place just now.

29 July
Today we lost one of our dogs, 'Julick', a good, kind animal. Heaven knows what happened to him; all we know is that he is lost without trace. [Meares imagines he has fallen into the water in some seal hole or crack – RFS]. This evening I beat Teddy at dominoes. The weather is superb, the aurora shining, and it is absolutely calm.

30 July
I have set foot on historic ground; I have today been on a skiing trip to Cape Royds. [I asked him to report on the open water – RFS]. I left the hut about midday in excellent weather, but cold with the thermometer down to – 40 °C. The going was pretty good, and I set out towards the red glow of the clouds in the north. Near Cape Royds, however, the ice was cracked and jagged, and it was difficult to ski – I had Finne bindings. I went into an inlet – Backdoor Bay – since I was not quite

sure of the direction to the hut, but I thought I could see a straight passage from sea to land. This proved correct, and I pushed ahead over the humps with my skis on my shoulder. Sir Ernest Shackleton's abode lay before me, alone and deserted, somewhat snowed in, but still standing proud in the violet light. It reminded me a little of a hut at Ulrikken.[13] Behind the hut was a knoll, and as daylight was beginning to return I put aside my skis and climbed it on foot. I kept on the south side but, when suddenly I reached the cairn [at the top], I was nearly blinded by the golden splendour in the north. The whole horizon seemed ablaze, as if the sun would appear at any moment.[14] Beneath me lay the sea, frozen over as far as the eye could see – a long way on this splendid, clear day. When he was with Shackleton, Day says, the sea was clear of ice a mile or two from Cape Royds. Today this was certainly not the case. [. . . for at least 5 or 6 miles past C.Royds the ice is old and covered with wind-swept snow. This is very unexpected – RFS].

I stood on the top quite a while, gazing at the approaching day. Then I climbed down and was soon inside the hut, something I had looked forward to since I first heard of it. It was cold inside, colder than it felt outside. I lit a candle and made out a confusion of cases, tables, and beds. To the left lay the dark room, to the right Shackleton's bedroom. Right at the back was the stove and, in the right-hand corner, a mound of provisions. I tried to make a fire but failed. I filled my rucksack with tinned stuff, mostly Norwegian (ptarmigan, salt beef, and peas), illustrated papers, etc., and then bade farewell to this ice box.

The dawn in the north had nearly disappeared and was now just a dark-red strip close to the horizon. Erebus was tipped with violet at the summit, and in the eastern sky a half-moon peered out over the mountain crags, joined by Venus shining cold in superb beauty. Then homeward bound with a backpack so heavy that it dug into my shoulders. But hunger kept my speed up, and at 5 [p.m.] I was again back in the nice warm hut at Cape Evans. It was Sunday afternoon and an atmosphere of Antarctic peace prevailed. The ptarmigan was delicious thanks to Thorne's[15] cooking. This evening the whole hut have their heads in the magazines I brought from Cape Royds. Any pictures from the outside world are priceless in these parts.

31 July

After all the activity yesterday life has returned to normal today with

13 In Norway.
14 The sun itself did not reappear until 22 August.
15 A company of Norwegian suppliers.

just a ski trip with Atkinson out to the thermometers. I heard from Teddy Evans that I shall probably go on a trip with him and one other (probably Wright) to 'Corner Camp' on about 15 September. These spring excursions will probably be unholy cold, but I look forward to them. It will be a chance to prove what the skier can accomplish.

1 August

A wonderful display of aurora this evening; it stretched like a thick, wavy veil over the hut from north to south. It seemed so close that it could have been just a few hundred metres above us.

(*Later, 10 p.m.*) I am writing this in my bunk. The Crozier party have arrived. I was half asleep when the watchman shouted: 'The Crozier party is coming'. [They looked more weather-worn than anyone I have yet seen – RFS]. They had had an adventurous journey; the tent had been blown away from over their heads and the temperature [went] down to –63½ °C. The going had been heavy, and they had taken nearly three weeks to cover the 100 km to Crozier. They had been there only ten days, and the weather had been bad almost the whole time. Wilson considers the journey to have been fruitless as regards, in any case, study of the [emperor] penguin, for they had only been able to get to the nesting place on one day. They are now eating and really enjoying the food. The hut rings with discussion about the low temperature and the weather. 'Poor Amundsen', I hear them say, but he will make it. [. . . it is difficult to see how he will keep his dogs alive – RFS].

2 August

Last night's great event has naturally occupied our day. Without doubt the three Crozier men were in bad shape. [The main part of their afflictions . . . arose from sheer lack of sleep – RFS]. Cherry and Wilson were nearly all in, and Bowers was pretty bad too. Their sleeping bags had got in such a state that it took hours to shove themselves into them. Cherry's bag was too big, and he didn't really manage to get warm. He therefore suffered quite a bit during the journey. Cherry had lost 5 lb[16] and the others 3. Wilson is so thin it's almost frightening to see; the sight of him brought to mind a starving, dying wretch during a famine. He was all skin and bone. [He (Wilson) says there is no doubt Cherry-Garrard felt the conditions most severely . . . we both conclude that it is the younger people that have the worst time; Gran, our youngest member (23), is a very clear example, and now Cherry-Garrard at 26 – RFS].

16 According to RFS, 1 lb.

3 August
Weather has been threatening, bitter and windy the whole day, and we have kept indoors as much as possible. Deb and I had a discussion this afternoon on 'the object of life'. Naturally I made myself out ten times worse than I am, and Deb came to the conclusion that I must either be mad or a scoundrel. Cherry today let it be known that the second edition of 'S.P.T.' will be published on Sunday 10 September; I must be sure to make a contribution this time. [By this time most of the diarists had lost their original enthusiasm . . . Gran and I were probably the most voluminous writers - TGT].

4 August
Lectures have begun again. Tonight Simpson devoted himself to wind and weather. During the morning I went out to Nelson's igloo and chopped the night ice from the entrance hole; it was 4–5″ thick. The air was snow-laden and we could only just make out Erebus and Tent Island, but I like such weather – calm and snowy, it is so much like home and one is not so affected by the desolation of this icy, God-forsaken wasteland. It's somehow more closed-in and tranquil. After lunch we all gave Day a hand with his motor sledge, which yesterday was dug out and today lifted out of snow-drifts. The weather is snowy tonight too.

5 August
Snow-fall tonight; and now it lies thick and soft. This afternoon I helped Day to build a garage for his motor sledge. It looks like a storm.

6 August
I went out with Ponting to South Bay tonight. The weather was superb with moonlight, no wind, and only –27 °C. Otherwise there has been snow in the air today, and we have stayed indoors. When I lie and muse these days before dropping off, I dwell on the question whether I should go home next summer or remain one more year. Bowers advises me to stay. It really is a difficult question and one that I have decided to leave open until the last moment.

7 August
It has been a wonderfully beautiful day – calm, not particularly cold, and sparklingly clear. Most of the day I helped Teddy Evans with his observations, and tonight too I will 'shoot' the stars. It is wonderful out of doors, by the way, moonlit and still. Ponting gave a talk on Japan tonight; it was most interesting, and of course the photographs outstanding. I must go to Japan.

8 August
Ponting and Taylor have announced officially that they will sail home with *Terra Nova* [in 1912]. Otherwise I think the rest rather want to stay on. We are doing famously, and the spirit of comradeship is ideal. It will soon be time to write letters. Spring will bring work, and there won't be much opportunity for such chores.

9 August
By midday the northern sky was aflame with rosy light. In a week or so the sun will be on the mountains. It will be lovely to sun oneself.

10 August
'Titus' Oates gave a talk this evening on horse training. He's really no speaker, but there is a lot in what he has to say and he often has his listeners helpless with laughter. We've been discussing snow-shoes [for the ponies] again; it is the difficulty of binding them firmly that causes problems. [. . . Petty Officer Evans has been making trial shoes for 'Snatcher' on vague ideas of our remembrance of the shoes worn for lawn mowing – RFS]. This afternoon I worked on the 'S.P.T.' [article] – hope it won't end up in the wastepaper basket.

11 August
Nelson and I thought we would be daring today, and despite a thick snow-storm and 30° of frost we set off towards the igloo. We got what we deserved – [we were] frozen through. One thing is crystal clear; foolhardiness never pays off here in the South.

12 August
After the bad weather of the last few days there has been a change for the better today. It has been calm and sparkling, the sun's red shadow has risen higher, and the snowfields reflected its approaching rays. This morning I went out to help Nelson. His trawl had become tangled, and it was impossible to get it up. We went out again after lunch, joined by Deb and Wright. But no luck – we had Mother Antarctica on the hook!

13 August
After divine service, I went out with Clissold to Cape Royds – I on skis and he with dog sledge. The weather was splendid and tranquil, and it was a successful trip in every way. We lit a fire in the hut and spent a couple of hours inside. And of course we helped ourselves to the provisions. The return trip took several hours. Clissold had one of Shackleton's old ski-sledges and a case of kitchen utensils, and I his old

toboggan and illustrated periodicals. We got back at 5 p.m. I almost wished that I could go to bed at once, for I must confess to being a bit tired, but I am on night watch. From what I have seen today of the co-operation between skier and dog, I believe Amundsen has a very great chance of getting good results with his animals. The dogs are stimulated by the swish of the skis and get the feeling they have a goal to aim at. A competitive spirit is a very strong factor.

14 August

It was an effort to keep my eyes open during night watch, and it was marvellous to drop into the bunk at 7 a.m. I've spent the whole day abed, except for lunchtime. The weather has been excellent. Tonight Wright gave a talk on radium, learned but short. 'Lady' gave birth to a litter this evening – we don't yet know how many.[17]

15 August

Despite the full-blooded effort of four men we still have not succeeded in loosening Nelson's tide plumb line. The weather is good but hazy.

16 August

After spending most of the morning writing, I went with Taylor at 11 to the top of Inaccessible Island to take some readings with the theodolite. The weather was superb, the sky flamed and flickered, and the polar landscape glowed with a strange blush. It was windless, but all the same we felt cold standing still in a temperature of –40°C. We were wearing ski boots, but it didn't take long for our feet to fall asleep. We stayed in for a bit after lunch, and I spent the afternoon doing calculations for Simpson.

17 August

For the first time in many months Erebus and the Western Mountains are today touched directly by the rays of the sun. Perhaps we'll see the sun ourselves tomorrow, if the refraction is strong enough. We can at any rate celebrate the fact that the long winter night has passed and spring waits at the door. The winter night has not been anything like as harsh and unpleasant as I had expected. The winter months have been among the nicest of the whole expedition. This morning I fixed a binding on a pair of skis belonging to Dr Wilson. This afternoon Bowers and I made a fine skiing trip, hunting for Simpson's balloons. We followed their lines[18] for hour after hour, between the bergs and over the humps towards

17 None of the six or seven puppies survived.

18 Trailing threads.

Tent Island and then to Razorback. Then came the shades of night, and Inaccessible Island and the bergs to the north rose like black shadows against the fiery red of the evening sky. The lines became more and more difficult to follow, and eventually we had to give up our search and return to base. Atkinson gave a lecture this evening on scurvy.

18 August

It is Day's 27th birthday and we drank a toast in his honour. He is a splendid companion – always cheerful and helpful. It's a pity he's got involved with the operation of the motor sledges – it will only bring him disappointment.

19 August

High wind and drift all day, so definitely not the day to venture forth. Bowers is occupied these days with the job of weighing out pemmican for the sledge journeys in the coming summer. [The table resembled a grocer's shop from now on – TGT]. The plateau ration will be 12 oz as against 9 oz on the Barrier. A good sensible ratio, I think.

20 August

During the night the wind gusted to hurricane force – up to 160 km.p.h. But it moderated a good deal in the course of the morning, and when I went to South Bay before lunch it was fresh but not stormy. This afternoon I have had a longish conversation with Dr Wilson. I asked his advice on what I could relate in my letters home about Amundsen, his prospects, etc. We both agreed that I should be cautious. Dr Wilson has begun to believe less in Amundsen's chances. He lacks faith in dogs.

21 August

Several of us went out to see the sun today, but we were disappointed. The cliff wall towards Cape Royds shut out the horizon. At 11 some of us went out to the igloo to give Nelson a hand with his confounded nets. [. . . 'Trigger' Gran started long after us, and 'flapping' along on his ski easily caught us up – TGT]. Strong in numbers and muscle as we were, we managed to break the rope, luckily at the bottom. From there I continued on to South Bay; I was on skis and made my way home *via* Inaccessible Island. The Western Mountains were sunlit. Ponting gave a lecture this evening about India; his illustrations were of course first-class.

22 August

We have been celebrating the sun's return this evening, though we haven't seen it because the icy wastes and mountains are shrouded in one huge snow-storm. So there is not much springtime to see. Nevertheless, it's there and we have therefore had champagne. Scott said a few words. He was happy to see the good health and spirits of the expedition during the past winter months. He is right; no expedition could have had better comradeship and health. Not one case of sickness the whole time. The dinner table was very animated.

23 August
The weather has not been fit for living beings today; we didn't even look forward to putting our heads out of the window. During the winter months my weight has gone down several kilos, but my condition has improved considerably. I now weigh 80 kg[19].

24 August
The bad weather continues, and only Nelson and I have ventured outside the hut. We went to the igloo and dug it out. Taylor gave a talk tonight on glaciers – mostly those in Switzerland – with illustrations by Ponting. Afterwards Ponting let the rest of his slides 'run through the projector', as he said. As usual they were excellent.

25 August
Simpson saw the sun today one-third over the horizon near Barne Glacier. He saw it from Windvane Hill. I went out with Atkinson this morning to South Bay. The bad weather has blown itself out leaving a stiff breeze. After a storm the going is never good and usually sticky, just as it was today. This afternoon I was out again, first to the thermometers in North Bay and then with Ponting on the slopes behind the hut. The sky to the north was fiery.

26 August
We had our first real spring day today; the sun shone on the mountains, on McMurdo Sound, and right into the hut. It was really lovely outside. This morning Teddy Evans and I went round setting up triangulation points for the geologists. During the afternoon Ponting and I took a trip out on the sea ice beneath Barne Glacier. We played like children in the snow-drifts, gambolling and somersaulting (this was only me – Ponting just stood there wishing for his camera). There was a new moon to the north this afternoon. This evening Evans and I played dominoes. It is beginning to look as though the fair weather is coming to an end; it is overcast and blowing hard.

19 *Compare* Gran's weight on 18 June 1911.

27 August

'Julick'[20] has returned – unbelievable, but true. By chance it was I who first welcomed the poor brute back home.

At nine o'clock Ponting and I went out for the weather had begun to improve after being windy and bitter all day. We went westwards until the new moon vanished behind the mountains. We rested on top of an ice-fall for a while, watching the stars twinkling in stark clarity. Then we turned back; above Erebus the aurora glittered ghostly and white. The bergs cast their huge shadows and, in on the shore of the bay, lay the hut with its light at the windows. A dog came towards me. It looked like 'Julick', but was it possible? Ponting and I had talked about 'Julick', and I had suspected one of the other dogs of doing away with him. Yes, it was 'Julick', long-haired, black-and-white, thinner than before, stinking of seal, and bloody too, but otherwise in good shape. I went in and awakened Meares. Scott got up too, and we talked in the quiet midnight hour of the strange return of the prodigal son. 'Julick' had been away a month. [I cannot but think the animal has been cut off, but this can only have happened by his being carried away on broken sea ice – RFS].

28 August

Meares gave an unusually interesting lecture tonight about his travels in southwest China. It was unquestionably the best and most entertaining of all the lectures we had heard so far.

It must be pretty bad form to admit I have had enough of the cold – I have been out in the wind today. In the morning I went up on The Ramp with Taylor and hacked through one of the many cone-shaped mounds.[21] [. . . We definitely proved that this symmetrical cone was solid, and was piled around a core of kenyte blocks (TGT). This gives a great 'leg up' to the 'debris' cone theory – RFS].

This afternoon with Teddy Evans on skis to Cape Barne. At the foot of the ice we left our skis and climbed to the summit. There we built a cairn with a flag atop for use in future survey work. The weather was superb even though a fresh breeze was blowing.

29 August

The weather has been good today too, with sunshine and a cloudless sky. It seems as though activity in the hut is proportional to the amount of sunshine reaching us. I helped Simpson release a balloon this morning. It went up alright towards the north, but we may have lost it. I shall

20 *See* 29 July 1911.

21 To see if it was ice-cored.

probably go after it on skis; we know the direction but that is all. This afternoon I went with Hooper over towards the Barne Glacier. At the spot where I nearly managed to knock myself senseless last year, I set about chopping away at the icefoot to make an even ski slope. Demetri came to help us and we really made good progress, so much so in fact that I was able to try it out. After a couple more days I hope to have a first-class slope suitable for jumping, not least with a view to taking some film.

30 August

After lunch I worked some more hours on the ski slope. It is promising but not quite ready. This morning I had a talk with Scott about the forthcoming spring journey to see to the depot at 'Corner Camp'. We shall have double tents and eiderdown sleeping bags, if we want them. I take the eiderdown with pleasure, for I really do want something to fill out my large reindeer-skin bag. Scott gave me his 'patent [ski] shoes' prepared by Evans; I shall take them on the spring journey. Bowers has given me new *finnesko*, and I must repair my others. Taylor and Debenham are working on a geological map of Cape Evans.

31 August

The last day of the month. Tomorrow we begin outdoor training for the summer sledge journey. Today I began to get together my things for the trip which will start about 10 September. I went up to 'Holmenkollen ski jump' after lunch and worked for a few hours. The whole day the weather has been rather threatening, though we are not expecting an immediate storm. But while I was standing there pondering, a sudden gust of wind hit our position and before I could count ten a snow-storm blotted everything out. Without lingering a second I took off for home, and I may say the short trip back was not much fun.

1 September

I went out just before lunch to try the 'patent shoes' with satisfactory results. Meares left at 11 for Hut Point with Demetri and the dogs. He will be away about ten days, hunting seal for dog meat. [There is no real reason for Meares' departure yet awhile, but he chose to go and probably hopes to train the animals better when he has them by themselves – RFS].

The wind dropped during the morning and Ponting and I went over to the 'hill' this afternoon. We made good progress. Scott was there and of course was sceptical – too steep [for skiing], he thought.

2 September
Skiing on the flat so much certainly means that I shall be unsteady on the downhill runs. Today I tried out the Antarctic 'Holmenkollen Hill'. Good heavens, how I fell! Ponting witnessed the spectacle and regretted not bringing his camera. Weather fine, sunshine and –30 °C.

3 September
Sunday, and the inhabitants of the hut are occupied with their own affairs. Ponting is reading an exciting love story, Oates is studying his great hero Napoleon [. . . over his bunk his sole picture was a reproduction of the great French warrior – TG], Deb and Wilson are reading scientific works, Day is making his sledging flag, Teddy is writing letters, Bowers is using his bunk as a writing desk, Scott and Atkinson are playing chess, Taylor is loafing about and Simpson is upholding the Sabbath. For myself, clothes washing is the order of the day, and when that is finished it will be sewing patches on underpants.

4 September
The day began stormy; Teddy Evans and I stayed indoors. I have spent the time working on the skis, mounting bindings and with Wilson trying to devise a better heel-strap for the new 'patent shoes', about which we have different ideas. Deb gave a talk tonight on geology in Antarctica.

5 September
Teddy Evans and I have covered 40 km on skis today. We have been over to the other side of Glacier Tongue, to Turtle Island where we took some sights with a view to triangulating the area. We spent two hours at Little Turtle Back.[22] We had our thermos flask with tea and helped ourselves when our fingers or toes began to freeze. I made a nice little collection of rocks for Deb. On the way back I got some frost-bite in the face, and that was because I was foolhardy and thought I could be out in 30° of frost with face uncovered. However, I had my new fur boots on and my feet were good and warm. We got back at eight, and it was dark and the moon shone.

6 September
If the weather holds, we'll start on Saturday – Forde, Teddy and I. [E. Evans, Gran and Forde will go out to find and re-mark 'Corner Camp' (RFS). Scott consented to our application (to make this journey) with the following remark: 'If you people want to suffer, for Heaven's

22 Both names refer to Turtle Rock, 2 miles south of Erebus Glacier Tongue.

sake, Go!' – TG]. Forde has had little opportunity to use skis; he may have a difficult time. These September journeys are reckoned to be the worst that polar explorers have to go through. We shall see.

7 September

Vile weather and, as yesterday, we spent the day within the walls of the hut. We have a lot to do; for myself I find that even a small trip requires considerable preparation.

8 September

The sledge is packed and ready down on the ice, and now there is only one question – the weather. The day passed in preparation. I shall take about the same gear as on the depot journey with the addition of the eiderdown. The 'South Polar Times' was published today, and I have only just managed to glance at it. Scott read something from it aloud, and it looks as if it's as good as it was the last time – certainly the pictures. There were toasts at dinner, one for the publisher and one for us, the sledge party: 'We have opened the big season.' Ponting gave a talk tonight about his travels in China, but it is late and we shall be up betimes; so now to bed.

The spring journey on the Barrier, 1911

9 September
It takes all my strength to grip this pencil. T. Evans, Forde, and I arrived here[1] after over 12 hours' hard sledging. I am lying in my sleeping bag writing this; it is –42 °C with a southerly breeze and moonshine. The two others have settled down into their sleeping bags; I am holding the candle in my left, fur-covered fist and the pencil in my right. We left Cape Evans at eight this morning in superb weather and reached the *Discovery* hut by three. All in all we have covered 30 km, and are now[2] bivouacked right under the Barrier. It blew as we rounded Cape Armitage and we had to look after our faces from time to time. [. . . whilst Gran cooked the supper I applied what warmth I could to Forde's nose to bring the frozen part of it back to life – ERGRE]. These double tents are excellent. With the primus going they are really warm. [. . . (PO) Evans has made a lining for one of the tents; it is secured on the inner side of the poles and provides an air space inside the tent. I think it is going to be a great success – RFS].

10 September
Again in the sack. On arrival 45½ and now certainly 50 degrees of frost. It was cold in our sleeping bags during the night because we had sweated so much during the day's march. We broke camp at 10 a.m., the weather icy with some drift. After a good hour's march we reached the Barrier; the passage over from the sea ice was not as even as last year, and I am therefore inclined to believe the summer's ice in 1910 did not break up as far south as in 1911. We arrived at 'Safety Camp' at noon, dug out the depot, ate lunch, and then continued the march in calm but hazy conditions with overcast to the south. The surface was not too bad.

1 Southeast of Hut Point.
2 Before 9 p.m.

11 September

(*8 a.m.*) When the primus is purring, it is comparatively warm in the tent. We're now at breakfast. The night was savagely cold, –55 °C. Forde and Teddy say they haven't slept a wink and I can thank the eiderdown for my rest.

(*12 midnight*) We covered 20 km during the day. The wind was moderate this afternoon, and we were about to start when suddenly it blew up so hard that we were afraid we should not be able to control the dismantling of the tent. In the end we just managed it – a tough job. We must have pitched camp near a crack, for beneath us the ice rumbled.

12 September

We have covered the ground to 'Corner Camp' but have not found the depot. It is hazy and pretty dark. I believe we are just a little short and too far south. It was better in the sleeping bags last night. Drift continued throughout the morning and we did not break camp until 2 p.m. It was blowing and foggy. By 8 p.m. we decided to bivouac, for it would be a waste of effort to push on, dark as it was. This type of life is interesting in a way, but disagreeable. My finger tips are frozen and I can hardly write. I have not been feeling quite fit since we left 'Safety Camp'. It's difficult to hold a course in these hazy conditions where there's nothing for the eye to fix upon. The going has been extremely laborious.

13 September

(*6 a.m.*) We hardly closed our eyes last night for it was –60 °C. I spent the night building 'bridges' in the sack, i.e. arching myself on heels and head, then letting 'the bridge' drop and getting a spot of warmth from the operation. We're starting now on our hunt for 'Corner Camp'.

(*2.30 p.m.*) We have reached 'Corner Camp'. We started at 8 a.m. Drift and fog had returned, and it really was impossible to maintain anything like a proper course. After some hours we decided to bivouac; we had got the tent up and were just going to start brewing up, when suddenly the sun broke through the fog and threw its rays over the endless ice desert. I gazed around – what was that? In the far distance I thought I could just make out a heap of snow. I hastily cleared the ice from my eyebrows. Yes, it was a cairn. We have found 'Corner Camp'. We got the tent down and were off. It took us an hour to reach our goal; the bamboo pole still stood but the flag was in tatters. We've now built up the depot again; a new flag flutters at the pole and we're sitting round the primus enjoying a well-earned meal. Building up the depot was a pretty hard job.

14 September

(*Midnight*) We have covered 18 km and will push on when we have appeased our hunger. The weather is good but foggy. The wind dropped soon after we had left 'Corner Camp'. It was difficult to hold our course; I was leading and felt great eye-strain.

(*4 a.m.*) We made camp[3] while dawn was breaking. Since then we have navigated exclusively by the stars, but the fog has been particularly thick to the northwest and we are somewhat uncertain of our position. We shall be able to take our bearings when day comes. These last hours we have travelled over large hummocks and patches of *sastrugi*, and I am inclined to believe we have come too close to White Island. We're beginning to get sleepy but would rather press on than turn in to our 'ice sacks'. The night's march was splendid. Over our heads the stars shone bright in the night sky. The Southern Cross, Canopus, and the Big Dipper twinkled large and clear, just like in a story book. Then the aurora began its play; from Ross Sea to the sound near White Island great heavy glittering bands of light shimmered and wavered like huge organ pipes. The whole pattern was in constant movement and changed from one moment to the next, rising and dying in turn. It was a superb sight. There were one or two shooting stars as well, falling through the background light of the aurora to die out, it seemed, just above our heads. The night was calm; now the light of day is creeping in from one snow-drift to the next and dawn's red light shows in the eastern sky.

(*10 p.m., Hut Point*) Back in the hut, near the fire in my old place. It was a tough march; we were on the go nearly 24 hours. We have covered 62 km, which is the longest distance anyone has hauled a sledge on the Barrier. For my part it would have been quite alright to carry on to Cape Evans; the others also wanted to but I got them to see that it would be sheer folly to continue in the dark night, exhausted as we were. It has been a considerable march, in such cold, without sleep for several nights, and with vile going like today's. We must be quite content with our achievement.

When we broke camp this morning, it was clear and we were more or less able to get our bearings. Instead of being too near White Island as I had thought, we had in fact come round further out towards Erebus. Before us we could see Observation Hill and set course for that. Then the sun came over the Barrier casting a golden glow over everything. In these everlasting icy wastes, distances can seem absolutely endless and it appeared that we were making no impression at all on the stretch separating us from the hills at Hut Point. Forde, whom I must admire for his strength and energy, began to weaken, to feel the cold and show

3 For a short stop.

other signs of exhaustion. In other words I began to foresee yet one more night on the Barrier. As the sun rose higher mirages began to swirl and dance, and our eyes and imaginations to suffer. A hundred times we 'saw' 'Safety Camp', but it always disappeared the next second. However, everything comes to an end, even the Barrier, and we gradually worked ourselves past 'Safety Camp' (seen only as a mirage) and down to the sea ice. Evans now began to weaken; hunger and exhaustion had taken their toll. But the surface on the sea ice was better, and we pressed on to Cape Armitage. It began to blow from the southeast, and soon the whirling drift-snow chased out to us from the land. Hunger began to plague me too; my guts seemed to be flapping with emptiness and I had to eat snow. The hut was not far away and slowly we moved on – I with thoughts of kitchen and food. The wind blew and the snow drifted. The wind was on our cheeks and our faces began to freeze. But we reached Cape Armitage, kept on round the shore, and then over the bay towards the hut, which I made out through the drift-snow. A last effort and we were at our goal. Meares was not in the hut, and we threw ourselves over the remnants of the last meal like hungry wolves. Then we got the fire going, Forde made some pancakes, dead tired though he was, and things began to look a lot better. We got in about 3 [p.m.]. As I said, I am lying in the sack by the fire. I have dried it a bit and have taken out the eiderdown to use as a mattress. [We cooked ourselves a tremendous meal, which we ate steadily from 4 to 5.30. . . . Gran remained sitting at the stove, as his bag was in such a shockingly iced-up condition that he could not yet get into it. He awoke us about 10 p.m. with more food, cocoa and porridge, both of which were excellent. I full well remember that he put about four ounces of butter into each bowl of porridge, which we mightily enjoyed – ERGRE].

15 September. At Cape Evans

Thank goodness – we are home again. It was a long and hard march. We left the *Discovery* hut at 2 [p.m.] and arrived here after seven hours on the go. We got too close to Tent Island and the going was atrocious, just like crossing waves of ice. It's lucky we didn't give up last night. Scott, Simpson, Bowers, and Boatswain [PO] Evans left this morning on their trip to the west; they will be away about ten days.[4]

16 September

It feels good to get back to our cosy hut. It is really quite strange to lie in a warm cubicle and to be able to drop off to sleep without waking

4 The party made a depot of supplies at Butter Point for Taylor's western journey.

the next instant from the cold. Forde's fingers are much more frost-bitten than anyone realized. [I am annoyed at this, as it argues want of care – RFS]. Atkinson says he is horribly afraid two fingers may need amputation. My own fingers are covered with blisters, and I have a good deal of frost-bite in the face. Teddy's leg has given him some trouble too.

17 September
The weather has been wonderful and I have had a quiet day in the hut. I have had enough fresh air for the time being on the Barrier. Forde's fingers are still causing anxiety.

18 September
We had a discussion today about our Barrier trip. All agree that the use of skis has an enormous significance. [The Norwegians use different kinds of paraffin wax and compositions of tar and other ingredients (on the ski). . . . Gran had brought from Christiania the best of these compositions – ERGRE]. Whether or not the double tents are worth while is another question. It often happened, even in the lowest temperatures, that our ice-covered clothes melted and we got wet through. When we stuck our heads out again, they refroze and got so stiff we could hardly move about. A journey like this in such low temperatures is excellent for our training as polar explorers. One simply has to be on the watch every moment, or things can go badly wrong. There had been some talk among our people that Amundsen will make his bid for the South Pole in winter time. Now I can see the absurdity of such a conjecture.

19 September
Have occupied myself with the ski bindings. The weather is superb. In a few days Teddy and I will make our way along the coast on a survey trip.

20 September
Meares and I have talked about Amundsen's chances. He, as a dog man, thinks Amundsen's chances are golden, always provided he lasts out the winter alright. The weather is stormy and horrible.

21 September
I saw Scott's plan for the journey today. My goodness, it is an involved proposition. The thought behind it is no doubt marvellous, if only he can carry it out. [This entry was underlined in the original diary].

22 September

I have spent most of the day composing a piece for the 'South Polar Times'. This time I have been luckier and the publisher has complimented me on the following verses:

Spring Night on the Barrier

Night has come – the distant mountains
have lost their golden fairy glance.
The Barrier lies cold and endless
– the wind is sighing in the South.

Night has come – the stars of heaven
are sparkling wonderful and bright.
The frozen sea is calmly sleeping,
the wind is sobbing in the South.

Camp is broken – muffled figures
bending – faces homewards turned.
Ski are moving, creaking, sliding,
– the wind is singing in the South.

Night is there – but what is happening,
a golden mist – a band, a curtain,
is playing on the dark-blue heaven,
the stars are fading, dying out.

Mysteriously mist is waving,
the curtain stretches out its tongues.
Rays are coming – growing – going
– the wind is whistling in the South.

Forward – forward frost-rimed shadows –
day is rising far behind.
Stars are dying – mist is fading,
– the wind is blowing from the South.

Day has come – the lofty mountains
shine in pink and golden flames.
The frozen sea is sparkling – glistening
– the wind is shrieking in the South.

Forward – forward muffled figures –
land is rising to the West.
Behind the Hill the hut is lying
– the wind is howling in the South.

Spring Equinox today – things are beginning to move at last.

23 September

We have arrived back at the hut after a day's work. T. Evans, Deb and I started at ten from the hut and dragged our gear up to Inaccessible Island, where we bivouacked. Deb went about his geological business, while Evans and I climbed to the top and spent the forenoon there. It was blowing from the north and pretty cold despite the sun and the high temperature (about 0 °F). At six we broke off, packed the sledge, and pulled it a short way towards Tent Island. Here we left it and set off home. Our arrival back at the hut gave rise to a verse of poetry:

To Tryggve

Three bold Explorers
marched them forth
for to survey the Plain.
Although so bold
they found it cold.
So marched them home again.

[The . . . scurrilous rhyme pinned to Gran's diary affected them not a whit – TGT].

Survey and departures, spring 1911

24 September
Again in the sack. T. Evans, Deb and I are bivouacked at Tent Island. We departed from the hut this morning in splendid weather and made it here after an hour's march. We were busy all morning and would have gone on into the afternoon, but the sun disappeared and a thick, heavy fog came down. There was nothing for it but to take to our sleeping bags.

25 September
Foul weather tonight with storm and drift. But we can look back on a good day's work. The weather has been menacing all day and now it's blowing so hard the tent is almost carried away.

26 September
During the past few hours I thought the tent would lift like a balloon, so stormy has it been. I am alone; Evans and Deb returned to the hut at lunchtime. I preferred to stay. The tent is nearly buried and the drift-snow swirls about the camp like steam from a boiling cauldron. I have had a quiet, lonely meal of porridge. The storm is howling but the primus is purring, and I am writing this by the light of it's flame. I haven't an earthly idea what the time is, but it must be nearly midnight.

27 September
If the weather remains so vile, I shall set course for home as it is rather wearisome here alone. The tent is nearly buried and it is quite dark inside. There is little improvement [in the weather]. The night was appalling and the storm blew worse than I had ever heard it before.

(*The Hut*) Again back in the hut; I got in about 4 a.m. During the night the wind rose to 39 metres per second. The storm is raging tonight too, so I am glad I decided to come in. I had to force the tent flap open from inside and dig myself out, [as] it blew so hard. Forde's fingers are bad. [For months his right hand was bound up, and he was unable to use it fully right through our western journey next summer – TGT].

28 September

The bad weather continues; it was a good job I left the tent. When you've been out a couple of days, it's pretty good to laze around in the hut.

29 September

Scott's party returned at 1 a.m. On the whole they had had a good trip and encountered bad weather only in the last few days. Their minimum temperature had been –41 °C. There was a terrific commotion when they arrived. Evans, Deb, and I left the hut at six, and after a delightful and interesting day, bivouacked on the sea ice on the south side of Cape Evans. From Tent Island we set course for Razorback.

30 September

A snow-storm blew up this morning, and we've hibernated the whole day. It is absolutely amazing how you can sleep the whole day round.

1 October

We have moved our camp east along the coast. This terrain is utterly wild, covered by moraine and ice cliffs. We have bivouacked in a little bay; on one side is a glacier and on the other a savage scree slope. Teddy has named the place 'Tryggve Bay'.[1]

2 October

It was pretty lively in the camp tonight. A violent storm suddenly sprang up, and we woke to find the tent practically blowing away from us. We got a grip on the tent cover at the last moment and held on until our fingers almost seized up with cold and fatigue. At last I managed to crawl to a spot of bare earth, and we at last succeeded in anchoring the tent with heavy stones. The wind conditions here in Tryggve Bay are extremely peculiar. Every gust from the south returns, after a minute or two, from the north. It is a dangerous camping site. The weather has forced us to stay in our sacks the whole day; now darkness is falling and it is bitterly cold. Our hands are freezing.

3 October

We are beginning to run short of food and I have returned to the hut.

1 Now Turks Head Bay.

A fearful snow-storm is blowing, and finding the way back was a pretty desperate task.

4 October

Lying in the sack. Left the hut again after breakfast. It was an exhausting trip, laden as I was. The weather was brilliant, the sun shining, and mittens nearly superfluous. I found the bivouac deserted; Taylor, who had left the hut half an hour before me, was with Deb on the ascent of Turks Head. Evans had gone off east along the coast. I found his spoor and followed it for an hour between frozen ice floes and icebergs. Caught sight of him, met him, and together we made our way back to the camp. After lunch Teddy and I struck camp, and we have now arrived at Glacier Tongue. [It is worthy of mention that Gran could easily carry sixty pounds weight in a 'rygsaek', and hung about him whilst keeping up a speed on ski that made the best of us sweat – ERGRE].

5 October

We were awakened this morning by a howling storm. It was clearly impossible to do any useful work outside, and we therefore decided to make for Cape Evans. Here everything is quiet and peaceful. Outside the storm is still shrieking.

6 October

Bowers gave me half a bottle of champagne on midwinter night, and Teddy and I have enjoyed it today. We left Cape Evans for Glacier Tongue at 6 a.m., in superb weather and relative warmth. When we had pitched our tent I asked Teddy, 'What would you give me for half a bottle of Heidsick?' 'Five pounds,' replied Teddy without hesitation. An hour later an unusual sight confronted us – half a bottle of frozen champagne melting gently in a saucepan. The primus purred away and soon the big moment arrived – the ice had melted. We made toasts for the future, and for the ladies who had left us in peace so long. We had a good time.

Afterwards we went out on survey. Teddy along the base of the glacier and I on top. I had not gone far when suddenly the snow gave away under my feet and down I went. This surprise descent lasted only a second or so before I reached bottom. A gentle fall like this into a crevasse was not an unpleasant experience. The bottom was covered to a depth of a metre in drift-snow and I sank up to my waist. I took stock. To climb back up was out of the question. There was only one choice: to crawl along the bottom of the crevasse and follow my nose wherever it led. And so I set off. It really was rather a tense moment. As I progressed, it got quite dark and I bumped against some large icicles which tinkled as they broke and fell to the floor. Then came a curve and it began to lighten again. Before I knew what was happening I was out on the sea ice. I could hardly believe my own eyes – there stood Teddy with his sextant. [If I looked surprised, he was astonished. When he saw a man coming out of a hole in the glacier, he thought the half-bottle must have given him delusions – TG].

7 October
Snow-storm the whole day, and Teddy and I have passed the time telling stories. [Gran kept us alive with his reminiscences, which were always amusing, and he certainly possessed the liveliest imagination in the expedition. He ought to have been a brigand chief – ERGRE].

8 October
We have moved our camp to Turtle Island. In the night it was pretty rough in our sleeping bags – they were sopping wet and we just lay there, our teeth chattering. This evening is clear with 30° of frost. We're having rice pudding for supper.

9 October
We are in *Discovery* hut, have spent the afternoon here and are in good shape. Demetri is alone as Meares went over to Cape Evans this morning. (We saw him in the distance). It's great the way they have fixed the hut up. It's warm and cosy. We left the tent at Turtleback and made our way direct here, for the weather was nasty and threatening and our primus had developed a choked jet. We had began to tire after all the bad weather and our 11–km return trip from Turtleback seemed endless. In the last day or two a telephone connection has been established between Hut Point and Cape Evans;[2] you can hear quite clearly.

10 October
The telephone link between Cape Evans and the hut is splendid. They have had heavy snow-falls at Cape Evans lately. Here at Hut Point we have had a howling storm of wind but little drift or snow-fall.

11 October
Today we have walked along the coast between Turtleback and Hut Point. It blew hard and was really vile. We left the hut at 9 a.m. and were back by four. Meares arrived this afternoon. He tells us that Clissold was out with Ponting climbing an iceberg on Sunday,[3] had

2 The line was laid on the sea ice by Meares.
3 While posing for photographs.

an ugly fall and nearly killed himself. He was unconscious for several hours. How sad, for he was to go south with the motor sledges. Meares brought some cutlets with him, so we have had a good meal.

12 October

Spent the whole day in the [*Discovery*] hut. We have sat at the blubber stove listening to the incessant shriek of the wind.

13 October

Back again at Cape Evans and as usual it feels good to be in more civilized quarters. After helping Meares with the dogs [at Hut Point] and seeing him well on the way to 'Corner Camp', Evans and I turned for home by way of Turtleback. The weather was superb. We arrived at 9 [p.m.]; the surface was rough and we had a heavy load, so we were rather tired. Clissold is better but has to stay in his bunk.

17 October

The outlook is not particularly promising; one of the motor sledges broke an axle today. After supper they were ready to drive it out of the 'garage', and the whole hut turned out to witness this great moment. We stood there waiting a longish time; then there was a bang and out came one sledge. Great jubilation but ah, woe! A second later it ground to a halt with a thump. Perhaps the cold makes the metal brittle; it shatters like glass.

18 October

We awakened to a snow-storm which has continued the whole day through. I have had a big wash day; I intend to leave behind as few dirty bits of clothing as possible. Day has been working on the broken axle. It is repairable, and he is optimistic as usual. This evening Scott described what he intends to take south in the way of clothing; it is more or less what you walk around in, about 10 kg. Scott has no faith in the motors. [I am secretly convinced that we shall not get much help from the motors, yet nothing has ever happened to them that was unavoidable – RFS].

19 October

Night watch. It is nearly midnight and clear daylight. Meares and Demetri returned from Hut Point tonight. They had the wind at their backs and covered the 25 km in two hours. Stormy weather and drift the whole day.

20 October

Wilson spends the morning hours nowadays writing letters. I think he has given up all hope of getting home this year. The rest of us nourish the quiet thought that, if Scott returns before *Terra Nova* has left for the north, all plans will be thrown overboard and the whole lot of us will set sail for New Zealand. Assuming no accidents, Scott should easily manage to be back before 10 March, and the vessel can wait until then. Played football tonight.[4] Oates acted the clown – great hilarity. Deb twisted his knee. [We shall start west with Forde's right arm useless and Debenham's leg crocked! – TGT].

21 October

Deb's knee is pretty bad, and it'll be at least a week before he can get out and about. Tomorrow the motor sledges start. There will be four men: Teddy Evans, Day, Lashly, and Hooper. [. . . Scott gave me my sledging orders (for the western journey). The method of our relief by the ship seemed rather comic. We were first of all to find Granite Harbour. . . . Here we were to await Captain Pennell in mid-January. No one on the ship had seen Granite Harbour either . . . the harbour was a dozen miles wrong latitude. . . . We rendezvoused there as required but our letters and flag on the bluff remain undisturbed to this day! – TGT].[5]

22 October

The motor party did not make an attempt today, but took a well-earned rest instead. Day has worked terribly hard lately and deserves success. The weather is superb today, and while divine service was on Taylor and I went out and chopped wood for exercise, so as to be in better form when we start. This will probably be our last Sunday in the hut. Nelson and Simpson went over to Cape Royds today; it was bitterly cold on the way back. They had seen three penguins, newly arrived – a sign of summer here in the south.

23 October

At ten this morning they got the motor sledges going, but for one reason or another Day had to call a halt when they'd only got as far as the end of Cape Evans. [Just off the Cape was a belt of smooth sea-ice with a thin layer of snow over it, and the (tractor) belts churned rapidly over this without moving the sledge forward. . . . After some delays and

4 The game was filmed by Ponting.

5 Various items were recovered from the site by a United States geological party under Dr. Robert L.Nichols in 1958–59.

readjustments they got the sledges well under weigh to Big Razorback Island – TGT]. The party are sleeping in the hut. The weather was splendid this morning but by lunchtime had begun to cloud over, and this evening a fresh northerly wind is blowing.

24 October

The motor sledges have got away; bulletins have arrived every hour. The last at 6 p.m.: 'All well, we are between Razorback and Glacier Tongue, 7 km from Cape Evans.' What speed! They started this morning at 10 a.m. The strength of 14 horse-power seems to have diminished sadly during the winter. Today's weather has been fine and clear but windy.

25 October

I am just waiting for Simpson to go with me to Hut Point during the night. The telephone connection has broken and Scott is eager to hear news of the motor sledges. They were seen this evening near Glacier Tongue, but through the glasses it looked as though something was wrong. Someone had been running from sledge to sledge. Simpson and I are off; we shall try to repair the telephone connection.

26 October

After a rather strenuous 30-hour journey we are back again at Cape Evans. It is quiet and peaceful here. We met Scott and seven men on our way back. They were going to the help of the motor party. The party had bivouacked for the night near Glacier Tongue. We came upon them and greeted them in their sleeping bags. Although nothing [mechanical] was wrong, because the blue ice had worn smooth the sledge tracks would not grip, and the men had had to haul the sledges themselves. We arrived at Hut Point at 3 p.m. We detected no break in the telephone line; so no doubt the fault was caused by leakage of current through the ice. During our trip the sun was on the horizon the whole time and only disappeared occasionally behind a peak or summit. It was a superb night. Telephone message just received that the 'motorists' have now camped at Cape Armitage. What progress!

27 October

The Scott party were back by nine this evening. They had seen the motor sledges well on the way up to the Barrier. Everything looked good. Nice for Day; Deb was up for one hour today, but Atkinson says it will be some time yet before he's off the sick list, perhaps Thursday or Friday next week.

28 October

'Christopher' and 'Chinaman' have just gone for each other in the stable. It was a terrific fight and the whole hut was woken up. It was a wonder I wasn't kicked to death. Oates came to my help, and in the end the brutes tired themselves out and could be chained up.

29 October

With Nelson today to Razorback to slaughter some new-born seals. It was horrid, bloody work, done in the name of science. These poor, innocent creatures had to be wrenched from their mothers who then ran round in desperation to other seals, hoping to find their missing young. We had to knock the mothers unconscious for a moment with a blow to the skull. Meares returned today and will take Ponting with him to the Barrier the day after tomorrow. He related that Evans had returned to the hut on skis for a bag he had forgotten. Evans had said that a ball-bearing had broken just after [Scott's] party had returned to Cape Evans. They had succeeded in repairing the damage during the night. The weather has been nice but there was a light wind from the north. The southern party will set off on Wednesday.

30 October

Hard wind and drift. Weather permitting, Atkinson, whose pony[6] needs a head start, accompanied by Keohane, sets off southwards tomorrow. After taking it out for a while in the winter, I wrote of this pony, 'I'm glad to get it back to the hut alive.' Its condition doesn't seem much better now.

31 October

The day dawned rough, but by lunchtime it was fine and Atkinson and Keohane set forth. Meares departed too, taking Ponting with him. Ponting will accompany the southern party to the Barrier. The main group leaves tomorrow, and I have asked Dr Wilson to report my presence to Amundsen, should they ever meet (which seems unlikely to me). We of the western party have had to make do with rather short commons of sleep these last few nights. I doubt if we'll get away before Saturday. The weather is brilliant tonight. Midnight sun and temperature about 0 °F.

1 November

By an irony of fate, I am to carry the Union Jack, at any rate for a short distance towards the South Pole, for the southern party, which started

6 Named 'Jehu'.

today, forgot to take the flag. Scott telephoned from Hut Point, and I shall dash over there after them as soon as the weather clears. It was all right in the morning, but the wind got up after lunch and now there's a blizzard. The ponies will have had a hard start to their journey. I doubt whether such a sharp transition from stable to snow-storm will agree with them. Scott has decided to travel by night, and the first stage will begin tomorrow night, weather permitting. I took the night watch, turned in at 6 a.m. and slept until the party departed. Scott was rather more than a little nervous. [I naturally felt rather uneasy when I saw my comrades make their departure for the south. I felt denuded and cheated as I stood there with tears in my eyes. I almost cursed Amundsen at that hour. It was he who had complicated life for me (TG). All the ponies arrived at Hut Point by 4 p.m. – A CG].

2 November

[*At Hut Point*] The polar party have gone; the last member has just disappeared behind Cape Armitage. They left in three sections, the first with the slowest horses. Atkinson, Wright, and Keohane at 8 p.m., Scott, Wilson, and Cherry-Garrard at 10 p.m. and lastly the 'Express' at 11 – Oates, Bowers, Evans, and Crean. This section was to cover a regulation 18 km without stopping. Ponting went down to 'Safety Camp' by dog sledge and will return by breakfast. It's been lively in the camp today. The weather was so bad yesterday that they took the ponies inside the hut – the stable we built earlier takes only six. I arrived here at Hut Point at 5.30 p.m. after three hours march from Cape Evans.[7] The going was on the whole good but I had to battle against a strong head wind, especially from Cape Evans to Razorback. The polar team were in the best of spirits and full of optimism. Meares and I are now alone in the hut, which we have tidied up a bit.

3 November

After a hard four-hour march I'm back at Cape Evans. The snow was terribly broken up and I had to carry my skis part of the way, but the weather was very nice. Ponting and his lot arrived [at Hut Point] in the morning. They report 'all well and good' on the Barrier.[8]

4 November

This morning I helped Clissold and Forde to dig out stores. Both are

7 The time given for Scott's departure (10 p.m.) suggests that the flag – the gift of Queen Alexandra – was handed over at Hut Point. This is at variance with the following: "Post-haste I dashed off and overtook the party about 40 kilometres from Cape Evans near 'Safety Camp'." (TG). *See also* p.17 above.

8 Where Ponting had filmed.

just fit for work again, though Clissold is still weak and Forde still has two useless fingers.

5 November

After lunch Taylor, Forde and I went out about 5 km in a westerly direction, and Nelson came with us a bit of the way. The weather was nice and mild. Several newly arrived penguins lay dead on the ice, killed by the dogs. Two of the hounds, 'The Lady' and a dog paying court to her at the moment, cornered a seal and kept up their attacks on it until I turned back to where they were. I was in a harsh mood and the dogs felt it when I set about them with the ice-axe. Deb is still sick, and it is doubtful whether he will recover this year. Taylor has decided to undertake a depot trip over to Butter Point. Nelson will accompany us. We shall leave tomorrow and be back again on Friday the 10th.

6 November

As we turned out this morning Anton came in. He told us that after an utterly exhausting march Ponting and he had bivouacked at Razorback. He himself had had stomach ache, fatigue, and 'God knows what', and had begged to be allowed to go to Cape Evans. Nelson and I went out to find Ponting, whom we came upon in deep sleep. We brewed up tea, and then struck camp and set a homeward course. Ponting was weary but otherwise alright. Anton is a tough, energetic lad; it was his first trip out with a sleeping bag. It's blowing hard tonight; we must see what the morning will bring.

7 November

We quit Cape Evans this morning and kept going westwards all forenoon. While we ate lunch, heavy drift began and by evening had turned into a blizzard. However, our spirits are high. Taylor is turning out to be a really agreeable leader of the party.

8 November

The weather improved during the night and today we journeyed 17 km westwards. The Ross Sea coast is beginning to disappear [and] Erebus is taking a pyramidal shape, while the Western Mountains wax in beauty and might.

9 November

We are about 40 km west of Cape Evans.[9] We shall turn back tomorrow

9 About 15 km short of Butter Point.

and hope to reach the hut during the course of the afternoon. The weather has been perfect the whole day, but it has thickened up again this evening.

10 November
Blizzard the whole day and we have slept the time away. We start as soon as the weather lifts.

11 November
[. . . we packed the tent and one meal on the small sledge and left a large flag on a bamboo by the larger sledge – TGT]. After a long hard march we're back at the hut. Struck camp at 3 a.m. and returned here by 4 p.m. Deb's knee is worse and now there's some doubt whether he can remain a member of the western party. There's some talk of Nelson going as the fourth man. We shall set off next Tuesday; Nelson and Anton will probably take part, at any rate for the first two days, to take Deb back if necessary.

12 November
Sunday has passed peacefully in a family atmosphere and the sound of music. Clissold went out with Simpson after a balloon at lunchtime; he returned completely done-in – a sign that he's still weak. I went out and helped him in the last bit. The plan for our journey is as I had thought. I fear Deb will not be fit to march – a great pity. Weather has looked threatening all day. Strong wind from the south and occasional drift.

13 November
A year and a half since I left Norway. I wonder how things are at home. Weather nasty and heavy with snow. Spent the day preparing for tomorrow's venture.

14 November
We[10] got away at lunchtime but, thanks to a forgotten can of spirit, I'm spending the night in my good old bunk in the hut. Our bivouac is about 10 km out in McMurdo Sound. Deb's knee is awfully stiff and he had to ride on the sledge most of the way. [Gran slept in the bunk above, and as the result of some salmon and a recent perusal of Jules Verne's 'Mysterious Island', suffered from nightmare. He explained next morning that he thought Erebus had overwhelmed the Cape with red-

10 Griffith Taylor, Debenham, Gran and Forde, with Nelson and Anton Omelchenko in support for the first four days.

hot lava, wherein Simpson had been engulfed, but the geologists had calmly climbed up to the crater! Was this a forecast of his own escape on the summit a year later, when Gran was nearly choked by the fumes? – TGT].[11]

11 *See* 14 December 1912.

The summer journey to Granite Harbour

15 November

Cape Evans is 25 km behind. Taylor and I left the hut at 8 a.m. and reached the bivouac by ten. We struck camp at once and set course for Butter Point. [We started at 10 a.m. and did nine miles by 5.30. I camped early to prevent Debenham over-straining his leg – TGT]. Our team makes an extraordinary procession, something like a family on a Sunday's promenade: Deb limping along at the sledge side, Anton dwarfish and stocky, Taylor lean and gaunt, Nelson in his tatters, and Forde old and grave. We look like anything but a group of brave explorers.

16 November

The wind and weather were not particularly promising this morning but this evening, as I write, the sun is shining and warming us. There was a thick snow-fall this morning and we had to steer by compass. By lunch we reached the sledge that Taylor, Nelson, Forde, and I had dragged there some days before. We shall need all our strength to pull the combined load. But the going is better than we had expected and we covered a respectable 17 km. Temperature tonight, –15 °C.

17 November

After a wearisome day we're in our sacks near Butter Point. We have dug out the depot – both Shackleton's old stores[1] and those we laid down last year. They were all in cases, and we spent several hours tonight breaking down the provisions into smaller bags (of pemmican, cocoa, etc.). The weather is perfect – a hint of wind but sparkling clear, and the mountain range looms large above us. The landscape looks a bit like Norway. Fjords, deep valleys, and glaciers break up the coastline, while the peaks resemble the crags and tops of Jotunheim. A bit cold in the night; we had been sweating rather a lot, and it doesn't take much

1 From the *Nimrod* Expedition, 1907–09.

of that to make you feel cold in the sleeping bag. Tomorrow begins the trudge up the coast.

18 November

Nelson and Anton bade farewell after lunch and set off for home. The combined weight of the two sledges is now 800 kg. The going is hard and we have to haul the sledges one at a time.[2] Such sledging is extremely enervating and the distances covered small. We are now on a rise in Ferrar Valley.[3] It was hereabouts that Captain Scott made his way up on to the plateau on his first expedition.[4] [Transporting the half-ton over a mile meant a hundred minutes of very hard labour, which with a light load we could cover in twenty-five minutes – TGT].

19 November

I've never had a heavier grind than this. We're dragging and heaving over vile going, and are all more or less exhausted.

20 November

The grind continues – four miles only today over *sastrugi* and loose snow. At lunchtime we laid down a depot of one week's provisions [at Cape Bernacchi] – just in case we had to return [to Cape Evans] if the ship was not there [at Cape Bernacchi]. [Captain Scott had ordered us to leave a week's provisions at Cape Bernacchi, for we should need this if the bay ice went out, and we had to return overland. So we carried up a half-tin of biscuit, and filled it with butter, pemmican, and chocolate. This was reared on end, and protected by a cairn of granite. We surmounted it with one of our precious bamboos carrying a flag. I left a note informing the finder as to our progress and immediate plans. This was the first of our post offices, of which we established four more during the summer – TGT]. The landscape here is just like Norway – granite and grey stone glittering, so that you could almost imagine the smell of wet flint. Deb has begun to give a hand with the hauling, but he must be careful for the *sastrugi* are nasty and cracked. At the last haul before each meal he stays behind and prepares the food, so that he has it ready when we go back for the last sledge. The sun is blazing down on us; we are as brown as berries. Our spirits have risen again – back to normal.

2 The relay method.

3 In fact, crossing pack ice in New Harbour, off the Ferrar Glacier, en route to Cape Bernacchi.

4 In 1903.

21 November

The weather looked a bit threatening as we set out this morning, but it cleared up as the day wore on and now it's brilliant. The going has also improved and, despite a longish halt, we advanced eight miles north. We have bivouacked this evening beneath what the geologists call Gneiss Point. I climbed to the top; the sun was shining over the rock-strewn waste, and sea-gulls flew around like attacking aircraft. Towards the north one could make out a deep bay several miles wide, containing a unit of Antarctic 'cruisers'[5] which have sought lee and anchored. In the sunshine their whiteness was dazzling. Ice conditions in the north look promising; as far as the eye could see no cracks and no open water either. The fear that the ice would break up by now seems to have been groundless. Tonight there is 12° C of frost.

22 November

[We started off relaying as usual, but as I was returning I felt this was just the time to test our outfit as an ice yacht! A steady south wind was blowing almost directly behind us – TGT]. We 'set sail' this morning and it has gone well even though we nearly turned over several times. Our rigging is extremely simple: tent poles as mast and crossbeam, and the floor covering as sail. It's incredible how this sail helps. Whereas before we could hardly get one sledge moving, today two were no great strain for us.[6] We hope this wind will hold.

23 November

Passed a barren little island[7] today. It was as flat as a pancake and consisted entirely of loose rocks. The wind has helped us again today, for despite appalling going we covered 10 km.

24 November

It is only 3 p.m. now, but we have bivouacked so as to change to night travel. The sun has made day travel quite impossible. In the tent here it's so baking hot that I find it difficult to grasp that I am only a few hundred miles away from the Pole itself. [There were plenty of opportunities to get a tan – both by night and day. The sun roasted us when it was at its zenith, and the tent often smelled of sweat as we lay nearly naked on top of our sleeping-bags in semi-tropical warmth – TG].

We started at the normal time this morning and kept going until lunchtime. It's not just the hard going that is having its effect – our

5 Icebergs.
6 The bay crossed was named the Bay of Sails.
7 Dunlop Island.

strength has been sapped by the over-exertion of the last week. Deb with his bad knee can only pull half his weight. [Night marching commenced about 9 p.m. – TGT].

25 November

After a really grinding night's work we are lying in our sacks. The going was better but there was not a breath of wind, and we had to haul the sledges one by one. We have therefore covered only 8 km. At midnight Forde and I pushed on a few kilometres to try to make out whether what we could see to the east was an island or an iceberg. It turned out to be an iceberg. We didn't get nearer to it than a couple of kilometres, but in the brilliantly clear weather and with the glass we were able to inspect it throughly. Strange how some icebergs look like land. [Our 'island' was merely a stranded berg coloured brown by the large amount of silt included in the ice – TGT].

26 November

We are approaching Granite Harbour and can make out with naked eye the hills surrounding the fjord. Some kilometres to the north lies Cape Roberts and, as we crept round it this morning we could at last see the 'promised land' at our feet. The weather tonight has been simply marvellous – calm and sunlit. The going has also been a bit better and, although we had to haul the sledges individually through the worst of the *sastrugi*, we have had a good day's march. The coast has been less interesting in the past day or two, with mountains only in the far distance and nothing to break the monotony of the eternal ice slope down to the sea. The scenery is at last picking up. There are masses of bergs around us, sparkling and glistening, and to our front rises the massif of Granite Harbour's mountains.

27 November

We have bivouacked among the ice mounds about 2 km west of Cape Roberts. We have made a lengthy halt on this foot-hill. Gulls are wheeling about us, busy building nests. From a point[8] that rises about 50 feet above the sea, we have a splendid view into Granite Harbour. To the northwest lie high mountains which appear to plunge directly down into the fjord. In these calm midnight hours they are covered with a reddish hue. In fact the composition of these mountains is essentially red granite, with dolerite at the summit. The play of colours is therefore exceptionally rich. A sort of glacier tongue[9] descends to

8 First View Point

9 Mackay Glacier Tongue.

occupy the middle part of the fjord, and the south side is encompassed by precipitous mountain faces, mostly covered with ice. We cannot yet quite make out what lies at the end of the fjord.

The weather has been superb most of the night, but towards morning a most penetrating wind sprang up. It looks as if the weather's going to change. The temperature is –4 °C. But now it really does not matter if bad weather arrives to break up the ice, for we have practically reached our goal. There are lots of seals around. A baby seal is lying squealing just outside the tent. Its mother is out looking for breakfast.

28 November

We have again gone over to day work. There is a great deal to explore and to map. Our halts last for hours and it's best to take advantage of the sun at its warmest. [We cut out breakfast and kept comfortably to our bags all the morning, having lunch at 1.30. Our last meal had been lunch also! Gran caused some amusement by demanding two cakes of chocolate, as due from the missed meal – TGT].

Taylor and I went inland this evening, climbed a crag, and got a superb view over the Ross Sea. The ice lay in one compact mass as far as eye could see. [Gran and I walked to the root of the ice tongue to examine it. It was a mile and a half long and was fed by a well-defined overflow from the Wilson Piedmont, which had cut its way through granite cliffs some 200 feet hight. There were several 'chimneys' offering tracks up the cliffs. One had a rough rock figure at its base, and led Gran to remark, 'This is an ome.' I realized he meant 'good omen', and accordingly we tackled the chimney indicated – TGT].

29 November

We had rather a fright this morning. Taylor, cook for the week, could not get the primus to light. We all tried but it was no good – the gas hissing out would simply not burn. By chance I got a whiff of the gas and instantly solved the mystery. Taylor had filled the stove with alcohol. This mistake arose because he had been unable to sleep and had walked about all night. We were woken at 5 a.m., but it was after nine before we got away. The weather has been splendid. The mountains were bathed in sunshine, and good weather clouds sailed before a light breeze over the tops. We set course for Discovery Bluff. The way there was longer than we had thought, and it was midnight before we hauled both sledges up on the icefoot. There are masses of young seals hereabouts; they make a frightful din when their mothers are out hunting.

30 November

We have reached our goal and are bivouacked behind the bluff, 3–4 km from the end of the fjord. The place is excellent as a camp site. There are stones for the hut, sand for the camping place. seal and birds to eat, and a delightful view. In the innermost part of the fjord the Mackay Glacier descends to the sea. It is a stupendous mass of ice and its great tongue of ice extends several kilometres into mid-fjord. Another glacier emerges from Mount England's steep walls, but it is different – more even and apparently without cracks. This was called New Glacier by the *Discovery* people; it is divided from Mackay Glacier by just a small belt of [ice-free] land. We shall doubtless use New Glacier as a spring-board when we want to make our way into the land that looms in the distance.

We sunbathed the morning away, and it was nearly 1 p.m. before we set out in search of a camping site. We left the one sledge beneath the bluff and made our way westwards about 4 km. Here we came upon a point that we have christened 'Cape Geology' and by 3 p.m. we were sitting in our tent, and our goal achieved. We have begun building the hut this evening; it is snowing and just like home.

1 December

It is Taylor's birthday today. We have celebrated by hoisting the flag. We have also inaugurated the blubber stove, for Deb prepared seal steak this evening. [Debenham said he had no present for me, but he could not allow me to cook my birthday dinner. I noticed that the others seemed overjoyed that I should be relieved of my cooking duties for one meal! (TGT). I gave him a present – a hermetically sealed bottle of plums I had slipped into my personal effects – TG] The stove was placed in the skeleton of the hut and the test was reckoned a success. It smoked but we don't mind being chimney sweeps. Taylor, Forde, and I today went to fetch the sledge we had left on the icefoot beneath the Bluff. The weather was perfect until this evening when a slight snow-fall began. There is a cheerful holiday-like atmosphere; both Deb and I feel it – it was the same on Scott's birthday. We have a ration of chocolate tonight. Temperature, –5 °C.

2 December

Forde and I spent the afternoon building our hut. The walls are finished, the sledge will form the roof beams, and sealskins will serve for the rest. [Buttresses of granite crossed the beach, and between two of these was an area where our kitchen was almost half built. Surrounded on three sides by solid granite walls three feet high was an enclosure which we managed to roof in well enough to hold the blubber stove. Forde and Gran were especially keen on this edifice, which they called Granite House from Verne's 'Mysterious Island'. It was a day or two before the house was finished. Forde was master mason and Gran chief labourer. He used to delight in bringing to the site great cubes of granite which we others could hardly move. There was a most uncomfortable block of granite projecting into the hut but, by repeated dropping of huge blocks on to it, Gran finally managed to remove this excrescence . . . Gran is going to sow sea-kale here, so that our vegetables . . . should be plentiful . . . Gran and I went off on a fur-hunting trip. . . . About half a mile away was a big seal, and I determined to secure him. . . . We managed to roll the heavy hide onto the sledge, but it would not stay there. Just like a slow-moving glacier, it slipped off everywhere. 'Trigger' took off his belt and lashed it on – TGT].

3 December
My spell as messman has nearly brought me to the filthy state I was in at Hut Point. After a couple of hours making the hoosh, I really don't feel like turning into my clean sleeping-bag, but I simply have to. This morning Taylor and I climbed 500 feet up the bluff. We planted a flag and deposited a note about our plans. [I wrote a note to Pennell (in *Terra Nova*), and lashed it to the mast, telling him we were going inland until January the 8th – TGT]. We killed a seal on the way back. We returned to Cape Geology at 4 p.m. to find that Forde had completed the roof with a sealskin. The weather has been marvellous.

4 December
Just back from a two-hour evening walk after supper. Taylor and I climbed to the top of the ridge above our camp. A savage, penetrating wind was blowing down below, but on the summit, 1500 feet up, the sun shone warm and it was almost calm. Beneath us we could make out the camp, dark and shadowy. Far away to the southeast, over the ice-ridden McMurdo Sound, shimmered Mount Erebus; the inland ice glistened to the northwest and north, and above us almost in the eye of the sun we could discern the white mass of Mount England.

5 December
We set out from Cape Geology after lunch and are now bivouacked beneath the tip of the Mackay Glacier Tongue near Mount Evans;[10] it is higher[11] and more broken up [in this area]. During the morning the sky was gloriously clear but has taken on a more threatening mien this afternoon. The barometer is falling fast and thick, ugly, blue-black storm clouds hang over Ross Island. This bivouac won't really do in a blizzard – the ground is soft and the site exposed to the wind.

10 In error; actually Mount Marston.
11 The glacier tongue.

6 December

(*2 a.m.*) The blizzard blew up and continued long into the morning. [We had a meal about 11 a.m. Gran cooking a good bovril-pemmican, with a large supply of biscuit therein – TGT]. By midday the wind dropped, but the snow-fall with thick flakes continued and now by evening our tent is nearly buried. The temperature is unpleasantly high, –3 °C., and we are almost swimming in mud. We lunched late so that we could skip supper and, when the primus was going at full blast, water positively poured down from our sodden tent.

7 December

The snow-fall continued throughout the night, and when we awoke the flakes were as thick as they had been the previous day.[12] We lay in our sacks until lunch. Later in the afternoon the sun broke through the cloud cover, and put a stop to the snow-fall. The temperature was up to freezing point for the first time in a year. Inside the tent all was awash, and our sleeping-bags like sponges. [There was a puddle by the door, but Gran and my bags have absorbed most of that, and Deb's is wetter – TGT].

Outside the snow lay feet deep, the sledge had disappeared, and we sank to our waists in the snow-drifts. The new snow sparkled, the sun shone like summer, and little by little the clouds sailed away westwards, revealing the mountain tops and driving away our ill humour. The tent came down, the sledge was packed, and away we went, but oh! how slowly. It seemed that it would take more than manpower to haul the sledge through the deep snow. It sank in, and we sank in, and our tracks must have looked more like those left by a plough than those of a sledge.

8 December

There is something to write about for once! In the day that has just passed things have happened which are no normal feature of Antarctic life. In a word, we nearly drowned. During our march towards the coast on the north side of Granite Firth,[13] the way became impassable, and we had to dump the sledge and continue with our gear on our backs. [Gran went first with his very heavy bag (half water) and the tent poles – TGT].

For hours we struggled against snow up to our waists. I took the lead and set the pace for the others. In our path we came across masses of seals lying sunbathing and wallowing in the snow. They looked so idle

12 The party was camped in the bay on the north side of Mackay Glacier Tongue.
13 Granite Harbour.

that I simply had to bombard them with snowballs. The animals jumped and looked astonished – no doubt imagining they were dreaming – and then relaxed again. Suddenly I lost my foothold and went in the next second; only my nose was showing over the ice. [Gran had laid the poles up against the floe and left his bag just behind, when the mush gave way and in he went to his waist – TGT]. Round about me the ice was brittle and, the more I struggled, the bigger the hole became. Luckily the tent poles were only a few metres away, and I broke my way through towards them. They were my salvation. I managed to get them under me, and crawled in until I reached the solid icefoot at the coast. Meanwhile, the others had come up. Taylor got too near my bathing spot and fell in to his waist. The ice was in a frightful condition, and it looks as if it will only last a few more days. We decided therefore to return [from Point Retreat] to Cape Geology at once. [First . . . we had to get Trigger off the ice-foot. . . . He threw the tent poles on to the mush and then launched himself full length on the stuff, gripping the poles . . . the poles kept him up, and he got across to us without further mishap – TGT].

The return march was as heavy as lead and thoroughly depressing. My feet had no feeling in them for hours at a stretch. We have now bivouacked about 10 km from Cape Geology.

9 December

We are back again at Cape Geology; it's been a tough day. The snow was deep and so sticky that it seemed like treacle. When we started this morning, we could hardly move the sledge, so we just waited for the sun to dry off the runners. This helped and we managed to cover 2 km before lunch, and then came on here. The weather was perfect and beautifully warm. On this side the storm has created havoc. Our signal flag on the bluff has disappeared, and here in the bivouac the flagstaff is broken down. 'Granite Hut' is half-covered in drift. The gulls have been at our gear; for example, they have managed to make a hole in my clothes bag. [The first duty before us was to replace the flag on the rendezvous. Gran decided it should be of a bolder pattern, and so he inserted a white specimen bag in the middle of a black depot flag, which made a very showy standard indeed . . . We had a merry meal that evening, at which we decided to have a sweepstake on the day of the arrival of the ship. . . . Gran had a brilliant idea, and suggested that the winner should have the *first bath* – TGT].

10 December

At about midnight half a blizzard blew up, but by mid-morning the foul weather cleared and for the rest of the day we have been sunbathing.

We are thoroughly enjoying ourselves. The little patch of sand on which our tent stands is redolent of sun and summer. The polar landscape has taken on wonderful colouring; it would be surprising if our spirits did not rise. We are all good friends and are having as good a time as anybody in the world. I have been doing some gardening tonight. Before we left New Zealand I got hold of a packet of seeds.[14] I have now sown them between the granite blocks. The earth is thin, but the spot sheltered and right in the sun. We are all looking forward to the results. [Gran swore the seedlings would be up in a week and edible in a month – TGT].

11 December

Taylor and I climbed to the top of the bluff this afternoon. We could see in the direction of Beaufort Island; a belt of open sea stretched eastwards towards Cape Royds. The ocean is on the move and it won't be long before the sound of waves can be heard along our shores. The weather has been superb – warm and summery. Melted water cascades down from the spurs of the bluff.

[The only thing I disliked was going out with Griff to slaughter seal. Although he gave the impression of being a sensitive soul, he was not in the least worried by the sight of blood. Although from necessity I helped to slay seals, it was a long time afterwards before I could swallow a piece of the meat – TG].

12 December

The snow is melting. I was out with Deb this morning, and we sat for a time sunning ourselves and enjoying the summer. Much moss is appearing; it's bright green and you can almost see it growing. And the streams ripple and murmur. On the way back I found the year's first gull's egg. Deb found the second this evening. I skinned a seal this afternoon, and butchered it at once for the meat and liver.

13 December

Deb and I have been up on Discovery Bluff the whole day. There is a marvellous view up there. The bluff is about 490 m high and we get a clear view of the open water. It looks as if the ocean has moved forwards along Ross Island right up to Cape Barne – that is, in sight of Cape Evans. We were back in camp by 5 p.m. Forde had found an egg – now we have three, just short of one to make a meal. The weather has been fine, but the wind has risen and the tent is flapping horribly.

14 Of rutabaga or sea kale.

14 December
I found the fourth and fifth eggs in the same nest this morning and we made our lunch of them. They tasted admirable – just like hen's eggs. [We lived high on gulls' eggs and had pancakes and egg nog at our meals (TG). It was amusing to see Gran's horror when a twelve-day chicken appeared in one of them – TGT].

After lunch Taylor and I went over to [Mackay] Glacier Tongue to set up a stake to measure the glacier's movement. We went in a little way, but encountered crevasses too wide to cross. [Finally, I got the theodolite set up, and sighted 'fore and back', until I got the cape and a crack in the Kar Cliffs (Plateau) in transit with my station. Here we planted the stake – TGT].

15 December
A month today since we left the hut – halfway to *Terra Nova*'s arrival. If the second half goes as quickly as the first, time will really fly. I'm now beginning to long for letters and news. Last night I dreamed that Amundsen had reached the Pole; I dreamed I had a telegram reading: 'Amundsen reached Pole, 15–20 December.' [I lay in the tent dozing in a kind of half sleep. Suddenly it appeared as though a picture materialized on the tent canvas of four men, at day-break, in front of a tent with two flags fluttering. The picture vanished immediately, and instead there was a telegram on which was inscribed, 'Amundsen reached Pole 15 December.' I jumped up and Taylor awoke. . . . 'The Norwegians have got to the Pole this minute' . . . Griffith Taylor hurriedly got hold of the chronometer, and the next moment noted down the exact time on the parchment of his scientific diary – TG].[15]

Went off hunting eggs this afternoon, and Forde was on the same errand for a time. Our combined haul: 23 eggs, of which I found 15. I had to kill one of the mothers, breaking her wing with my ski stick when she attacked me.

16 December
Plans for our summer activity have now been worked out. Soon after Christmas we are to go up over Mackay Glacier on a 14–20-day trip. On our return we shall move camp, if possible to Cape Roberts, and await the ship there. If she arrives before the end of January, we shall be transported north to Evans Cove, and spend some weeks there. If the ship does not appear, however, we shall make our way to Cape Evans overland.

15 TGT's version of this incident is similar, but he gives the date as 20 December. Amundsen did in fact reach the Pole on 15 December.

This week we are to reconnoitre the inner part of Granite Fjord, and we have made camp tonight on a small promontory, which Taylor for one reason or another has christened Cuff Cape. By the way, Taylor has a poisoned finger – the forefinger on the right hand. [Taylor had cut his right index finger during the seal slaughter – TG]. It's painful and seems to be getting worse. Our bivouac site is a mixture of ice, moraine, and granite. We had three eggs each for breakfast, but only Deb had the pleasure of consuming all his – the rest of us each found one had gone off. On our arrival here I went up to the knees through ice into a freshwater hole. Taylor had less to carry and managed to jump clear.

17 December

Taylor's finger was so painful during the night that he got no sleep. He has therefore spent the morning in his sleeping-bag. We doctored him as well as we could, and have poulticed the finger with porridge, which is soothing. After lunch I took a trip with Taylor, but his hand was too bad and after an hour we had to turn back. I found an insect just visible on a reddish-brown stone. We don't know whether it is a new genus, but we hope so. It's black and looks like a centipede, and moves its own length in half a second.[16] [He (Gran) also discovered 'gold'. This latter, however, was only golden mica, though it quite resembled the precious metal – TGT]. Taylor and I are sitting in the tent waiting for Deb and Forde who have been out surveying.

18 December

I went to the summit of Cuff Cape today. The types of stone there were remarkedly varied as regards colour; it was a real pleasure to the eye to see such strong tints. Taylor's hand is extremely bad and I carried out an operation this evening as best I could. We are all – Taylor not least – anxious about the outcome. He is feverish, and I have given him a dose of pretty well every medicine in the chest. Something should help. [Gran was our self-constituted doctor, though I am bound to say that the stories he told of deathbeds which he had attended on Norwegian ships were not at all reassuring – TGT]. This afternoon we moved our camp to a point called The Iron.[17]

19 December

We have struggled all day up the slopes covered with massive boulders. The weather is superb and we are enjoying our surroundings. This life

16 It was the springtail *Gomphiocephalus hodgsonii*, first reported by the *Southern Cross* expedition, 1898–1900.

17 The Flatiron.

reminds me of my boyhood, when Sigurd Heiberg and I wandered about the mountains near Bergen. How often at that time did we not say, 'When we grow up, we will go to the Pole.'

20 December
We struck camp after breakfast and continued on into the Devil's Punch Bowl. It took us an hour, and then we bivouacked on the beach in good, fine sand. This place is of enormous interest to the geologists, and Deb in particular is exceedingly pleased with the afternoon's exploration. He has found a rich variety of rocks. Because of his hand Taylor is out of sorts; it makes his journey a burden, and of course he can't write. [I became a fairly expert writer with my left hand in the course of time, but it was very galling to be incapacitated in almost the most interesting part of our journey – TGT]. But all credit to him – he does not show his impatience to others.

21 December
Taylor and I were over to Cape Geology this morning to fetch more provisions, for Deb wants to stay a day or two longer here in the 'bowl'. When we started it was snowing, then fog came down over the mountains and it really looked extraordinarily dismal. During the night some inches of snow had fallen which made it a tough march. All was in order at Cape Geology – the hut was snow-covered, the gulls had enriched the area with their eggs, and the seeds had begun to show signs of life. [The sea kale did not show that verdant growth which Gran had predicted – TGT]. I captured 8 eggs from the shrieking birds, and carried them with me. Tonight we are to celebrate mid-summer eve.

22 December
Mid-summer Day: the sun stands at its zenith. This afternoon Taylor and I took to the hills. We found a little lake on our way. Roundabout lay the glaciers, but the sun was so warm that a strong desire to bathe suddenly entered my head. Off came my clothes and in I went. We say farewell to the 'Punch Bowl' tomorrow.

23 December
Back again at Cape Geology where we shall spend Christmas. I have taken over mess duties from Taylor because of his hand which still troubles him. I spent several hours preparing supper. I served hoosh, and the hut was half full of ice and snow-water which trickled in. But all was well in the end, for the rest of the arrangements were all right.

24 December

Christmas Eve, the second in Antarctica and probably not the last. I am the chef, and spent the whole day cooking seal pemmican for our forthcoming journey into the interior. It is not really appropriate work for Christmas Eve, but it has to be done and better today than tomorrow when we intend to celebrate Christmas. Forde has given me a hand, and we have been sitting in 'Smoking Villa' talking about home and days gone by. What splendid weather today, sunshine on the mountains, on the glaciers, sun as far as the eye can see – calm and summery, not a breath of wind. I am now in my sack, dirty as anything, but smoking a cigar which Forde provided. I am off to dream-land to visit home thousands of miles away.

25 December

We have celebrated the day in a way which would have been quite acceptable in more civilized surroundings. Our sledge flags flutter proudly over the camp. The colours of England, Australia, Ireland and Norway are side by side. We are indeed a mixed brotherhood; Taylor is English, Debenham Australian, Forde Irish, and I Norwegian. [Gran's sledge flag was a beautiful piece of emboidery presented by Queen Maud, and contained the Norwegian arms – TGT].

For supper we had seal steak and fried egg to which Forde added an omelette. Some of the eggs contained chickens but despite my loud protests into the pan they went. However, it really didn't taste too bad, and for dessert we had the plum pudding we had brought with us.

26 December

We are continuing in the Christmas spirit, and it is Deb's 28th birthday. He is a heavy smoker and I have given him cigarettes. During the morning I went over to New Glacier to find an easy way up for the sledge. I believe, however, that we ought to proceed by the way of The Iron. Splendid sunshine the whole day.

27 December

The route *via* The Iron was decided upon, and we are now bivouacked 1,000 feet up the mountain. It was pretty rough work, for we had to carry our gear on our backs. [Forde and Gran carried the sledge on their shoulders . . . and had a most uncomfortable journey with this 'old man of the ice' to handicap their scramble – TGT]. From here we can see the blue of the sea, but no nearer than before Christmas.

28 December

The Mackay Glacier has turned out to be an easy slope and mostly flat. The newly fallen snow lies deep, and all the crevasses are hidden from sight. Taylor has lengthened the tow-rope and the rest of us haul in fan formation, thus diminishing the chances of one of us meeting with a catastrophe. We are suffering from the heat. We are walking almost naked and are getting very sun-burned. We have bivouacked for the night beneath an island surrounded by gigantic icefalls. This island is called Redcliff Nunakol.[18] [That evening we camped on Redcliff *Nunakol*. This latter term I invented with Gran's assistance to describe a rock island resembling a *nunatak*, but rounded by previous glacial erosion. The nunatak has properly never been below the ice; hence its name, from the Icelandic *nuna*, lonely, and *tak*, a jagged peak[19]. Nunakol is from *nuna*, lonely, and *kol*, a rounded ridge. . . . To the north-west is a mountain approaching seven thousand feet, which is capped by dolerite lava. . . . We called it Black-cap at first, but it is now officially known as Mount Tryggve Gran (Mount Gran) after our ever-cheerful comrade – TGT].

29 December

We have spent the day mapping the surroundings. [Debenham was our principal cartographer. He employed simple, readily understandable methods, and we could thereby follow hour by hour how the picture of the terrain was built up – TG].

This evening Taylor showed me one of his diary entries,[20] which I reproduce herewith with the author's kind authority: 'We carry a medical chest full of pills, and Debenham is our sledge doctor and knows as much about medicine as Dr Wilson could put down on a sheet of notepaper. He feels himself an expert on snow-blindness, frost-bite and so on, but my hand baffled him. However, Gran had served on many vessels in his naval training and at first I had great faith in him. He gravely felt my pulse, and then the armpit. "Do you feel any pain here?" I truthfully said no! "No blood-poisoning that finger", says Gran. Next day my hand was worse, and Gran proceeded to lance it with great gusto, with the result that the thumb and two fingers swelled [to] double normal size. For a week I could not sleep, and I tried all sorts of bandages and most of the pills – as expert opinion favoured frost-bite, rheumatism or blood-poisoning. Gran remembered aspirin as good for rheumatism – so the patient swallowed two [pills]. Then he said he meant salicylate, so I took two of them; and then he cheered us by telling us how a former invalid, with whom he had had medical dealings, died in his hands!'

18 Redcliff Nunatak.

19 TGT's etymology is spurious. *Nunatak* is an Eskimo word meaning 'the land it is'.

20 For 23 December.

30 December
Thick snow all day which we have passed playing chess, writing and reading. Our goal tomorrow is an isolated spur about 10 km towards the plateau.

31 December
The last day of the year. And so a year has gone by here in the South without our having the remotest idea what has happened in the great world. All things considered, time has passed quickly. On New Year's Eve last year, the polar continent was in sight and the weather dark and foggy; and that is just how it is today.

We are bivouacked on Gondola Island.[21] The march over the plateau and the sea was blessed by fine weather and the absence of cracks. It didn't take us long, either, to find a perfect camping place – an oasis of sand on top of a moraine. This afternoon we have been creeping around the tent, for the fog, thick and even, has blotted out visibility, and all the tops and crags have disappeared. It really is very dreary weather, but as recompense the geologists received an unexpected present on the last day of the year in the shape of seashell fossils – the first they have found in Antarctica.

The old year will ring out soon; I give thanks for new experiences, and thanks also to my comrades for their friendship. All honour to 1911!

1 January 1912
[The New Year's actual arrival was . . . celebrated by a moment of solemnity. We sat silent and stared pensively before us. 'God save Scott', said Taylor suddenly. We repeated his words and shook hands with one another – TG]. The New Year continues with fog and bitter weather and we are forced to stay near the tent. It cleared a bit this evening, and Taylor and I made a reconnaissance of the best route to the top. We shall have a go at the northern slope. [When Gran and I returned from our first survey of the ridge we found that Debenham had already been successful in the shales. He had found some vesicular horny plates. . . . On our return to Europe these were identified as the armour-plate of primitive fish, and probably of Devonian age – TGT].

2 January
The bad weather continues; it must be the approach of the ocean.[22] The others are suffering from rheumatism.

21 Gondola Ridge.
22 i.e. due to open water offshore.

3 January

Our march today was over moraine, scree, and snow. [Gran and I determined to circumnavigate Mount Suess – TGT]. To the southwest Gondola[23] falls vertically from its summit. It reminds one of an ancient weather-beaten castle or a Chinese fortress. There are good ski runs on the south side. Granite Harbour would be an ideal wintering place for a ship – no ice-falls, open water by March, and a dominating position over the 'untrodden uplands'. From what I could make out today, this would be a good place for an easy ascent to the plateau. If you kept to the south of the Gondola, along Sperm Bluff, and then in along the coast where the glaciers are not too serrated, you could go far, far in. Towards the south there are blue fjords, and the mountains are high and tempting. And to the north lies a chaos of deep valleys, which astonished Deb as he scanned them through his telescope. Deb, by the way, has come across some coal – so there must be a seam in the neighbourhood. There is not much movement from the sea. From a thousand metres up, we could see only the same blue strip we had spotted three weeks ago. It's time we had a storm. The weather has been sunny, but patches of fog remain and from time to time seem to take possession of the crags and crests.

4 January

Taylor, Forde, and I have climbed Mount Gondola.[24] We left camp at 10 a.m. and were at the summit by 2 p.m. I took the lead and kept to the scree towards the north, whilst the two others held a lower path. I had thought the northwest summit was the highest and climbed up it without difficulty. Taylor and Forde chose the south summit which to my mortification, turned out to be 50 feet higher. The twin summits were divided from each other by a 1,000-foot long ridge. After taking some photographs, I traversed it to join the others. The summit was 4,000 feet high.[25] At 6 p.m. we were home again, and I must say the trip had taken more out of our feet than our energies. We were lucky with splendid weather – even at the summit we were able to enjoy the sunshine. From the northwest summit I made out Cape Roberts. The ice seemed heavy and thick up to the coast, and it will take a good storm to produce navigable water for the 13th, 14th and 15th. [According to Scott's orders, *Terra Nova* would seek contact with us on 15th January near Cape Roberts – TG]. Otherwise McMurdo Sound was clear, blue water as far as eye could see.

23 Evidently referring to Mount Suess, which is joined to Gondola Ridge.

24 Mount Suess.

25 In fact, 3,900 feet.

5 January

This morning Deb and I went south nearly halfway round the island.[26] The weather was perfect, and we took it in leisurely style and chatted about everything from philosophy to the scarcest commodity in this neck of the woods – women. We got home at 4 p.m. Forde tended the stove and, while lunch was being prepared, we talked about the future.

6 January

We are now on our way back and have bivouacked at our old camp site beneath the summit of The Iron. The march over the glacier was wearisome and hot, but luckily there were no crevassses. We did not leave Gondola Island[27] until midday, for we had been delayed by the discovery of a 'coal mine' in the moraine close to the sledge. While Forde and I were packing, Deb took a last look round and found some lumps of coal. [It was undoubtedly derived from Beacon Sandstone beds close to our camp – TGT].[28] Forde and I also wanted some 'black diamonds' – the first discovered in Antarctica. After Deb had helped himself to what he thought was the lot, Forde and I took spades and soon found the coal seam. We filled a couple of sacks and Deb was delighted. [The geological collection far exceeded any reasonable sledge load for 4 men – TGT].

A small gale blew tonight and we thought it might have shifted the ice, but no, it doesn't seem so; it stretches all the way to Cape Roberts. We shall spend a day or two here at The Iron. The weather has been very fine all day.

7 January

Thick banks of fog rolled in from the sea today. Beneath us all is wrapped in the murk, but round about we can see the sun shining. It's a splendid sight this golden sea of mist through which the mountain tops are peeping. [It is impossible to find one's way in these fogs, and exposure to Antarctic weather is a thing to be dreaded even in summer – TGT].

8 January

Back at Cape Geology tonight. It's more summer-like here – the snow has gone and my little garden has begun to grow green. A dozen plants have pushed an inch or so up from the earth. [I imagine these

26 The nunatak comprising Mount Suess and Gondola Ridge.

27 Gondola Ridge.

28 Farther inland, from the work of the *Nimrod* expedition, 1907–09, these beds were known to contain coal seams.

(dictoyledons) are the first grown within the Antarctic Circle! They seemed thirsty, so I gave them some water. But, alas! the weather rapidly grew colder. Every day a few were blighted, and, finally, I gathered the remnants and placed them in my pocket-book as a record of Gran's well-meant experiment – TGT].

The movement of the tide can now be widely observed, and in general the ice is showing signs of summer's approach.

9 January

From tomorrow we shall begin to reduce our pemmican intake. We have plenty of biscuits and other provisions. The idea is to remain here until the 15th, and then to take advantage of the sea ice and move to Cape Roberts.

10 January

The weather was snowy and calm, like yesterday. We could really do with a couple of days of gales to break up the ice.[29] But it is one thing to want something and another to get it. We are passing the time bombarding the noisy gulls, but we are not very good as gunners.

11 January

Terra Nova in sight – hurrah! Deb caught a glimpse of her through the glass, and we all rushed out knocking over the cooking things and the primus. I got out first and Deb gave me the glass. Yes, there she was, tight into the ice edge, and it was clear that heavy seas had worked wonders during the night. Taylor grabbed the glass. 'I can see two ships,' he said. Forde poked his head out of the tent and echoed, 'I see the same, Sir.' Deb seized the glass and rush up the scree; I followed him. 'What can you see?' 'It must be a mirage,' he said slowly. 'Perhaps she's gone behind the headland,' I said optimistically. I took the glass, moved down a bit and took another sight, but the ship had gone and with her the mirage. Far out to sea I spied a seal; no, many, a whole flock. So Deb, that was what had made our hearts go thump!

When we had overcome our disappointment somewhat, Taylor and I climbed up Discovery Bluff to weigh up the situation. When we got to the top I was horribly disappointed; not a spot of open water was to be seen. Through the glass I could see that, although the inner [part of] McMurdo Sound was open, in the Ross Sea and along the whole coast around Ross Island as far as Beaufort Island and to the northwest, the pack ice was as thick as ever. The unbroken coastal ice stretched about seven miles east from Cape Roberts. All the floating ice must have come

29 So that *Terra Nova* could approach the shore.

from the south, so if only the southerly wind holds the fairway should soon be cleared, at any rate sufficiently for *Terra Nova* to come in. There is still no sign of the vessel. I walked up the bluff for a better view and saw seals, icebergs, and far distant leads, but no *Terra Nova*. Taylor did some surveying at the top, and I deposited a quantity of fat, paraffin, waste rags, etc., to be ignited as a smoke signal to attract attention on board once the vessel heaves into sight.

Taylor and I were back by 2 p.m. Forde had made his well-known Hut Point waffles with raisins. To his credit they tasted delicious. The weather was threatening and rotten the whole morning, but tonight it has cleared and grown colder. The glass has fallen sharply. Tonight Deb and I have had an argument about the relative strengths of England and Germany. I maintain that, if it came to a showdown, Germany would have a better chance because of her more highly developed scientific knowledge. [That evening we had a great argument about the possibility of a German invasion, Gran *versus* Debenham, in which Forde and I took sides to keep things lively – TGT].

12 January

If Taylor had guessed right, we should have been on board *Terra Nova* today, but as a prophet he is wide of the mark. My guess is the big day will come tomorrow. This morning Taylor and I went off to Mackay Glacier, where we had driven in a stake. [On this occasion we both wore spiked boots, and so had little difficulty on the glacier – TGT]. The glacier was covered with snow, and it was a miracle we didn't go through one of the many hidden crevasses. I led the way and I must admit that several times my life wasn't worth twopence, but luck was with us and we came over unscathed. The stake had moved 82 feet since our last observation, in other words, 3 feet a day or 365 yards a year. When the *Discovery* expedition was here, no [Mackay] Glacier Tongue was observed; it must have broken off a year or two before.[30] The gulls are getting cheeky, bombarding our tent at night and disturbing our sleep and making off with bits of Deb's collection.

13 January

My prophecy has fallen through too. No sight of *Terra Nova* from the bluff this morning. I went up there at 2 p.m.; it was quite hazy, impossible to see more than 20 or 30 miles, but it was clear that there was heavy pack ice in Ross Sea and firm ice seemed to stretch 15 km[31] out from Cape Roberts. [There was no possibility of the ship coming

30 And subsequently re-formed.

31 In a footnote in the diary TG records: 'The distance turned out to be nearer 60 km.'

in to us, and we could meet them as easily from the entrance (of Granite Harbour). On the other hand, there seemed no way out of the *cul-de-sac* at Cape Geology if the ship did not arrive, and the sea-ice broke away – TGT].

This afternoon I and the others have started to prepare for the start tomorrow. We have taken the roof off the hut, and taken down the sledges and loaded them with our possessions. We are taking to Cape Roberts only the necessities for our stay at Evans Cove. The weather has been fine today, if a little cold. My 'plantation' is frozen over, but at any rate it proved plants can grow here.

14 January
We have made camp at Cape Roberts, tired and worn after trudging all day right through to the evening. [The sledge was over-loaded – more than 100 kg per man – even though we had to abandon much of the rock collection of Debenham and Taylor – TG]. We struggled against a strong head wind the whole time and, when Deb suddenly thought he could see open water about a mile ahead of us, Taylor hurried on ahead. He went so fast that, when we eventually caught up with him, he was completely blown. [I had cramp from the pulling, and couldn't move for a time – TGT]. We have found a good [camp] site on a sand bank. It was held by a gull with young when we arrived. The young are now flapping around squeaking, for their mother has gone, probably glad of the opportunity to get away. You can't see open water from here, and yet tomorrow is meant to be the rendezvous [date]. It seems inconceivable in these conditions that anything will happen.

15 January
The rendezvous date has arrived, but not *Terra Nova*. There is only ice and more ice as far as the eye can see, and I am beginning to doubt whether anything will come of our stay at Evans Cove. [We were to be taken north on the ship to Evans Cove (to spend five weeks there during January and February) as soon as the *Terra Nova* could reach us – TGT]. Of course, much can happen in 16 days, but I don't think the coast will be ice free, at any rate not in time. It doesn't much matter to me what happens; time is passing. We need not worry about *Terra Nova* for the first week, as we are hardly likely to see her even if she does make an attempt to push forward to relieve us. We must prepare ourselves for a two-week wait. Went out therefore to kill a seal. The blubber stove is rigged up, and Deb is preparing our hoosh.

16 January
No *Terra Nova* in sight. These sea gulls are real birds of prey. Taylor carried the young from outside the tent to another nest. The gulls there

at once adopted the young, ate their own eggs, and seemed very pleased that their own brooding time was over.

17 January

You would have thought that here in the south we should enjoy the company of the animals, but one thing is certain: these gulls irritate the life out of us. The noise they make is indescribable. They have lost all our sympathy, and now we use them as targets. Clear weather, but no *Terra Nova*.

18 January

Gales and bad weather the past 24 hours, but no change in the situation.

19 January

I have begun to write a play 'Tangholmen's Light'. It is exciting. Taylor and Deb are very interested, [but advise greater attention to the action and less to the effects – TG]. In this vile weather one has to find something to do. [The place of (PO) Evans[32] as Society Entertainer was taken by Gran. His varied adventures in Arctic seas, among the Andes, in Turkey, Venezuela, and others of the less-known regions of the earth interested us much. He was, I remember, very anxious to experience the delights of (Australian) station life as experienced by Debenham – TGT].

20 January

It is my birthday and I have had a greeting from the outside world – *Terra Nova* is in sight, trying to push her way through the pack ice. When I first saw her, she seemed to be coming from the direction of Cape Evans, but now she lies to the south again. The weather is splendid, and the sun is really warming. After the somewhat low morale of the past few days of waiting our spirits are up and we are excited. Taylor has given orders for a big party to celebrate this double event. We are flying the sledge flags up on the glacier, and from 20–30 km., the distance at which *Terra Nova* lies, it may just be possible to make out our signals through a telescope. [The rest of my birthday passed in a carnival spirit. Dinner was expanded to include delicacies like pemmican porridge and cocoa with sweet condensed milk – TG].

As a birthday present Taylor has given me the following:

Ode to Tryggve
On his 24th[33] birthday, Cape Roberts

32 A member of TGT's western party the previous season.
33 Correctly inscribed by TGT on Gran's 23rd birthday. TG is one year out.

(Chanted at ye Full Pemmican Feast)

O Tryggve Gran, O Tryggve Gran,
I would Thou wert a moral man,
And yet since we
(The other three)
Are just as moral as can be,
A 'soupçon de diablerie'
Improves our little company.

O Tryggve Gran, a holy calm
Is most essential in a psalm.
But prose should be a thought less calmer
When elevated into drama.
And yet though we
(The other three)
Are critical to a degree,
We wish success some future day
To the first Polar 'Nature Play'.

O Tryggve Gran, Thou art a man
Who hath compressed within a span
Of three and twenty years, such deeds
That hearing which, each man's heart bleeds
Among us three.
And yet though we
Are kind to every girl we see,
I have no doubt each lovely creature
Would rather help you follow Nietzsche!

O Tryggve Gran, you should be dead
A-many years ago – instead
Of which, he saves you oft,
That 'Little Cherub up Aloft'.
And therefore we
(The other three)
In this new principle agree,
(As with your luck no man can quarrel)
'Twill serve us best to be un-moral!!!

21 January
Night-time. *Terra Nova* seems to have been driven northwesterly and all day it has been difficult even with the telescope to make her out. This evening she disappeared completely. Well, there is nothing for it but patience.

22 January

Nothing to do but sleep – just lying and waiting is utterly boring. Nasty weather and the air heavy with snow.

23 January

Terra Nova came into view again this morning. Just after lunch Deb and I climbed up to our flagstaff on the glacier, 450 feet up, and from here we had a splendid view of the ship's operations. Through the telescope we could see her clear and sharp, and could even make out the mizzen mast. Her course lay along the ice edge off shore; once or twice she ran into drifting pack ice and swung round with bows towards us. By 4 p.m. she seemed to have stopped. Taylor and I went up to the flagstaff again after supper; *Terra Nova* still lay there, perhaps a shade farther out from the ice edge. We couldn't make out any signals. I semaphored this afternoon, but in vain. I wonder if they can see our flag. [I did not entertain the idea of trying to reach Pennell across the screw-pack. We should get into more precarious regions each mile, and we could not communicate with the ship to ensure her awaiting us. . . . I was, however, very glad later to find that Pennell also considered the pack absolutely impossible for sledging from the ship – TGT].

24 January

This waiting makes us sleepless. It is nearly midnight and I am still tossing restlessly. Even so, of the four of us, I seem to know how best to pass the time. Weather splendid. Just this moment Deb has given the latest report on *Terra Nova*: 'Disappeared. Whether in cloud or in distance is not known.'

25 January

The situation is unchanged. We have slept more or less day and night.

26 January

We have seen nothing of *Terra Nova*; perhaps they have given us up.

27 January

[A strong southerly storm blew up . . . and we hoped it would blow away the worst drift ice, but when the wind abated and visibility improved we saw there had been no significant change – TG]. Deb, who went up to the flagstaff this afternoon, reported that *Terra Nova* was in sight near Cape Bird. McMurdo Sound is full of pack ice, so there must be a great break-up of ice somewhere. Taylor, who is now cook, abandoned the blubber stove tonight in favour of the primus. [Our rations had been cut down by half for a fortnight. We now had three or four biscuits a day; butter, every other day; chocolate, one stick; pemmican, one-eighth; sugar and tea, two-thirds a day. However, we had plenty of seal meat, and as we were not working we required much less food. . . . Gran spent all one afternoon making chupatties. The lid of the camera box was his pudding-board. He used the wheat-meal thickers for dough, and commandeered our allowance of raisins. The cakes were cut out with the rim of a cup, and then fried in a mixture of butter, fat, blubber and soot – TGT].

28 January
Ship has disappeared again. We must be an uncommon group of men not to tear out each other's hair in sheer frustration.

29 January
We seem to have come into a more windy period, perhaps autumn is coming. Deb and I went up to the flagstaff before supper, and we hoped the wind would have done wonders but, alas, the ice seems to be as solid as ever. But about a kilometre from the cape we've spotted a lead which seems to widen each day. I shouldn't be surprised if that's where our meeting with *Terra Nova* takes place, perhaps in a week.

30 January
An hour ago I went down to the icefoot to identify the source of some very strange sounds we had heard. Yes, it was there. The whole of the icefoot was groaning, and a strange whistling and wheezing arose from the tide-water cracks. Dark clouds lower over McMurdo Sound, and a heavy storm not far away must be the cause of this movement. Around us we have only had light airs, sunshine, and a cloudless sky.

31 January
More weird noises from the sea today, but apparently no change in the ice situation.

1 February
We discussed the situation and the future at the 'supper table'. According to Scott's sledging orders we now have a free hand. Taylor and Deb have given up Evans Cove, and we therefore discussed a retreat to Hut Point. It was decided that we should begin the return march about 6 February, provided no great change has taken place in the ice situation.

2 February
No sign of the ship today either.

3rd February

We[34] went several miles over the glacier this afternoon, towards Cape Bernacchi, to reconnoitre the conditions for a retreat. The snow was deep so that it would be hard work to haul a sledge there. We were 650 feet up and so had a good view over McMurdo Sound. We could see some open water, but it seems to me that the ice conditions are roughly the same as they were a month ago. [. . . a huge mass of ice-pack was apparent as far north as eye could see – TGT]. The weather was crystal clear and we had a superb view which, alas, did not include a ship.

4 February

Taylor and I took a 10-km trip along the coast this afternoon, and found several places where we could haul a sledge up to the glacier. On the ice towards the sea the going was very soft, but on land it was good. We were back at 6 p.m. We prepared for our journey tonight. I have changed into clean clothes and left behind the dirty. In general we aim to leave a good deal at this place, for we want to travel as light as possible. We are taking with us all the photographic plates and films, and are fully provisioned for ten days.

5 February

[I wrote a long letter to Pennell, which we all signed. We made a depôt on the highest point of the Cape and fixed a flag alongside, with the letter in a little matchbox. The journal for Captain Scott I left in my ditty bag. I remorselessly weeded out everyone's gear. We took nothing but what we stood up in, and our notes and the instruments – TGT]. We are on our way back – fancy it coming to this! We left Cape Roberts at 11 a.m., having depoted one week's provisions there.[35] The first 7 km were along the coast and, since Taylor and Deb were extremely uneasy about the sea ice, it was decided to continue over the glacier. We lunched on the icefoot. The glacier surface was better than I had thought possible. There were a good many bumps and we sank in a bit, but the sledge slid along easily and we managed to cover 7 km, though it took us over an hour or so to find our way round some horrible crevasses. We had lengthened our tow-line and Taylor, who led, used his alpenstock as a probe. When we set out this morning, the weather was wonderful and calm, and there were some remarkable mirages. The open water seemed so clear, and it was somehow strange to see McMurdo Sound mirror-like and calm with the ice floes gently sailing. The weather is still good, but now it is blowing a bit.

34 Taylor, Gran and Debenham.

35 On Scott's orders, in case the party had to return.

6 February

We have been making south over the glacier since 9 a.m., and it has been almost all uphill. Our lunch bivouac was 700 feet up and about 7 km from the night camp. From this point we climbed steadily upwards to the highest point at 1,200 feet. We have had a superb view over McMurdo Sound the whole day. From Dunlop Island and southwards the ice is broken up for several kilometres from the land, and *Terra Nova* could easily force a passage through the drifting floes. I am beginning to get the slightest bit worried that something may have happened to the ship. [We were now behind Dunlop Island, and about 1,250 feet up the Piedmont (Wilson Piedmont Glacier) – TGT].

7 February

Splendid weather all day. We have been toiling up and down and with good hard going on the northern slopes, but soft on the southern slopes and on the crests. [. . . we climbed up the snow hill behind Gneiss Point, about 1,350 feet above the sea – TGT]. Our two scientists move with the greatest caution [because of crevasses]. Our last night was disturbed. Forde was moaning from pain and is snow-blind. Taylor couldn't sleep because he was frozen. This evening it's Taylor's turn to be snow-blind, and I am beginning to wonder when something will happen to me. Mind you, I had my share of problems in the first half of the expedition.

McMurdo Sound is now navigable along the coastline for a couple of kilometres from the shore. If *Terra Nova* is all right, they must surely pick us up in a day or two. The ship should now be probing along the coastline; it is 11 whole days since we last saw her.

8 February

Arrived at Cape Bernacchi this evening. The air has been heavy with snow all day, and now this evening the weather looks very threatening. Taylor 'presented' me with a newly discovered mountain hitherto called Mount Black Cape.[36] It is without question one of the finest I have ever seen. It lies like an outpost to the plateau on the north side of McKay Glacier. It's height is the same as Galdhopiggen.[37]

9 February

The weather was vile this morning so we kept to our sleeping bags until midday. However, it cleared up and Taylor and I mounted to the top of what we have named Hjort's Mountain[38] after the inventor of the

36 Now Mount Gran (2,233 m). *See* 28 December 1911.

37 The highest mountain in Norway (2,468 m).

38 Hjort Hill.

primus stove. It is 2,500 feet high and an easy climb. [As we were climbing this hill, Gran swore he could see the ship off Cape Evans through the binoculars . . . but after an hour or so we decided it was only a mirage crack in the Barne Glacier – TGT]. We were back at the Cape by 9 p.m. There is a strong swell this evening, the ice floes are bobbing past, and the occasional iceberg drifts by on the tide. The temperature is –7 °C.

10 February

Today, all told, we have covered 18 km of which 15 were along an icefoot stretching right along the coastline here.[39] It's reminiscent of a broad country road, furrowed and undermined by water, with the interesting difference that one metre beneath us the sea was heaving the ice up and down with a sound like thunder. [We . . . camped below the Kukri Hills – TGT].

11 February

We have been weather-bound all day, but there is no hurry; the stay at Hut Point will be long enough anyhow.

12 February

A relatively exciting day. We have been following the coast which consists of cliffs leading straight down to the sea. As we came up to each headland, our hearts began to beat because we were afraid the open sea would lie behind it. But all was well; we were not halted, and the way to Butter Point and on to the *Discovery* hut now lies open to us. [We had lunch amid a colony of over forty seals, and then reached the southern side of the Ferrar Glacier, where we camped – TGT].

13 February

Reached the depot at Butter Point this morning. Nearby there is open water. There is a little drift ice, but not enough to prevent a large school of whales and dolphins swimming about and disturbing our friends the penguins. The weather is wonderful but cold. [The depôt had been blown over and wrecked generally. We took some pemmican, butter, and chocolate (TGT). . . . Debenham and Forde thought we ought to rest a few days. But Taylor and I wanted to push on with all speed – TG].

14 February

Our camp site tonight is on the bank of a dried-out river delta – a mile-

39 Of New Harbour.

long moraine.[40] The river runs out into a tarn which is frozen over, but not thick enough to stop us using it for cooking-water. Today's march over Butter Point Glacier[41] was enormously heavy going. There were hundreds of holes, and we seemed to be slipping and falling every second step. Close to the moraine the surface improves and tomorrow's prospects seem better, although caution may prompt Taylor to decide against the sea ice and follow the coast instead.

[We had the choice of two routes now: either to cross the snout of the Blue Glacier, or to take to the sea-ice and coast round the latter. . . . The latter might be quicker, though a great calved berg blocked the route about two miles ahead. Debenham preferred the glacier, the other two the sea-ice. I considered it unsafe to march on the sea-ice if it could possibly be avoided. I made a bet with Gran that we couldn't get the sledge between the calved berg and the glacier without unloading it. . . I decided to keep to land ice. . . . In a very short time we had all been in (crevasses) a couple of times, and it was evidently an unpropitious region for sledging. I deviated to the edge of the glacier to try and lower the sledge on to the sea-ice, for we were now abreast of the calved berg. . . . We had an argument as to who had won the bet, for there was a jumble of ice where the calf jammed the parent glacier. The other two decided in my favour. . . . Gran was dissatisfied with the court's decision, and kept glancing back to the scene under discussion – TGT].

15 February

At last! Again on board *Terra Nova*! We were plucked up at about 2 p.m., 4 km from the night's bivouac. We were just heading towards the Blue Glacier, which incidentally was full of crevasses, when I suddenly saw smoke rising above the moraine behind us. It was *Terra Nova*. [For a moment we just stood and stared: it were as though we could not believe it was true – TG]. Her masts soon hove into sight and we set off at high speed down to the edge of the glacier and onto the sea ice. [We fell, we rolled down a steep slope and got the sledge on top of us, but it did not matter – TG]. After a quarter of an hour's quick march, we stood on board good old *Terra Nova*. All was well. [. . . they had not been able to communicate with Cape Evans until a week before, and had been unloading stores every available moment before they came over to search for us (TGT). *Terra Nova* had never been nearer than 30 nautical miles to Cape Roberts – TG].

Scott's chances of reaching the Pole were very good. Atkinson and

40 The Strand Moraines.
41 Bowers Piedmont Glacier.

three others[42] had left Scott[43] on top of Beardmore [Glacier]. There had been no trace of Amundsen and all our spirits leaped. The motor sledges had reached a spot about 3 km south of 'Corner Camp'. In other words everything had gone as expected. Even the horses had carried out their work splendidly.

My share of the post is unspeakable. I had expected at least a couple of dozen letters and I received one, and that a bill! I had looked forward to news for half a year. I was very disappointed, and can only console myself that it will be a heavier post-bag next time. The ship has brought seven Indian mules. We shall remain at Cape Evans yet another year. Campbell has been set ashore at Evans Cove [whither Taylor, Debenham, Forde and I would have gone had we been picked up at the agreed time – TG].[44] He had passed a long winter at Cape Adare. He experienced exactly the same difficulties Borchgrevink had encountered[45] and it had proved impossible to get inland. The steepness of the mountains proved one barrier and the sea ice was never quite safe.

I am sitting by the fire in the wardroom. Taylor and Deb are buried in their mail. The Australians have sent an expedition this year under Mawson to the coast opposite South Australia.[46] The Japanese[47] are launching their attempt from King Edward VII Land and the Germans[48] from Coats Land – that is five Antarctic expeditions all at one time.

[Ponting came along and after complimenting us on our villainous appearance, begged us to remain picturesque until the sun showed enough light for a photograph! Luckily we had only to wait a few hours for this specimen of 'ponting' – TGT].

16 February

It is a good thing we were fished up yesterday, for we've had gales and snow all night and today. We have been hove-to riding out the storm some miles from Cape Evans. I spent most of the night reading newspapers, but the latest is dated 15 January 1911. That is over a year old. From these it appears that there are divided opinions about Amundsen's polar expedition. On board this ship people believe Amundsen has the best prospects. The fact that there was no trace of him at Beardmore [Glacier] suggests to me that he has taken another route. And that is probably best for both parties.

42 Wright, Cherry-Garrard and Keohane.
43 With Scott's and Lieutenant Evans' sledge teams.
44 Campbell was accompanied by Levick, Priestley, Abbott, Browning and Dickason.
45 On the *Southern Cross* expedition, 1898–1900.
46 King George V Land and Queen Mary Land.
47 Under Lieutenant Choku Shirase.
48 Under Dr Wilhelm Filchner.

17 February
Bad weather the whole day; we have just had to ride out the storm. The idea is to fetch Campbell as soon as the weather permits. *Terra Nova*'s homeward voyage last year had been pretty stormy and they didn't reach New Zealand until the end of March. They had employed the winter months surveying the north coast. The voyage back down here was blessed by the most delightful weather and only six days in pack ice.

18 February
This evening I have had a haircut, a shave and a bath, and look at least ten years younger. We are steaming through pack towards Evans Cove, but many diversions are slowing us down.

19 February
Through thick pack ice all day. Appalling weather and completely overcast. Mount Nansen came in sight in the afternoon, and by evening Mount Melba[49] loomed out of the fog. I stood watch at the engine telegraph this evening. A full gale blowing from the southwest, and the whole of McMurdo Sound lies in a whirlwind of spray and snow.

20 February
Gales from the south. We are keeping under way, clear of the ice. Perhaps my mail was sent to the *Fram*.[50]

21 February
Heavy rolling all day; my sledging companions are seasick. We have been driven far to the north.

22 February
During the night the wind dropped, but this evening the weather has set in with violent snow flurries. Autumn is on the way.

23 February
When we awoke this morning, we had a bit of a fright. The ship lay dead still in newly frozen ice, for all the world like huge pancakes. The prospect of a winter on board, imprisoned in ice, sent shudders through us. The relief of Campbell is not going to be easy. He will have to tighten his belt for a time, perhaps even for months. The ice broke up a bit after lunch, and during the afternoon we forced our way south some miles

49 In error, presumably, for Mount Melbourne.
50 Amundsen's ship.

towards Cape Evans. We are becalmed again this evening, but there is hope of movement in the night for we can see open water from the crow's-nest. If we can reach it, the course to the hut is clear.

24 February

It wasn't until mid-morning that the ice pressure eased and we could get the ship away from the floes. It was 'all on deck' to carry out the see-saw drill[51] to roll the ship adrift. We made good progress this afternoon, even though we were sailing through an ocean of large floes. The course is set for Cape Evans and, provided nothing out of the way happens, we should get there tomorrow. We have given up Campbell at any rate for a few days. When those for the landing party have been put ashore, and those for the ship's party brought on board, Pennell will attempt to force his way through to Evans Cove. I am afraid the prospects for success are pretty dim, but let's hope all goes well.

51 Sallying; *see* 21 January 1911.

Cape Evans again

25 February

At the hut again, big news. Teddy [Evans] is back at Hut Point with Lashly and Crean. Evans has had a bad attack of scurvy and had to be hauled from 'One Ton Depot' to 'Corner Camp'. From there Crean came over to Hut Point for help. Demetri and Atkinson went over with the dog team and fetched Teddy Evans back. There are five in the polar party: Scott, Wilson, Oates, Bowers, and PO Evans. Teddy Evans' party left them 288 km from the Pole. The party had provisions for seven weeks, so they could be sure of reaching the Pole. There was no sign of Amundsen on the plateau. Few of us are left in the hut: Meares, Crean, Keohane, Williamson, Archer, Nelson, Deb and myself.[1] Simpson, Day, Clissold, and Anton went on board with the boat, which landed us. [We found them all asleep, and by no means ready to come off – TGT]. Wright and Cherry have gone to Hut Point.

The day aboard *Terra Nova* was anything but pleasant. We entered Hut Bay[2] by lunchtime but there was such a storm that the anchor would not hold, and we repeatedly had to heave in the 7-fathom chain by hand because something was wrong with the steam winch. By 11 [p.m.] the wind dropped enough for us to go ashore. But it sprang up again before we had reached the hut, and now a full gale is blowing. All connections with the ship are severed, and indeed we can hardly see her in this thick weather. The skis have been a great success, and without them Beardmore [Glacier] would have proved a formidable obstacle. They have taken the skis to the Pole, hurrah!

26 February

We have spent the first day in the hut dozing and resting. The gale has been so violent that we hardly dared put our heads outside the door.

1 In a footnote in the diary TG records: 'Williamson and Archer replaced respectively Forde and Clissold, who went home with *Terra Nova*.'

2 North Bay.

When Meares leaves, the idea is that I am to look after the dogs of which there are 15 altogether[3]. If Atkinson has to accompany Teddy home in the *Terra Nova*, perhaps I shall take over one of the teams, which I should like very much. It is lighter tonight, but still blowing a full gale. *Terra Nova* has disappeared and I shouldn't be surprised if she had been driven 50 miles northwards. I went out this evening to look for my gear, and found the case from Hagen.

Simpson is on board[4] and we lack technical knowledge[5] here in the hut; even Nelson does not understand machinery. We do our best, pressing buttons and pulling levers until something happens. The more I hear about the Polar journey, the more I see it as a triumph for the skis.

27 February

I went out this morning and dug out the case from Hagen. The stuff I had ordered was in excellent condition, but I haven't been able to find the *finnesko*.

The storm has moved the ice 1 km out from Hut Point, and *Terra Nova* has been in sight all day in McMurdo Sound. Perhaps they want to get in touch with the hut. I have been taking [dog-driving] lessons from Meares this afternoon. It seems [that] the new dogs are not really first class. The mules, however, are good. They are handsome and a pleasure to the eye. [. . . seven superb Indian mules, the gift of the Indian Government – TG]. There are lights in the stable now, and several improvements have been made to the hut during the summer. A covered passage now connects the hut to the stable. It looks like snow again tonight.

28 February

According to last year's record, wind and weather in February and March were as bad as they could possibly be. It seems the same this year too. When we awakened this morning there was a gale and drift-snow, and we kept to the hut all day. I tidied up our cubicle; it needed it. We were nearly up to our knees in muck and dirt. Deb and I developed some of the photos of the summer journey this afternoon. Deb's are really excellent, and some of mine not too bad either. Indeed, one or two of them are outstanding. It seems that *Terra Nova* has taken refuge in Erebus Bay.

3 The new Siberian dogs brought down by the ship. Two dog teams remained from the previous season.

4 The meteorologist was on his way home.

5 To make meteorological and other physical observations.

29 February

We were roused at 3 a.m. by the sound of *Terra Nova*'s siren. We turned out hurriedly; the weather was superb, the sea slight and both ship's boats were making for shore at Cape Evans. The object was to put ashore the final load of cargo. *Terra Nova* came direct from Hut Point, and Teddy Evans was on board. Nelson and I went on board at 4 p.m. to say good-bye. Poor chap, scurvy has really brought him down; we could hardly recognize him. He was lying in his own old bunk. I had a long talk with him, and he tried to persuade me to go with him in *Terra Nova*, for he thought he would take command as soon as he was fit again, and in that case I could become Third Officer. However I felt I had to decline his very kind offer, grateful though I was. First, I just did not believe his condition would improve quickly enough for him to take command and, secondly, I thought I would be of more use here in the south. Teddy Evans has had really bad luck. It is interesting that he now says that it was the skis that saved his life. When he couldn't lift one foot in front of the other, the skis carried him a day's march of 30 km. *Terra Nova* will now attempt Campbell's relief. [My conversation with Evans had not lasted long, but from what I had heard it became clear to me that the prospects of our five-man polar party were not so bright as most of the members of the expedition imagined. Evans' frightful return journey was a pointer to what Scott and his men would be bound to undergo. There was also another matter which caused me anxiety. Since the Beardmore Glacier's suitability for dogs had been established, I took it for granted that Amundsen had reached the Pole before Scott. The consequence would probably be a fall in morale for our polar party. Of course I kept these dark broodings to myself for, as the situation was, my pessimism could only cause damage. There was nothing for us to do save wait and hope that the help (which had long since been despatched southwards) would prove sufficient. On 26th February, in accordance with Scott's wishes, the dogs had set off to meet the polar party. As Meares wished to accompany *Terra Nova* northwards, Cherry-Garrard had taken over his position. The dog-team party, Cherry and Demetri, had food for 24 days, plus 2 weeks' extra provisions for the polar party. How far south they would go was a matter which conditions and the two men would decide – TG].

1 March

There has been a sprinkling of snow in calm and mild weather and it has been quite summery. Today I nearly lost one of the new dogs which had become marooned on an ice floe in South Bay. Nelson and I went out after lunch to rescue it and, using a tow-line and some planks, we managed to get it back on dry land. I suppose the hound had been out hunting seal. There will be no repetition of this; tomorrow I shall chain them up. Lashly arrived with the ship yesterday; he now claims a world record for sledging. He is in good condition. Today we stacked away 50 bundles of fodder, which *Terra Nova* had brought. Here in the Antarctic we now have enough fodder for an army of horses.

Mr Archer, who has taken over as head cook in the hut, manages to make life into a great joke. It is not just his culinary skill that's done wonders for our well-being; his whole personality is enormously attractive. He did not really want to come over to us, for he felt at home in *Terra Nova* and the crew worshipped him. Williamson replaces Forde.

2 March

This morning we washed clothes. The weather has been beastly with gales and drift-snow. Have also developed some more photographs.

3 March

We had the animals out one hour today. It is a real joy to handle them; they are quick and willing from the time they emerge from the stable until they return to their straw. I have been acting vet today, for one of the animals was blown up like a balloon. We had no enema and used a football pump instead. It functioned perfectly, but only time will show whether my doctoring has been successful. Crean and I had a long chat tonight, and among other things he told me that, when he was sent from 'Corner Camp' for help, Teddy Evans had said he hoped the rescue team would consist of Nelson, Forde, and me.

4 March

I have driven the dog team today. Cape Evans is not exactly a first-class racetrack with all its stones and scree. I managed to tear my trousers, and this evening I detect a certain tenderness when I sit down. But my first attempt was well blessed, and during the autumn I hope to become skilled in handling the traces. I had only five dogs today, but when the sea ice arrives I hope to get the number up to 12. We were aroused this morning by the *Terra Nova* people coming in to the hut. They came from the north to report 'mission not accomplished'. In other words Campbell's prospects [of relief] are definitely not of the brightest. The ship could not approach closer than 35 miles from shore. After an hour they sailed to Hut Point with Atkinson and Keohane, who will wait there until Scott's arrival. [There was not time to say goodbye properly to those homeward-bound. I just managed to shake Griffith Taylor by the hand, but had to be content to wave to Simpson, Ponting, Meares, Day, Forde, Clissold and Anton, while the ship rounded Cape Evans – TG].

The ship is to make one more attempt to rescue Campbell, not because there is the slightest hope, but because it would look better in the world's eyes should the worst happen. The ship took freshwater ice on board at [Erebus] Glacier Tongue. The weather has been marvellous, though there has been a steady breeze from the northeast. [In the hut at Cape Evans were now nine men (Wright, Debenham, Gran, Nelson, Lashly, Crean, Hooper, Williamson, and Archer) – TG].

5 March

When I took the midnight readings, I saw *Terra Nova* on the horizon to the north – the last time I shall see her this season. Fine weather and calm. Fresh ice is gradually beginning to form. It is –12 °C.

6 March

We exercised the mules after lunch, and then I made a trip with the dogs. One dog was ill and breathed its last tonight; we dumped the corpse in the sea. The poor thing died almost in my hands. I was massaging its stomach when it gave up the ghost. I was a little surprised at this result, but I think it must have been doomed anyhow and my conscience is clear. Nelson and I had a violent argument this morning about the shape of the Antarctic continent. I compared it with South America – highest at the Pole, or a few degrees beyond, and an even declivity towards the Weddell Sea. The polar party shouldn't be far from its goal[6] now, if all goes well, but I have a funny feeling that Amundsen has already reached the Pole.

7 March

The polar party can now be expected any day, and we shall keep watch for a signal [from Hut Point] every night between 10 and 12. [When the ice broke up in inner McMurdo Sound, the cable (of the telephone line between Cape Evans and *Discovery* hut) was washed out to sea – TG]. The agreement is that as soon as they are expected back, rockets will be fired on two successive nights.

8 March

It is beginning to get much darker; by midnight it is half-dark. I stood on Vane Hill[7] tonight, looking for a signal from Hut Point. The stars were winking and the moon, big and yellow, shone over Erebus. The new ice in Hut Bay[8] glittered and the icebergs cast their shadows. But

6 i.e. Hut Point.
7 Windvane Hill.
8 North Bay.

I saw no signal. Hut Point lay dark and silent against the dwindling light of day.

9 March

Hooper has given me a description of the motor-sledge party's journey. To judge by this, it seems that for as long as the machines worked the inventor of such a useless means of transport was roundly cursed. The party had greeted with relief the break-down of the last machine 3 km south of 'Corner Camp'. The team had thereupon gone over to man-hauling and continued south to [latitude] 81°30′. Day and Hooper returned from this point on 25 November and reached Cape Evans on 21 December. The return trip had gone without serious incident, but one episode was worth mentioning. The dogs 'Stareek' and 'Cigan' had been sent home with them because they were more or less useless. On one occasion Day harnessed the dogs, but 'Stareek' would have none of it and Day dismissed him with a kick. But proud 'Stareek' would not put up with such treatment and vanished in high dudgeon back towards the south. Three weeks went by, and a frightful gale was blowing, when suddenly they heard barking outside and who should come in out of the storm but 'Stareek the Lost'. He was utterly exhausted and could hardly eat. The animal is here now, but has been pensioned off, for he is good for nothing. Pity really, for he is a fine animal.

Day and Hooper had not had long to rest at Cape Evans, but had left already on the 25th [December] with Nelson and Clissold – southwards again to 'One Ton Depot'. At the turn of the year, therefore, only Simpson, Ponting, and Anton had been in the hut.

10 March

Before *Terra Nova* stood north for the last time, Pennell declared that if he succeeded in rescuing Campbell and his party he would, between the 10th and 15th, attempt to push southwards again as far as necessary to exchange signals. It is the 10th today, and we have established a system of watchkeeping through the night. The air is heavy with snow and we can't see far.

11 March

Bad weather and stormy all day. All the newly formed ice has been washed out to sea. 20 degrees [C] of frost now.

12 March

A blizzard is blowing and it is almost impossible to move outside the hut; visibility disappears in a whirlwind of snow. At midday it calmed down a bit, and we were out with the mules for a quarter of an hour.

13 March
Out with the dogs this afternoon, but they chucked me off at once and hared off homewards. The surface is not really suitable for dog-sledging. The polar party should be back now.

14 March
Storm, snow-fall, and drift almost the whole day. Even so at ten o'clock I went up to our 'Observatory' to watch for any movement at Hut Point, but I could hardly make out Razorback Islands. If Scott maintains the same average speed as Shackleton, he *must* be back now. Teddy Evans, Lashly, and Crean covered 21 geographical miles down Beardmore Glacier on ski in nine hours. On foot they sank in knee-deep and could not have covered a fifth of the distance in the same time.

15 March
Kept watch for the ship but *Terra Nova* must surely be well on the way to New Zealand. [We concluded that the ice had been just as thick outside Evans Cove as before and that the ship, with her fast dwindling coal supply, had taken the fastest way home – TG]. Snow-storm and low temperature.

16 March
We've had a big discussion today on the meaning of dreams. I held that there is a distinction between ideas and images that merely float before the mind in a haphazard way, and dreams of extraordinary clarity and realism. As proof of my opinion, I wagered Nelson that the dream I had had of Amundsen reaching his most southerly point on 15 December 1911 would be fulfilled.[9]

17 March
St Patrick's Day, and we celebrated in the evening with some bottles of beer. Crean, Archer, Williamson, and I took a trip this morning to South Bay. The sea ice was quite solid, and some score of seals were stretched out on it. Crean and I walked on the ice, keeping close into land. One more week and the ice will stretch safely all the way to Glacier Tongue. It will be good to get a bit of exercise space for the dogs. Weather has been thick with light snow-falls. It is Oates' birthday.[10]

9 As, indeed, it was.
10 His 32nd.

18 March
A large picture of Piccadilly Circus hangs on the hut wall. It is a night scene and people in evening dress wander round the lighted buildings. Nelson and I often study this picture, which brings back memories and holds a promise. Indeed we have much to live for. A winter will pass quickly enough, and then homeward-bound to real life again. Snowfall and thick weather tonight.

19 March
Blizzard these last 24 hours. The temperature is –20 °C and the wind speed 100 km.p.h. I pity the dogs, lying outside in such weather.

20 March
I thought the hut would fly apart in the night, so strong was the wind. It can't be easy to travel on the Barrier in such God-forsaken weather.[11] Let's hope our people have reached Hut Point. Temperature, –18 °C tonight.

21 March
We are now experiencing the equinoctial gales – at any rate that's what Meares reckoned [last year]. He did not want anyone to go out until the equinox had passed. I wonder if he can advance any reasoning for his superstition. I suppose *Terra Nova*'s decks are awash in the 'roaring fifties', with endless setting and shortening of sail.

22 March
As the weather was fine, if windy, I took the opportunity to clean up the dog stable. The sun shone and the dogs seemed to be enjoying themselves. Yesterday we killed a seal quite close to the hut. I cut my hand slightly, and have therefore been treated with antiseptic. During the *Discovery* expedition one of the men cut his hand while butchering seal; it turned bad and he suffered from it for ten years, having many operations. But he must have been more than usually unlucky. Clear tonight and we should be able to see a signal from Hut Point, if there is one.

23 March
Waiting for this signal seems to last for ever. Last night and this evening it was apparently clear, but not a trace of life. Perhaps they are waiting for really perfect weather before signalling. Let's hope so, for if the polar

10 He was 32.

11 In a footnote in the diary TG comments: 'It was precisely during these days that Scott and his companions were fighting their losing battle for life.'

party are not back yet there must be grounds for anxiety. It looks like foul weather again; it has begun to blow from the south, and a thick bank of dark clouds has reared up over White Island.

24 March

We took the mules out for exercise, and then I harnessed the dogs to the sledge and they led me a merry dance till lunch was on the table. You take your life in your hands when you try dog driving at Cape Evans. My back is so bad I can hardly lie down, my eyebrows torn, and my fingers and clothes all scratched and torn. I slept this afternoon. Half a blizzard, and the wind howls and shrieks as though the wind god had assembled all his forces at Cape Evans.

25 March

We have begun to worry a little about the fate of the polar party. No one says anything but you can see it in most of their faces. When the watchman comes down from Vane Hill each night to report, everything comes to a standstill in the hut and every eye is fixed on him.

26 March

I had rather a shock this afternoon when I went up to feed the dogs and found one of them dead. It was the lead dog that had suffered so much from the bad weather. It will find its last resting place in McMurdo Sound. The weather has been vile, the worst for a long time. Snow has been driven by a wind which gusted up to 150 km.p.h.

27 March

At midnight, when I was up taking readings, it was so bad I could hardly crawl round the outside of the hut. The wind gauge was blocked and I had to climb on the roof of the hut to clear the snow from it. It is a wonder I wasn't blown right off into McMurdo Sound. [My hands were constantly in a state reminiscent of bad days and nights out on the Barrier – TG].

This morning the weather improved, and before lunch, after digging out the dogs, I took a trip round Cape Evans. A moderate gale was blowing, but the temperature was quite high and, after walking some way, I got up steam and enjoyed a good work-out. This evening it looks like bad weather again. There is open water as far as you can see – even in the bay beneath Turks Head. Communication with Hut Point [by telephone] will not be restored until next year.

28 March

Still and clear after breakfast this morning, but this calm won't last long.

I studied Hut Point through the telescope this afternoon but, although visibility was good, there was no sign of life. It is Hooper's 21st birthday and we drank his health this evening. Temperature, –11 °C.

29 March

Superb weather; quite summery this evening. I didn't need gloves for the telescope tonight on Vane Hill. No sign from Hut Point. We went out with the mules this morning. My animal, 'Lall-Khan', is a real high-stepper. She is lively and intelligent, strong and easy to handle, and seems to enjoy exercise thoroughly. To begin with she was a bit unsure of the snow underfoot, but is used to it now and we were round Cape Evans in a jiffy. South of Cape Evans new ice has formed and, if this dead calm holds, it won't be long before McMurdo Sound is safe to walk on. It is high time this happens, for both dogs and I are longing for room to run in.[12]

30 March

After feeding the dogs this afternoon Nelson and I walked over to Lands End.[13] The cloud was low and there was a snow-storm at Hut Point. We amused ourselves by shoving some enormous blocks of lava over the precipice down into McMurdo Sound. The sea, though ice-covered, was not strong enough to withstand the weight of these enormous boulders, which created an almighty splash. We were just like children at play. This morning I fixed the bindings on a pair of skis for Williamson.

31 March

Another Sunday has gone by in peace and quiet. Heavy, snowy, windy weather. Tonight we had a discussion about the relative merits of skis and snow-shoes. I always go to extremes, and Nelson and Deb went for me in deadly earnest. Wright understands my position and just smiles. Afterwards he and I had a serious conversation, and he is a supporter of ski *versus* snow-shoe for most occasions on the Barrier. He believes, however, and I with him, that snow-shoes would be fine for leading horses. Perhaps we can have a try with the mules next year. He also believes that the sledges could have larger runners without making them heavier.

1 April

We lead a strange life. Nelson, Deb, and I live close together one day after the next. You'd think we'd get bored with one another, but the remarkable thing is we become better friends as time goes on. For

12 In a footnote in the diary TG records: 'Captain Scott probably perished on 29 March.'
13 The head of South Bay.

example, we never lack for something to talk about. The same goes for the crew.[14] There is no doubt that Scott fully understood the trick of selecting men who get on with each other.

2 April

Fine snow has fallen steadily all day. My thoughts flew homewards, where now everyone is off for the Easter holidays.

3 April

The weather was fine today, and I therefore decided to give the dogs a good work-out. Crean and Archer accompanied me – a real joy ride. The surface was perfect, and off we went at top speed. Up in The Gap,[15] Crean fell off, shortly to be followed by Archer, whereupon the sledge capsized. I grabbed on to the chassis as best I could, and down we went towards South Bay. It was a miracle that I managed to get the sledge back on its runners, but my brake-iron had disappeared and the dogs just carried me away. We rushed towards the precipice leading to the sea ice, and at the last moment I chucked myself off to save myself. The sledge went over and with it the first two dogs, but the others had the sense to stop and the situation was saved. [It was a long time before Crean and Archer would accompany me on such a trip again – TG].

The temperature has begun to fall.

4 April

Ice is forming in McMurdo Sound, and I shouldn't wonder if it is safe by tomorrow. The weather has been calm and cold, and at midday the sun shone from a glittering sky. Tonight the moon is shining and a cold, northerly wind blowing. I could see Hut Point clearly through the telescope at 10 p.m., but no sign of life. We went out with the mules this morning, and I took the dogs out on a sledge drive in the afternoon. I am afraid it did not last long, for I had too many joy-riders and the sledge broke down.

5 April

Crean, Williamson, Hooper and I tried the ice in South Bay this afternoon and went out for some kilometres towards Razorback. The ice was on average one foot thick. On the way back we came round by Cape Evans, and although the ice was only a few inches thick in Hut Bay[16] we reached home safe and sound. The weather has been perfect

14 i.e. the ratings.
15 Behind the hut.
16 North Bay.

all day, calm and sunlit. The sun sets in the northwest now, at about 5 p.m., having been over the horizon about seven hours. But it is going downhill fast now, and in about three weeks sunlight will be only a memory. It is a month today since *Terra Nova* sailed north for good; perhaps the world has news of us now. I'd give a lot to know how Amundsen has fared and his route. Calm again tonight, with moonshine and 25 °C of frost, and so I shouldn't be surprised if Scott were to arrive on Easter Sunday.

6 April

Easter Eve, the moon is shining and there is a southerly breeze; it is getting autumnal. During the night and this morning big leads have opened in Hut Bay, and down towards Hut Point there is a thick sea fog which probably indicates open water. But our people could still get round by Hutton Cliffs, as we did last year. We were out with the mules this morning, and this afternoon was 'wash day' and time for a shave, etc. From time to time one must, I suppose, have a wash, though I personally believe that dirt falls off when its weight exceeds its power of adhesion. An Antarctic formula! I weighed myself a day or two ago and found I was 83 kg, i.e. a few pounds lighter than when I weighed myself last year.[17] I have become leaner than ever and feel better for it.

7 April

Easter Day has passed quietly, for the weather has been most unpleasant and none of us felt like going out. The ice in Hut Bay has pretty well disappeared, but there is no change to be seen southwards. This evening we talked about sending a party of four to Hut Point to discover their situation and to inform the people about the state of the ice. If the trip is on, the party will consist of Nelson, Crean, Williamson and me.

8 April

A storm sprang up last night and has continued all day with its howling and shrieking. I went up to Vane Hill this morning. As far as I could judge, there is ice between the island and Castle Rock.[18] At Hut Point there is open water, and it would not surprise me if the channel were navigable right up to Hut Bay.[19] They have rigged up a sort of billiards table, which has given us a few hours recreation.

17 *See* 24 April 1911, footnote 7.

18 In the inner part of Erebus Bay, presumably.

19 Near Hut Point.

9 April

Stormy and raw today. This morning I slept and this afternoon patched my trousers. But, in spite of the storm, I jogged round Cape Evans after feeding the dogs. I have to get a bit of exercise to keep in good shape. There is still ice between the islands and down to Glacier Tongue, and in all probability it will be firm from now on, for we are unlikely to have a stronger wind than that of the past few days.

10 April

Alas, our fears of last week are justified. The polar party have still not returned to Hut Point; their fate must be sealed. This tragic news was brought to us this evening by Atkinson, Keohane, and Demetri. [Meanwhile I was left alone at Hut Point, where blizzards raged periodically with the usual creakings and groanings of the old hut – A CG]. Cherry-Garrard and Demetri had waited over a week at 'One Ton Camp'. Bad weather and blizzards prevented all their efforts to push farther south, and finally they were forced to give up the attempt and turn for home. They only just managed to reach their goal of Hut Point. The dogs were utterly exhausted and Cherry-Garrard and Demetri ill – the former nearly at death's door. [Atkinson's position was extremely difficult. There was no contact with Cape Evans and at *Discovery* hut, apart from himself, only Keohane was fit for another journey into the interior of the Barrier. The chances of finding Scott, as Atkinson reasoned, were pretty well zero, but to sit there and not make the attempt, that he would not do. He therefore set out with Keohane on 26th March. They toiled on a way past 'Corner Camp', but everything now pointed to the fact that Scott and his party had perished, and on 30th March they gave up. Atkinson and Keohane reached *Discovery* hut towards evening on 1st April – TG].

11 April

I'll never get the events of yesterday out of my mind. I was standing outside the hut taking the temperatures when I heard someone shout, 'The polar party's coming.' I rushed into the hut to the gramophone to get out the National Anthem to greet Scott. I stood and waited long, but no one came. I went out again, and there stood three men,[20] bearded and coated with ice, dirty as sweeps. I took in all at a glance.

We have discussed the situation today. We feel the weight of responsibility that lies on our shoulders, and our thoughts and plans are deeply considered. Scott and his team must have met their deaths, given that they're still on the Barrier – that we are all agreed upon. We

20 Atkinson, Keohane and Demetri.

could rush on off southwards to try to find the dead, but an ounce of common sense tells us to stick out the winter in the hut, for spring will soon be here in the south. If we go now, I fear the remainder of us on the expedition will perish too. We have, after all, a certain duty to the nation whose flag we bear. Scott's goal was the South Pole and no one doubts his success; indeed we're all certain of it. But certainty is not proof, and it is our duty to find him and see whether documentary proof can also be found. Another factor must be taken into consideration. In all probability Campbell is still there, north up the coast. We have a duty to him too.

12 April

Tomorrow Atkinson sets off with Wright, Williamson and Keohane for the relief of Campbell. I'm afraid the party will soon have to turn back, halted by the open water. Demetri and I are to go as far as Hut Point.

To the land of the fallen

13 April
We left Cape Evans at ten this morning [man-hauling] in a biting cold wind, and when we had come right over Little Razorback the weather thickened and the drift started. We halted beside the island, and bivouacked on the icefoot to see the weather out. Strange, just a year ago we camped at this same spot. As it eased a little later, we struck camp and set course for Glacier Tongue. The going over the sea ice was really vile, and we only just managed to haul the sledges through 'Salt Lake'[1] at a speed of 2 km.p.h. We have now made camp on the north side of Glacier Tongue.

14 April
After a grim day of sledging, we have at last arrived at the *Discovery* hut. By the time we reached Castle Rock, Atkinson, Wright, and Williamson were utterly exhausted, and when we got to the hut Keohane, Demetri, and I were not much better off. A stiff southeasterly wind was blowing from the glacier [on Hut Point Peninsula] chapping our faces. The ice in Erebus Bay[2] was more broken up than in South Bay, and the sledges slid along more easily. By 11 p.m. we came to Hutton Cliffs and half an hour later reached a spot where we could get up on the glacier. We were confronted by a sheer rise of 20 feet, but Wright, Williamson and I held a sledge on our shoulders and the other three climbed up without difficulty. This sledge is in a pitiable state, its runners chipped and scarred. It was a miracle that we managed to keep up with the other sledge team, although unquestionably the weaker of the two. Of course we're not really in training – but even so. We took lunch halfway between Hutton Cliffs and Castle Rock. When we struck camp, a thick frost-cloud sailed slowly in from the north, and

1 A name invented by Gran and referring to the briny slush on newly formed sea ice.
2 On the south side.

the dying sun sank like a gigantic ball of cold fire in a sea of cloud. On our arrival at Ski Slope the fog lifted, and when, minutes later, we reached the *Discovery* hut the sky cleared and glittered, with the temperature below –40 °C. Cherry-Garrard was glad to see us. Not surprisingly: he had been alone five days. [Cherry-Garrard seemed more mentally than physically affected, and Demetri and I were left to cope with the dogs' welfare – to fetch in seal meat and fodder for the ravenous animals – TG].

15 April
We're back in the swing of hut life from last year. It's true conditions are not quite so primitive, but Hut Point is just the same – smoke, half-darkness and the smell of blubber. [In spite of everything, however, the place had a certain mysterious charm – TG]. We have rested today. Our legs were stiff this morning but are better now. Keohane's pancakes for lunch were of a size and quantity that left us gasping. The relief party will depart tomorrow.

16 April
As the weather was perfect, Demetri and I went seal hunting. True, there's blubber in the hut for some weeks, but we don't know how long we shall stay at Hut Point, and it seems a good idea to use the good weather to get in supplies of fuel. Without a fire, life in Antarctica is impossible. But our hunt was fruitless; there were no seals along the coast to the south and we returned empty-handed. This afternoon I helped Demetri tend to the dogs; they are thin but otherwise in good condition. 'Cryst' is really lean but as usual beautiful, 'Lappa' wild and playful, 'Kumogay' dispirited and melancholy, and 'Vaida' growling and snarling with well-being. He has grown, has a new coat, and is nearly unrecognizable. Before supper a walk down towards the Barrier. A raw, cold fog lies over the ice-field; I froze just at the sight of it. The party [to relieve Campbell] leaves tomorrow. It will take four weeks' provisions from here and can also get supplies at Butter Point.[3]

17 April
The party set out this morning leaving just Cherry-Garrard, Demetri and me in the hut. [With my knowledge of the northern coastal strip, I reckoned (the journey) a hopeless enterprise – TG]. This afternoon the weather has been perfect; brilliant, white, good-weather clouds sailed

3 Atkinson, with Wright, Williamson and Keohane, planned to start over the old sea ice south and southwest of Hut Point to reach Butter Point, thence to sledge up the western coast.

north towards the sun, which glows fiery-red low in the sky. Erebus was extremely active today. Smoke poured out, straight upwards at first, but then spreading eastwards to form a column of golden mist.

18 April

Cherry-Garrard has told us of fearful, indescribable days and nights out on the Barrier. As soon as the sun went down, the temperature would at once sink to –50 °C. How on earth could the polar party hope to succeed in such conditions, sick and worn out as they must have been after a journey of 2,600 km? Poor Dr Wilson, you deserved a better fate.

19 April

I had a bit of a fright today. I was working over my pots this morning while it was light. The blubber stove was spluttering, the chimney pipe glowing red-hot right up to the roof, and outside a blizzard was blowing. Suddenly there was a bang at the door. I stopped day-dreaming and sat up and listened – yes, there it was again. A wild idea rushed through my head. Could the impossible have happened? Could Scott have returned? I rushed out of the hut into the blizzard. Something loomed up and I ran towards it. Ugh! A big emperor penguin was paying us a visit. It paid for its cheek with its life. Temperature has risen, and it's cosy and warm in the hut.

20 April

The ship had landed some sacks of coal here, and today I proposed to Cherry that we should try it out in the blubber stove. We did so this afternoon, and the hut is hardly recognizable. Pieces of coal burn beautifully, giving off an even, pleasant warmth without smoke or smell.

21 April

We have been a bit short of seal recently, but today was a truly 'Bloody Sunday'. Six whole seals have fallen to my knife. Demetri and I killed two before lunch, and Cherry and I four, soon after. We now have seven seals out on the ice, and our stock of blubber should therefore last till the middle of May.

There have been some marvellous light effects today. Some long, pink clouds hung over [Minna] Bluff and Demetri compared them to ladies' silk stockings. The weather looked pretty threatening this afternoon. Above Cape Evans and the slopes of Erebus there was an extraordinary reflection, bluish-green and ghostly in tint. The sun has not appeared, but we have seen blood-red streaks in the northern sky.

22 April
Bad weather all day. It's been impossible to venture out, and we have just sat chatting by the fire.

23 April
The rescue party returned tonight. They hadn't been very far. They had reached Butter Point, but found the ice conditions to the north absolutely hopeless and had to give up the idea of going forwards. The party had had foul weather pretty well the whole time. And it had been cold too, with a minimum of –43 °C. They have reached the conclusion that Campbell is wintering north, near Evans Cove. If this is the case, I feel sorry for Campbell and his people, who must be having a terrible time. [The probability was that only divine miracle would bring the northern party, without shelter, without food, through the cold, long stormy night of winter – TG]. But I cling to the possibility that this eastern party[4] may no longer be in Antarctica.[5]

24 April
I was a bit surprised this morning when Atkinson, who is now Commandant at Cape Evans, asked me if I would agree to become Bowers' deputy [in charge of stores] and at the same time take over meteorological duties from Charles Wright, so as to release him entirely for work on ice problems and magnetic observations. Of course I accepted, and so it was arranged. With Simpson's work and Bowers' duties I shall be kept fully occupied this coming winter.

25 April
I have been busy all day taking stock of our supplies of provisions at Hut Point. It was all in a terrible mess, but I put some order into things. The weather has been superb, nearly calm and round about –40 °C. Weather permitting, Wright, Keohane, and I intend to set off for Cape Evans the day after tomorrow. This evening we exchanged signals with Cape Evans, and could clearly see the fire at Vane Hill.

26 April
Glittering clear weather, but a terribly cold wind has kept us indoors. This morning we rigged up the sledge for our trip back to Cape Evans; this afternoon we have been sitting round the fire gossiping about this and that. Among other things we discussed the possibility of war between

4 As it was originally designated.
5 i.e. that it had been picked up by *Terra Nova*.

12
Tryggve Gran

13
Releasing a meteorological balloon at Cape Evans

14
Mule at exercise watched by emperor penguins,
Cape Evans, 1912

15
Mid-winter dinner at Cape Evans, 22 June 1912, (left to right) Cherry-Garrard, Wright, Atkinson, Nelson, Gran

16
Gran as clown, mid-winter dinner, 22 June 1912

17

Some members of the search party, October 1912, (left to right) Gran, Williamson, Nelson, Crean

Germany and England. One thing I now understand clearly: the seamen of England are deeply suspicious of the *Vaterland*.[6]

27 April

The journey to Cape Evans had to be postponed because the weather was simply vile. Let's hope it'll improve tomorrow so that we shall be able to set forth; I long to get going with my new duties. For every day that passes the meteorological readings are piling up, and even as things are now it will take me months to get up to date.

6 German: Fatherland.

Back at Cape Evans

28 April

Wright, Keohane, and I arrived at Cape Evans in a blizzard. We left Hut Point at ten this morning and got here at 6 p.m. We have struggled for dear life all day. Shortly after leaving Hut Point we ran into a belt of thin, new ice, and it seemed for a time we should not be able to go on. But close to the land we found a strip of stronger ice, and we proceeded cautiously along the coast beneath Castle Rock, led by Wright on a 60-foot tow-line. Since morning the sky had been snow-laden and by midday thick snow began to fall, and then the wind came. We kept close inshore, but suddenly the ice began to give. My left foot went through and, to save the situation, we began to run. Turtle Back[1] came into sight, and we were soon safe and sound on old sea ice. We set course for Glacier Tongue, hoisted a sail, and rolled along at 10 km an hour. On the north side of Glacier Tongue we camped for lunch. It was the iciest bivouac ever. We froze in every bone in our bodies. [We really ought not to have stopped. . . . The wind had increased to full storm, the temperature was minus 30 °C and all of us were so icy cold by the time we had pitched the tent that we could not light a match in the ordinary way. Keohane had to use his teeth. Boiling hot pemmican and tea work wonders for frozen limbs, but my left foot had been so badly affected when I went through the ice that a short break was not enough to cure it – TG].

29 April

There wasn't much sleep for me last night; my hands and feet hurt terribly. Nelson has operated on my foot, cutting holes in some blisters on the sole. I don't know how I got them. I got frost-bite in my fingers when we bivouacked at Glacier Tongue. When we got to Cape Evans, it was nearly dark. The visibility was bad too and ashore there was

1 Turtle Rock.

heavy drift. We therefore didn't find the best place for climbing the icefoot, but just pushed on up at the spot where we first made landfall. I must say this wasn't an easy ascent either, but the hut was near and that helped. I have rested most of the day, washed myself, and played the gramophone.

30 April

Today I have begun the task of trying to get some order into the expedition's gear and equipment. It is all in a terrible mess. I have also begun to look through our housekeeping inventory; it will take me a bit of time before I get to the bottom of this particular mystery.

The weather has been pretty good and there is moonshine tonight. I began my [four-hourly] meteorological observations this morning. Keohane has started to construct a dog hospital. I participated in a billiards tournament tonight; it was quite fun. Signalled tonight [to Hut Point] but no answer. [We lit a bonfire on Vane Hill to let Atkinson know that the sea ice was all right for the dogs – TG].

1 May

It's May again, and spring and sunshine back home. Out here the storm is howling, and the hut is in a whirlwind of drift-snow. Tonight we are all assembled again; that is we who are still alive, for the five who are out on the Barrier can, alas, no longer be counted among the living. The dog-team party[2] came in tonight after a heavy haul over the sea ice. It was hard on the dogs. Little 'Noogis' had to be abandoned on this side of Glacier Tongue, when he could no longer keep up. It's an open question whether we haven't lost him for good. One animal ran ahead of the party. 'Rabchick' escaped from Hut Point last night and was found by me this morning, having spent the whole night out in the lovely moonshine. I have taken stock of all our clothing today; we have a good supply, except for underpants. [It was sad to think that so many were absent and it pained us to see the empty bunks. Nevertheless there was no point in our going around feeling down-hearted and anxious; for our own well-being we felt it our duty to push aside sad thoughts. Mourning does not bring the dead to life – TG].

2 May

Gales again today and this evening too; the wind velocity is round 50 km.p.h. It was bitter cold taking the readings up on Vane Hill this morning. Some decisions were taken about the future today. The 'South Polar Times' will be published on midwinter's day, and we shall

2 Atkinson, Cherry-Garrard, and Demetri.

have one lecture a week. Mine[3] will be entitled 'Lall-Khan'. She's a wonderful animal, so clever and beautiful. Incidentally, I shall give two talks, the first on skiing.

I have been playing the barber. After cutting my own hair, I then attended to Nelson, Cherry, and Wright. It was my first attempt with the scissors, and I must admit that Wright's head looks rather strange.

3 May

Another day of high wind; tonight the ice in Hut Bay[4] has moved northwards. The moon is at its maximum declination and, according to Nelson, this is the main reason for the break-up of the ice. A sad job today – tidying up in Wilson's and Scott's cubicles.

4 May

Tonight a terrible gale is whipping up the snow. A bombardment of projectiles on the roof awakened us at 4 a.m. The storm had lifted up and transported stones from the heights above. The noise, like a cannonade, was repeated several times. The wind velocity was a record 180 km.p.h. I could hardly make my way against it this morning, when I turned out and fumbled my way up to Vane Hill. [I established a 'there and back' record of 3 minutes. It was impossible to stand up in the wind, and I had to creep out and back on all fours – TG]. It was a bitterly cold and very difficult job, and I was heartily glad to get back to the hut. Storm and drift-snow all day. The wind gauge keeps getting blocked by snow, and it is my job as meteorologist to keep it going. It is not much fun up on the hut gable in a blinding blizzard of wind and snow, so thick that it is like being in a foaming trough of waves. Some improvement this evening, but it is still blowing hard.

5 May

These night watches can seem a little tedious. I have dropped off [to sleep] twice sitting by the stove. It was clear with moonshine outside, but the wind kept up its concert all night. Towards morning clouds began to form, and this afternoon we are enjoying a full-throated storm again. A game of billiards is going on in the mess quarters. The one who gets the smallest score gets the 'Jonah Medal'. Gave a talk today on 'How to take meteorological readings.'

6 May

At last a spot of fine weather. There was beautiful moonshine and near

3 Gran's article for the 'South Polar Times'.

4 North Bay.

calm when I went up to Vane Hill this morning. Daylight is receding. We didn't much notice this during last week's bad weather, and I was therefore quite surprised when I came out to find the moon shining with such a strong light, which was reflected in the sea. We took the mules out after lunch, and they clearly enjoyed the exercise after being cooped up so long. At 6 p.m. I went up to Vane Hill. Full moon and twinkling stars. To the north the sea shimmered in the blue distance, to the south the white snow glittered, and beneath me lay the dark shape of the hut. I could see the light shining out on the snow-drifts and a thin column of smoke rising easily from the chimney. The dogs were roaming about apparently enjoying the fine weather. Let's hope it stays with us a bit.

7 May

Wonderful moonlight these days. I don't know why but it makes me homesick. I feel I am so very far away. Today is Mother's birthday.

8 May

Spent the day calculating wind velocities. My brain is a bit out of training with figures, and it is therefore not surprising that I have a bit of a head tonight. It now turns out that for two hours in the morning of 4 May we had an average wind speed of 144 km.p.h., i.e. a hurricane. Readings at Vane Hill the same morning show even higher figures, for in the three minutes I took the readings a figure of 52 metres per second was recorded. One thing is certain – I had an awful job staying on my feet, though I had no idea it was blowing that hard.

9 May

We had the billiards final today. Crean won and Keohane was 'Jonah'. Two prizes were given: the winner received a bottle of beer and 'Jonah' a medal, with orders to wear it at lunch in a week's time and say in a loud voice as he sits down, 'I am Jonah'. [A never-failing source of amusement after dinner every night has been a form of bagatelle which is played on a mess table – ELA].

10 May

Splendid weather all day. Went out with 'Lall' in the morning. She is beginning to recognize me.

11 May

'Lall' and I went out this morning. She was a bit wild, her lead rein broke, and off she went. But she seemed to regret it, and came back and put her head on my shoulder. It was so touching that I couldn't resist giving her a hug. [Suddenly the beast grabbed my cap and wind hat in her teeth, and dashed off towards the hut before I realized what was happening. There was nothing for it but to hurry after her and, when I got to Cape Evans, I found a triumphant 'Lall-Kahn' in her stall – TG].

12 May
I am preparing a lecture on skiing in general. I have photographed some pictures from text-books and Debenham is making slides from them. They should help.

13 May
Two years since I left Norway. It is a long time, but somehow it has gone pretty fast. This time next year I hope I shan't be far from my native shores. However, it does seem that this long sojourn away from civilization has somehow weakened my longing to see it again. I have become fond of Cape Evans, and I shall always want to return to the volcanic heights beneath the peak of Erebus. The weather is clear and still, and the aurora flickers with a mysterious and ghostly light. Went out with the mules this afternoon. 'Lall' was limping a bit but I couldn't see the cause, so I hope it will soon pass. One of the dogs died this afternoon; as usual the cause is unknown. It was one of our new dogs and a good one. We are into another 'Jonah' tournament in the evenings.

14 May
More storms tonight; the masses of snow round the hut grow larger and larger. I am on watch and sit musing by the fire.

15 May
It is amazing that the ice is not forming in Hut Bay[5] this year. A couple of hundred metres from land the sea is free of all trace of it.

16 May
I have become 'Jonah'. If anything goes wrong in the hut now, I am to blame. Ponting was unanimously elected to the 'Grand Cross of the Jonah Order',[6] an honour he will certainly much appreciate.

17 May
Once again Norway's day of freedom. The flag waves over my bunk and 'Lall' boasts a rosette. The animal likes the decoration very much, at any rate enough to try to eat it. We shall have a party tonight.

5 North Bay.
6 *See* 5 January 1911.

18 May
We had a wonderful supper last night. Demetri presented me with something he called Vodka-Zubarowsky. [I thought the drink tasted awful, but drank for the sake of politeness with the result that I fell sound asleep while my companions went on merry-making – TG]. Archer had kept aside some penguin eggs and served the world's best vanilla ice-cream. In short, a jolly party. I felt cold all day.

19 May
The weather has been marvellous; 'Lall' and I have been on a long trip in the starlight. The thermometer is dropping.

20 May
Today the mercury approached – 40 °C. It has been blowing too, so it's no fun to go out.

21 May
Scientific work passes the time. The days roll by incredibly quickly.

22 May
Great excitement in the hut tonight: Archer *versus* Hooper in the final for the medal. Archer won amid great applause. I was Master of Ceremonies.

23 May
The wind vane on Vane Hill is connected to the hut by wire, so that we can read the wind velocity inside the laboratory at any time. This evening the wires were knotted somewhere, and there was nothing for it but to dress up and go out to try and find the fault. There was a high wind and drift, and it was as black as pitch; before this job was done, our fingers froze. Being a scientist in these parts isn't all that easy.

24 May
Cherry-Garrard gave a talk tonight about rowing. He himself was in an Oxford eight. Frightful storm the past 24 hours, and all ice has disappeared from Hut Bay.

25 May
We had a bit of a fright this afternoon when there was a fire in the hut. I was sitting working in the laboratory, when there was a sound like a shot and a fierce jet of flame spread across the hut. [Twenty places were alight immediately, clothing, bedding, papers and patches of burning oil were all over the table and floor – A CG]. I rushed out and

grabbed some blankets to damp it down, and went 'into the flames'. All the occupants of the hut took a hand, and it wasn't many seconds before we extinguished the flames. Like proper firemen, we sprayed the chemical foam everywhere. This fluid burnt holes in the mats and our clothes, took the skin off our faces, and temporarily blinded several of us. In short, it was a wonder-worker and those who used the spray had every reason to be proud! The cause of the whole thing was one of the English primuses. Wright and Nelson were experimenting and had pumped it up until it exploded.

26 May
Wonderful moonlight and almost completely calm. Fresh ice is beginning to form and is reflecting the light as far as eye can see. All day long the dogs have been singing a horrible chorus of howls, probably because they can scent seal in the neighbourhood. Four men have gone hunting.

27 May
The hunting party killed two seals, so the dogs have had a feast today. Demetri is 21.

28 May
One day passes like another. Thank goodness my time is fully occupied, so that the hours fly by. Of late the temperature has been rather high, but tonight it is down to –30 °C again.

Crean told me about the following little episode that happened up on the plateau [on the polar journey]. The tent was full of tobacco smoke and Crean coughed. Suddenly Scott stuck his head in through the door and said, 'You've got a nasty cough, Crean, you must be careful with a cold like that!' Crean replied, 'You think I can't take a hint, Sir!' Scott laughed, but all the same next day Crean received orders to turn back with Lieutenant Evans and Lashly. Clearly it must have been difficult for Scott to choose his teams, when there was so little difference between them. Crean's 'cough' was an excuse for Scott, but Crean understood his Captain and saw through him.

29 May
It was calm and moonlit in the morning, and Nelson and I went out with our mules. Fortunately 'Lall' was almost fit and seemed to enjoy the outing. We went on the sea ice, which is beginning to look better. Tonight it looks like snow. Otherwise I've spent the afternoon preparing my talk [on skiing].

30 May
One of the dogs has taken a fancy to me. Every time I go out and he hears my voice, he comes running and follows me around everywhere and back to the door. He's a handsome dog but rather thin.

31 May
Last day of the month, and we've nothing to look forward to for weeks but night and winter. Not that the winter nights scare me – I am experiencing an odd feeling of calm and content. The darkness somehow works like a protecting wall against all the cold and emptiness that surrounds us. From today onwards I shall only write up my diary on Sundays – so little is happening.

Nelson and I went out with the mules this afternoon. The weather was perfect and the icebergs glittered and glowered in the wonderful moonlight.

[On June 1, the ice appearing sound, Demetri and Hooper with a dog team went to Hut Point, doing the journey there and back the same day. One of the dogs 'Noogis' had been lost on our return to Cape Evans; but no trace of this animal was found on arriving there and he was never seen again – ELA].

2 June
The last few days' fine weather has created something of a sensation in our little community, and everybody is enjoying a few hours' fresh air every day. The moon is up 'night and day' and, even out by the icebergs, we can move about without falling head first. Latterly the temperature has held steady in the [minus] thirties, but tonight it looks like falling to the forties. But it is still, and we hardly notice the cold. [During the first few days of June . . . our spirits rose as the thermometer dropped; we wanted permanent sea-ice – A CG].

9 June
It doesn't take long to record last week's events. The weather has been variable, but bad weather has had the upper hand the past few days and, as meteorologist, I've had quite a job to keep my instruments functioning. The 6th was Nelson's birthday. Last year it was a day of double celebration for it was Captain Scott's birthday as well. Nevertheless we celebrated the day this year too. Nelson's a strange chap, but a fine one too. I've seldom met a man with a clearer brain and, moreover, he is equipped with a first-class physique.

I gave my talk on skiing the night before last. I began with the elementary techniques, and then we 'went on a trip' in the Jotunheim mountains, and ended up with jumping and the Holmenkollen overland race. Today an appalling snow-storm. I am now giving my companions a weekly report on the meteorological conditions of the preceding week. The average temperature has been –30 °C and wind velocity 13 metres per second.

[June 10 . . . All the ice in North Bay has gone. The part immediately next to the shore, which has now been in so long, and which was over two feet thick, we had considered sure to stay. . . . But if the ice in South Bay were to follow, it would be a calamity, cutting us off entirely from the south and all sledging next year – A CG].

16 June

Since my last entry we've had constant drift and storm, and it's been impossible for anyone to go out. The temperature has been relatively high (about –15 °C), but the wind has been so strong that at times it has been impossible to stand up. The average wind velocity shows 22 metres per second, a record so far as I know. The electric wires to Vane Hill have kept breaking and my hands are covered with frost-bite. It's no fun being a linesman in this God-forsaken place.

On Friday [14 June] Atkinson gave his talk on the expedition's future plans. He spoke clearly and modestly, and everyone had a chance to express an opinion. Roughly his theme was as follows. There are two alternatives to choose from: first, to strike north to relieve Campbell, and second – which he personally thought best – to drive south to see what had happened to Scott. The goal of the expedition was the Pole, and its success depended entirely on finding out whether the [polar] party had reached it. There was also a duty to the polar party's relatives to obtain news of their fate. To these reasons could be added that *Terra Nova* could rescue Campbell, though a few (perhaps three) weeks later than a party from Cape Evans.[7] It was also just possible, though he doubted it, that the eastern party[8] had already reached civilization, in which case a whole year would be wasted for nothing. Campbell's fate depended on the winter; if he survived it, his chances would improve each day the sun rose higher in the sky. However, Atkinson wanted to hear everyone's view on these questions. In fact all shared his assessment, and the journey south was decided upon.

[On the 19th preparations were begun for our celebrations of Midwinter Day on June 22. Debenham was busy making the slides for a lantern lecture. Gran and Williamson were busy behind a blanket making a Christmas tree.[9] This consisted of a central bamboo with lateral

7 Because of the difference in sea ice conditions.

8 Now the northern party.

9 This was Bowers' tree refurbished from the previous year.

stems and the whole imbedded in a pot of gravel. . . . On June 22 . . . Cherry-Garrard, our editor, presented us with another number of the 'South Polar Times', and the remainder of the afternoon was spent as a holiday in reading this, playing bagatelle, or making preparations for a happy evening – ELA].

23 June

Midwinter Day, and now we can look forward to the return of daylight. We had a lively party last night and thoroughly enjoyed ourselves. We even had a Christmas tree – a better I've never seen in civilized latitudes. It was bowed down with decorations and tinsel, and the electric lights twinkled in all colours. I rigged up a clown's outfit and dished out the presents. [His acting was splendid, with a joke for everybody and sometimes a piece of poetry which he declaimed to the men as they came forward to receive their presents. Gran made an excellent clown, and the whole entertainment went with a roar from beginning to end – ELA]. We had a marvellous meal too, and the clown stuffed himself with ice-cream. Praise be to Mr Archer.[10]

Half the winter has passed. Our comradeship is splendid, and truly unbelievable when one thinks we are now in our third year of extreme propinquity. The two new men whom the ship brought, Archer and Williamson, were a fortunate addition to our community. Both are men of excellent temper and humour, who make the best of everything. Williamson is the ring-master for our billiards tournaments, and they provide outstanding entertainment . . . [the very best medicine against low spirits – TG]. Each evening, until far into the night, the balls have rolled and clicked for months now, and the interest and excitement of the game have quickened rather than the reverse. We're all united on one thing – here south it's no good hanging one's head. 'Mourning brings not back the dead', says Ibsen, and so say we. It's been stormy and horrid all the week.

30 June

A glimmer of sunlight seems to tantalize us. Perhaps it's wishful thinking but truly the sun is on its way back. We 13 lead a strange life. One day passes very much like the next, and our routine is as regular as a chronometer. Hooper, Lashly, Archer, Wright and I are up first. The rest emerge one by one from their cubicles, and by ten Nelson has

10 According to ELA's account, it was after this dinner that he outlined his options for the coming season. He thought it most likely that the polar party had been lost in a crevasse on the Beardmore Glacier and that the search might have to extend as far as the upper part of the glacier.

usually finished his breakfast. I spend the morning calculating my readings and, if the weather is fine, Nelson and I take 'Sahib' and 'Lall' out for a walk. After lunch the others exercise the rest of the animals. In the mornings they are usually occupied with preparations for the summer's sledge journey. Cherry-Garrard spends a lot of time drawing. Deb does too, and usually takes a nap in the afternoon. I spend afternoons on difficult things – taking readings, making calculations, writing, etc. Atkinson is the seal hunter and also makes endless plans. Wright keeps busy with his work. In the evenings, all except Lashly assemble round the billiards table. I often take part in the first game, then write up my diary, then turn in and read for a bit, before sinking into the world of dreams. So pass 90 per cent of our days at Cape Evans.

Shaved this afternoon – a superfluous activity really – but I have to keep up appearances. It doesn't take long. Cherry has grown a beard; Deb and Atkinson shave, but Wright and Nelson don't need to.

7 July

This last week storms and bad weather have surpassed anything in our experience. Interesting from a meteorological view point, but if this keeps up I'm not sure my fingers will last. The average wind velocity has been 24 metres per second with an average temperature of –16 °C. I've tried several times to get up to Vane Hill, but the blizzard took my breath away. One morning I was awakened by the night-watchman, and he advised me not to go out, so bad was the weather. [As he put it, 'it's blowing broken glass' – TG]. I took no notice of him, grabbed an electric lamp and stepped outside. I fell immediately, lost the lamp, and stumbled along a few steps. What happened then is almost unbelievable. It took me nearly an hour to get back to the hut. We have now rigged a line up to Vane Hill. We have recently been putting provisions in sacks in preparation for the summer sledge journey. There's no harm in being on the early side.

14 July

When it cleared, by about midday, the sun made its presence felt for the first time during this long winter. It really was light for a time. Packing of provisions now proceeds apace, and we the 'volunteers' are helping all we can. Everybody is looking after their own sledge ration. The hut is a hive of industry. The weather has been better, and we've been able to take strolls outside. Snow fell during the week. [On the 19th the plans for the Southern journey were laid before the other members. Debenham, who had been suffering from an old knee injury at football, and Archer were the two members who would have to remain by the hut – ELA].

21 July
For the summer sledge journey we're trying something new in the way of provisions – an onion a day for each member. I think this is a good idea, not only as a prophylactic against scurvy but also as a food-stuff. At any rate the men will get the impression that they're not just on a slimming course. At the moment the whole hut smells of onions.

The past few weeks the temperature has been quite mild, but today the thermometer fell to the [minus] forties. Crean had his 35th[11] birthday yesterday.

28 July
A blizzard with hurricane-force winds blew up in the night. Such vile weather I have never seen. The wind gusted to 50 metres per second. In these conditions our thoughts fly to our comrades north up the coast. It must be hellish for them with such slender resources. They have scant provisions, and their clothes must be in shreds by now. Let's hope they've been able to kill some seal; otherwise I fear the worst. Tonight the weather has improved slightly, but dark shredded clouds race each other low across a moonlit sky.

4 August
This winter the aurora has had little chance of displaying its splendour. For the most part storm-clouds have obscured the sky, and only now and then have we been able to see the stars. In the past few days ice has been forming in Hut Bay and we can now make longer trips northwards. It is my watch tonight, and I am sitting reading in the centre of the hut. The days are beginning to lengthen and in the middle of the day Erebus's smoke plume takes on lovely colours.

11 August
Spring is in the air. Throughout the week it has been really warm and the hut walls have begun to drip. We've been skiing several days now up on The Ramp [behind the hut], where life has been cheerful. We've jumped and held competitions; the atmosphere has been very sporty. We've been on long trips with the mules too, and both men and beasts have benefited from the exercise.

18 August
Last Monday [12 August] for the first time, the smoke plume from Erebus was properly lit by sunshine. It was really quite a solemn moment. On Tuesday we expected the sun to reach the summit, but at

11 In fact 36th.

midday there was a thick snow-fall and we could scarcely see more than 100 yards. Today too the bad weather has persisted first as a thick windless snow-fall, and finally as a blizzard, which completely buried the hut. To be outdoors was virtually impossible, and you came in to be met by a pack of frightened dogs – scared, that is, by a wind with enough force to blow you off your feet, if you weren't careful. Poor dogs, their shelter is pretty skimpy in such God-forsaken weather.

We cleaned up our cubicle this morning. We dumped Taylor's bed and a couple of tons of rubbish into the Ross Sea. The amount of stuff we seem to collect is beyond belief, but this time we have really cleared up.

The bad weather ended today. Sunlight is reflected on the Western Mountains and was playing on the slopes of Erebus for a whole hour. Theoretically the sun should be over the horizon tomorrow, but for practical purposes we can't expect it until the 21st because Cape Barne [to the north] is in the way. We went south on a long ride with the mules this morning. Williamson's 'Gulab' stumbled, which it often does, and threw him on his head in a snow-drift, and then ran off home on its own.

25 August

We still have not really seen the sun, even though we celebrated its return three days ago with a party that nearly burst the hut's seams, We acted like a pack of schoolboys who had just been set loose on holiday. Nelson and I danced a 'mixed cakewalk Fandango'. Wright was the judge of the dance, the last part of which ended as follows: a somersault by Gran knocked Nelson out of the dance, causing the judge Wright a paralysis of laughter which resulted in his making acquaintance with the floor of the hut. His hilarity was uncontrollable, and we the artists didn't find it easy to help in this situation. Wright was therefore carried off to bed where he laughed himself to sleep. After this manoeuvre we went over to vocal exercises. Keohane, Williamson, Nelson, Atkinson and I began the rehearsal, but Deb soon got up to join us and, by midnight, Mr Archer had entered the choir. It was 2 a.m. before the fun came to an end.

We had some splendid side-effects of the sun the day before yesterday. Some cloud above Barne Glacier cast a shadow over Cape Evans, and we had to content ourselves with watching the play of sunlight in the distance. We could see the roseate light on Inaccessible Island creep down to the icefoot and the sun shone on Hut Point, Castle Rock, and Mount Discovery. Nelson went up to 'Dreadnought'[12] at 1 p.m. and

12 A knoll above the hut.

was rewarded by a glimpse of the sun god in person. I took 'Lall' out in the afternoon near the iceberg down in South Bay. From the foot of the iceberg the horizon to the north was clear and the sky ablaze with light, so that even the impatient animal seemed to stop and admire this magnificent sight. This delayed us a bit, and the others got about a mile ahead. We set off as fast as we could. 'Lall' is eager when needs be, and we ploughed on fast through snow a metre deep behind the iceberg and beneath Lands End.[13] Then we turned north again and caught up with the others at the door of the hut. Both mule and I were sweating hard, and I gave 'Lall' a lump of sugar as a reward. If weather permits, we shall begin a methodical programme of training for the mules on 1 September. It was a nasty spring day yesterday and, if spring is like winter this year, it will be horrible at Cape Evans in September and October.

The hut is pretty well snowed-in, much more so than last year, and I shouldn't be surprised if the year's snow did not bury our dear hut completely. It is a terrific struggle just to keep the entrance clear enough to get in and out. The smallest snow-fall seems to produce metres of the stuff [because of drifting].

1 September

The ice in Hut Bay has again been driven out to sea. Nelson's theory is that the break-up is caused by the moon and that it often happens at the maximum southerly declination. Wright agrees with Nelson and the rest of us have to be satisfied. Spring has arrived. The sun shines warmly and casts a rosy light on everything, including our tempers. The mules and dogs also seem to enjoy the light. Activity at Cape Evans is proportionate to the sun's strength, so it is pretty lively now. [This spring we have done a lot of skiing. Nelson was the keenest, both in jumping and *langlauf*, and ended up by achieving real competence – TG].

[On the 6th, with the idea of giving the members exercise, Nelson, Gran, Crean, and Archer started for Cape Royds over the Barne Glacier. Gran made a complete list of all the stores at Shackleton's quarters – ELA].

8 September

Some of us have been over to Shackleton's old hut at Cape Royds this week. It has become a sort of place for outings. There are plenty of supplies there, and we run some risk of eating too much. I revel in all the Norwegian tinned stuff when I am over there. [One large tin had a

13 The head of South Bay.

label reading, 'Wild Duck, Tornoe and Co., Moss, Norge', and this I thought would be a masterpiece. I therefore placed the can over the primus stove in a pan partly filled with snow, having first made a hole in it (the can). It normally takes about half an hour to warm one of these tins through and, as the wild-duck can was the biggest I had had to deal with, I sat myself calmly down to stuff myself with one of Archer's dishes, which had already been served. Then suddenly there was an explosion, and millions of particles of tin-plate flew round our ears. The primus was slung to the floor, the oil ran out, caught fire and threatened to set fire to the hut. . . We managed to put the fire out pretty quickly. . . it turned out that the pan had leaked and that the big wild-duck tin had an inner container which the knife had not reached – TG].

I returned today in wonderful sunshine all the way. Last Thursday the hut looked like going up in flames once more. [We were bagging pemmican in the hut when someone said, 'Can you smell burning?' At first we could not see anything wrong, and Gran said it must be some brown paper he had burnt – A CG]. The problem was two years' soot in the chimney-pipe running from the galley to the middle of the hut. The pipe became red-hot, and the flames broke through and soon spread, with almost an explosion of soot and ashes as well. It took us nearly a couple of hours to get on top of the fire. [We then did what we ought to have done at the beginning of the winter – took the piping down and cleaned it all out – A CG].

15 September

Seven peaceful days have passed, mostly in packing pemmican rations. This time last year we were on the Barrier. Thank God, I don't have to repeat the spring journey this year. Once, such a trip can be an interesting experience, twice is too much. The weather has on the whole been fine of late, but Cape Evans is itself again tonight. It is blowing a hard storm with heavy drift.

22 September

Our 'Indian friends,'[14] must have had good training in their native mountains. They take quite naturally to sledge work and even their snow-shoes don't disturb them. Last year's ponies were quite different.

A whole flock of emperor penguins is swarming about Cape Evans. It is almost impossible to keep the dogs under control and even 'Lall' went wild at the sight of these weird creatures. We are now all trying to dig the hut out of the enormous snow-drift. [On September 18 to 22

14 The mules.

18
Camp below summit of Mount Erebus, December 1912

19
Mount Erebus in eruption, December 1912

20
Approaching the summit of Mount Erebus, December 1912

21
Pre-Christmas dinner at Shackleton's hut, Cape Royds, December 1912, (left to right) Dickason, Priestley, Williamson

22
Outside Shackleton's hut, Cape Royds, December 1912, (left to right) Debenham, Williamson, Dickason, Priestley

23
The arrival of
Terra Nova
at Cape Evans,
January 1913

24
Norwegian 40 øre stamp (blue) commemorating
Tryggve Gran's North Sea flight of 30 July 1914,
issued 30 July 1944

a party went (to Hut Point) with dog teams, taking down a load of stores and with the idea of putting the hut in order – ELA].

29 September

A month today and our imprisonment in the hut at Cape Evans will be ended. It will be marvellous to be on our way south with the knowledge that every hour that passes will reduce our last hundred days in Antarctica. Two years is a long time to spend in this icy desert, but all the same it will be sad to say farewell to the animals, our comrades, and the hut.

6 October

The heat wave we have experienced in the past few days is almost disquieting for these regions. It has been summery even with the snowfalls – just a few degrees of frost, wet and sloshy everywhere – and the drip, drip of the snow melting from the roof has been almost like civilization. I am afraid it will end with a hurricane and a blizzard any moment now. Atkinson and Demetri will set off southwards with provisions. The dogs will leave in a week for 'Corner Camp'. [The plan was to provide enough provisions to enable two parties, each a unit of four, to ascend the Beardmore Glacier, and two dog teams with a unit of three men to return from some point not as yet settled. Of the men ascending the glacier, four were to remain at The Cloudmaker[15] and collect geological specimens, photograph and do survey work. They would then proceed to the foot of the glacier and continue doing this same work until the return of the others, for all this time they were needed as a support by the advance party. This advance party, the other unit of four, would ascend to the top of the glacier if it were necessary to go so far. . . . At this time it was believed by most of us that an accident had occurred to the Southern Party . . . and that sickness had nothing to do with the disaster. . . . As there was no food either for dogs, mules, or men in any of the depôts, the initial starting weights would have to be very large. To help as far as possible some small depôt journeys would be made in the spring – ELA].

13 October

The flocks of penguin round Cape Evans seem to grow despite the dogs' harrassment. We've been out on a trip with the mules and on the way back met a big flock. They are strange creatures but beautiful in their black-and-white uniform. 'Lall' attempted at first to scrape up an acquaintance, but they rejected her advances and 'Lall' soon took fright

15 A mountain rising to 2,680 m on the west side of the lower Beardmore Glacier.

when some of them pecked her snout. There were about 15 birds altogether. It must be open water that brings them here, or perhaps they come from [Cape] Crozier via 'Corner Camp'. A problem for the scientists.

Atkinson asked me a few days ago whether on the journey south, I would like to remain at The Cloudmaker and participate in the mapping of Beardmore [Glacier]. I naturally accepted. There will be four in my party and our goal will be to climb The Cloudmaker, or at any rate get as high as possible for a view of the whole area. I am grateful to Atkinson for the offer, which really gives me a big chance to make a contribution to scientific discovery. [When the sun had risen high enough in the sky, I started work with the theodolite. . . . I was delighted to be given this task (on the southern journey) and tried my hardest to prove that I was ripe for it – TG].

Atkinson, Cherry, Deb and Demetri left Cape Evans at 10 a.m. yesterday, the first and last named to make for 'Corner Camp'. So the season has opened. Now that plans for The Cloudmaker bid have been laid, I'm beginning to worry lest the party will be brought to a halt on the Barrier, thus frustrating the attempt. The weather is now as fine as it could possibly be. The sun warms you, and I have a real feeling of summer. I have spent the past few days taking readings. The sun is still too low for much of this work, but I am doing something at any rate.

'Kumogay' [a dog] got loose in the night and today we found the corpses of four penguins. Beating does no good; [preying] is too deep in the nature of the brute. 'Stareek' went sick and was withdrawn from the team for the southern party, but now seems better. Goodness knows whether the illness was put on; this creature is more human than animal and doesn't want to face the Barrier. The other dogs have departed and, the danger over, the animal can risk 'recovering'.

20 October

This past week has been marked by nothing save snow-storms and bad weather. 'Stareek' is dead, so he was really ill after all. Today[16] the weather improved, and some of us took the mules over to Hut Point. 'Lall' pulled like a hero. [On October 19 four of the mules came down from Cape Evans to Hut Point, bringing loads; they did the journey splendidly and gave great promise of their future usefulness – ELA]. In the morning, before we left for home, Demetri made a new sort of pancake. It tasted so good [that] I must have set a new Antarctic record! The return trip was arduous – 'Lall' wanted to run but her master didn't feel like it. [On October 25 Cherry-Garrard and Demetri with two

16 Yesterday? *See* following excerpt from ELA.

dog teams went out to 'Corner Camp' taking with them a further supply of dog biscuits and fodder – ELA].

27 October

It is our last Sunday [a short Divine Service was held – TG] in the hut, and we set forth southwards the day after tomorrow. Let's hope the journey will bear fruit. The fate of the polar party must and shall be cleared up. The sun has recently been shining gloriously. Erebus has been bathed in the rays of the midnight sun, while golden-white summer clouds sailed along its lower reaches. It's nearly summer. The sea-gulls have arrived, and young seal lie squalling along the coastline.

Southward bound in search of Scott

29 October

We arrived this afternoon at good old *Discovery* hut. The surface was good, and the mules[1] pulled their loads very well. Everything is all right at the hut. Cherry had returned from his Barrier trip on the 27th. He had wonderful weather throughout. 'Lappa' had cut its leg and, despite violent protests, had been loaded on a sledge. The animal felt wounded in its pride as a sledge dog and had to be restrained in a sack.

30 October

The splendid weather is holding, and we push on south this evening. It will be good to get away from the hut, which is not particularly kind to our clean clothes. [It was decided to march at night as we had done the previous season. . . . At 7.30 p.m. . . the seven mules and eight men making up the Pony Party started south. C.S.Wright was in command, as he was a skilled navigator. The mules and their leaders were as follows: E.W.Nelson, leading Khan Sahib; T.Gran, leading Lal Khan; W.Lashly, leading Pyaree; T.Crean, leading Rani; T.Williamson, leading Gulab; P.Keohane, leading Begum; F.J.Hooper, leading Abdullah. Wright . . . went ahead, setting the course and standing by to give any help he could – ELA].

31 October

We are camped about 31 km in on the Barrier. It's about –30 °C, and the animals don't seem to like it. 'Lall' pulls like a hero, but her thick pelt makes her sweat a lot and, as soon as we halt, the animal stands shivering like an aspen. There's a fresh southerly breeze and our noses are white. During the climb up to the Barrier, 'Sahib' fell into a crevasse and hung there. It was fortunately narrow, so we managed to haul the animal out with a tow-rope. A frosty fog covers the Barrier, and dark and threatening clouds have appeared in the south. It began to snow this morning, but luckily it has started to clear again. Our animals have not lost their ravenous appetites in spite of everything. When we had to

1 All seven.

turn a hand to the job of rebuilding their snow-walls[2] this morning, we found they had begun to chew away at the putties we have wrapped round their legs to protect them against the snow and cold. They don't know what's good for them.

1 November

The bivouac site is enjoying the most delightful sunshine. The mules certainly need a day of rest in the sun. It was pitiful to see how the ice had formed on their bodies, as soon as we halted tonight. Long icicles flecked with blood hung from their nostrils, and their eyes were coated with rime. Poor 'Gulab' has a nasty sore from the chafing of the harness and seems to suffer especially at the start of each march. We have crossed several crevasses. [The two dog teams, with Cherry-Garrard, Demetri, and myself, started to follow the mules – ELA].

2 November

We have made a bivouac at 'Corner Camp' after a particularly dreary 10- km march. Because of the crevasse danger our mules were linked together.[3] Our section was led by 'Sahib' and her dreadfully slow speed necessitated incessant stops for the other animals. The cold in the neighbourhood of 'Corner Camp' is incredible. The last time I was here the temperature was down in the [minus] sixties, and now it's in the [minus] forties. We had midnight sun for the first time tonight. We're lying in our sleeping bags having 'breakfast in bed'. Our thick, steaming hot stew tastes delicious. Williamson is at present acting as cook.

3 November

High wind and drift with intermittent sunshine; our horses are relatively snug behind their snow-walls. We have bivouacked at 'Demetri Depot'[4] and the dogs should have joined us by now. But I don't believe they will find the way in this thick drift.

(*Evening*) Still stormy, and the animals are half-buried. 'Lall' worked loose and stood in 'Gulab's' lee. We are now about to strike camp and toil on southwards.

4 November

Another horrible night with strong wind; we're getting frost-bitten.

2 The mule party also built snow cairns every two to four miles to assist the dog teams in following their tracks.

3 Alpine rope was used between the leaders of the mules.

4 Twelve miles south of 'Corner Camp'.

'Lall' hasn't touched her feed of late – just stood and sniffed at it. She can eat sugar and biscuits, so perhaps the beast is suffering from a little devilry. If things don't pick up, we shall be in big trouble. The animals are dragging very heavy loads – 350 kg per sledge.[5]

(*Evening*) Still bad weather. The animals are pretty well done for. [The cold, the wind and the awful uniformity of the ice desert broke them down all too soon – TG]. I've given 'Lall' three of my biscuits; they vanished like mist in sunshine. We strike camp soon.

5 November

(*Midday*) We've had a rest day. The dogs arrived just as we were preparing to break camp, and for obvious reasons we decided to stay on. The weather is relatively warm; it will do the mules good to have a 'drying-out day'. We gave them warm mash last night, but oddly enough they didn't seem to take to it. 'Lall', that rogue, hardly touched her food. The animal has barely eaten 10 lb of oats since we left the hut about a week ago.

6 November

We had a good night's march with fine sunshine and excellent going. The dogs have taken some of the load, and the horses seem to notice the difference. It is about –20 °C but calm.

7 November

During the night we covered over 20 km on the southward track. Perfect weather and 30°C of frost. 'Lall' has become pitifully thin and I fear she will not last long. 'Gulab', on the other hand, seems to put on weight from day to day, despite his bloody side. He's as fat as a pig and eats everything. Crean is now cook. [At lunch Atkinson thought he saw a tent away to our right – the very thought of it came as a shock – but it proved to be a false alarm – A CG].

(*Evening*) A lovely warm night in the sack, but I'm not in good humour for my good comrade 'Lall' has sunk to her hindquarters and refuses to eat anything but sugar and biscuits. But even so the animal still works satisfactorily and, so long as that's how it is, we mustn't worry overmuch.

8 November

The beautiful cold weather continues. At 4 a.m. it was –37 °C and

5 New 12-foot Norwegian sledges, with tapered runners, were brought down by the ship for use this season,and were considered an improvement on the broad-runner sledges used in the previous season.

because of the low temperature the going was rather heavy. We've passed 'Bluff Depot'[6] and are now on the right side of 79 degrees [past the 79th parallel]. 'Lall' has eaten very little and showed signs of snow-blindness during the day. [It was then that their snow-goggles were tried for the first time. We found that they were of the greatest use and generally stayed on while the mules were on their lines – ELA].

9 November

We can't complain about the weather, when we can cover 21–22 km every night. It's true it is very cold, but without wind we can take it. [Our surfaces were so hard and good that the mules did not with their small hooves sink appreciably into the snow – ELA]. 'Lall' is beginning to look awful – she's shrinking to nothing. Well, in a couple of days or so, we shall be able to kill the animal with a good conscience. We'll soon need meat for the dogs.

10 November

A light mist rests over the Barrier, but otherwise the weather is glorious. We haven't many miles left to 'One Ton Depot'. All in all the situation isn't bad. 'Lall' has been condemned to death, and 'Gulab' ought to go too – otherwise we have no serious problems. We get on famously together in the tent; it will be really sad to split up.

11 November

We reached 'One Ton Depot' at midnight, after covering five miles in an atrocious wind. [Our hearts beat a little faster as we drew near, for in spite of everything there was a tiny possibility that the polar party had reached the place after the dogs had left. But no; we found the depot quite untouched – TG]. We couldn't avoid frost-bite and Nelson's nose is rather bad. There's masses of food and oil in the depot, but unfortunately one of the paraffin tins has leaked and spoilt some of the food. [There was no hole of any kind in this tin – ELA][7]. The weather looks threatening, and it's blowing and drifting. [I decided to give men and animals a half day's rest here – ELA].

(*Evening*) It's been awful all day but looks a bit better now, and we shall shortly push on south towards Beardmore [Glacier].

12 November

It has happened! We have found what we sought! Good God, what a

6 Off Minna Bluff.

7 Similar leakage at depots farther south had contributed to the disaster that overtook the polar party.

twist of fate. Barely 20 km from 'One Ton Depot', we have come upon the snow-covered tent with the bodies of Scott, Wilson, and Bowers. [Somewhat towards morning, just when we had begun to look forward to food, drink and the sack, Hooper made out a pyramid shape almost 45° from our course. I plucked my ski-sticks from the sledge, and made off as fast as I could go. Barely ten minutes later I stood before a partly visible tent. It was almost completely covered by a two-metre high snow-wall, just like boulders in the mountains in winter. The door was partly snowed-in. At that moment the mule caravan had stopped, and a dog team (party) came towards me. It was Atkinson and Lashly (TG). We with the dogs had seen Wright turn away from the course by himself and the mule party swerve right-handed ahead of us. He had seen what he thought was a cairn, and then something looking black by its side. . . . We came up to them and halted. Wright came across to us. 'It is the tent' – A CG].

Captain Scott lay in the middle, half out of his sleeping bag, Bowers on his right, and Wilson on his left but twisted round with his head and upper body up against the tent pole. Wilson and Bowers were right inside their sleeping bags. The cold had turned their skin yellow and glassy, and there were masses of marks of frost-bite. Scott seemed to have fought hard at the moment of death, but the others gave the impression of having passed away in their sleep.

The main news is that Scott reached the South Pole on 17 January this year, only to find that Roald Amundsen had been there on 15 December – a good month earlier. Amundsen had four men with him – he had taken a new and better route. A splendid feat, and I congratulate him. [I was served up this significant news in the following manner. Tom Crean came over to me and said, 'Sir, permit me to congratulate you. Dr Atkinson has just found Scott's diary, where it is written that our people found the Norwegian flag when they came to the South Pole'. I grasped the outstretched hand, shook it and gazed into his tearful eyes. Then I too was overwhelmed with emotion – TG].

Of our own polar party there is only the most tragic news. I have only glanced through Scott's diary but, from what I have seen, it is clear that misfortune accompanied my dead comrades. It was a bitter blow for Scott to reach the Pole and find it vanquished. His lifetime dream was shattered and he felt himself wronged. On the return journey, during the descent of the Beardmore Glacier, Petty Officer Evans fell down a crevasse and was injured. Right from the Pole itself they had noticed a great change in this big, strong man, and the fall seemed to take toll of the rest of his vitality. The fact that Amundsen was first at the Pole in a way meant more to Evans than to the rest. Had Scott been first, Evans would have achieved financial independence. But now the future must have seemed uncertain and unattractive.

Petty Officer Evans died at the 'Lower Glacier Depot'. On the Barrier itself the party encountered tremendously low temperatures. Snow became like sand, and then came the wind against them. Oates was badly frost-bitten and gradually became completely helpless. He begged Scott several times to leave him to his fate, but without response. Finally he took the matter into his own hands. On the 80th parallel a snow-storm halted the party. Oates crawled out of the tent, to save his companions and to end his own days there in the abominable waste of snow and ice. Thus died Oates.[8]

On 21 March the other three arrived at the camp here. They had provisions for two days. Atrocious weather prevented them from pushing on. Day in and day out the wilderness presented the same picture – a howling, whirling chaos of snow and storm into which no man could venture. Food and fuel ran out, and on the 29th Scott wrote, 'I do not think we can hope for any better things now. . . . For God's sake look after our people.'

We buried our dead companions this morning; it was a truly solemn moment. [We never moved them. We took the bamboos of the tent away, and the tent itself covered them – A CG]. It was moving to witness 11 weather-beaten men standing with bared heads singing. The sun flamed through threatening storm-clouds, and strange colours played over the icy desert. Driving snow whirled up around us and, when the hymns came to an end, a white mantle had already covered the dead. We have erected a 12-foot cairn over the graves and atop a cross made of a pair of skis.[9] We have slaughtered 'Lall' and 'Sahib', but it took five bullets to kill poor 'Sahib'. We shall now push on south in search of Oates.

13 November

(*Morning*) We have covered 15 km southwards. It blew hard and was horribly cold. Before we left, I took stock of the polar party's *impedimenta*. It was incredible how much they had crowded on the sledge. Apart from the geological specimens [from the head of Beardmore Glacier] which weighed about 20 kg, there were masses of empty sacks and tattered clothing. I think they could have saved themselves the weight.

14 November

After a long, hard march in vile going, we have bivouacked on the 80th

8 On or about 16 March.

9 They were Gran's.

parallel. This will be our southward limit this time. We shall search for Oates and then set course northwards and, if possible, go to the relief of Campbell. I don't like the idea of giving up, of turning my back on the mountainous country in the south. I console myself with the thought of returning some time in the future.

15 November

We didn't tarry long at our most southerly bivouac. It blew with a driving force which whipped up the snow and ruled out a proper search for Oates. [All we found was his empty sleeping-bag[10] (TG). Inside the bag was the theodolite, and his finnesko and socks. One of the finnesko was slit down the front as far as the leather beckets, evidently to get his bad foot into it. This was fifteen miles from the last camp, and I suppose they had brought on his bag for three or four miles in case they might find him still alive (A CG). And so it was at this spot where this noble man had sought death that we raised a cross bearing the inscription: 'Hereabouts died a very gallant gentleman, Captain L.E.G. Oates of the Inniskilling Dragoons' – TG].

Atkinson and Demetri will stay behind a while to see if the weather clears. The rest of us have covered 21 km of the return march. With the wind behind us we have made great speed, even in this foul weather.

16 November

During the night we reached Scott's last camp and have bivouacked some hundred yards north of it. I believe our monument to the fallen will long endure, for the ice and drift is already building a protective wall round it. Today a blizzard – the snow swirls and eddies around us, and it's next to impossible to stick our heads out of the tent. The temperature is high, and inside the tent the moisture is dripping off the walls and making everything wet and clammy. This graveyard seems barren and depressing; let's get away from it as quickly as we can. Perhaps some people at home will ask why we did not bring back the dead. But we would all answer as one: Scott's wish was to lie at rest in the land of his life's work.

17 November

Back to 'One Ton Camp'. The bad weather disappeared yesterday and we had a pleasant march. The going was soft and we used our skis, which went well – just like home for once. I am using Scott's skis; they at any rate will complete the 3,000-km trail.

10 This sleeping bag is preserved at the Scott Polar Research Institute, Cambridge.

We overhauled the sledges tonight before striking camp and, as a result, Williamson and I discovered by pure chance, among the things we were going to dump, a bag containing a letter from Amundsen to King Haakon. Scott had found it in his tent at the Pole. [. . . on the envelope was written: 'H.M.King Haakon, Slottet, Kristiania'. No explanation was needed. It was Amundsen's triumphant greeting to his King. How strange that I should have found this proof that both Amundsen and Scott had reached the South Pole. . . . An hour after this event our caravan was on the march again, and soon the cross disappeared over the flaming horizon – TG].

I have been able to read a little more of Scott's diary. For 15 January he writes: 'It's wonderful to think that 2 long marches would land us at the Pole. We left our depôt today with nine days' provisions, so that it ought to be a certain thing now, and the only appalling possibility the sight of the Norwegian flag forestalling ours.' The following day Scott continues: 'The worst has happened, or nearly the worst. About the second hour of the march Bowers' sharp eyes detected what he thought was a cairn. . . . Half an hour later he detected a black speck ahead.' Scott now realized it could not be a natural snow feature. 'We marched on, found that it was a black flag tied to a sledge bearer; nearby the remains of a camp. This told the whole story. The Norwegians have forestalled us and are first at the Pole. It is a terrible disappointment, and I am very sorry for my loyal companions. . . . All the day dreams must go. . . .' [This paragraph may have been added later.]

18 November
Foul weather, snow-storm. The mules are wearing themselves out in this soft and heavy going. We, on the other hand, sail like the wind on our skis. It would have gone quicker without the mules; we could have set sail and rushed along. Temperature high.

19 November
After a long period in sheer fog, with nothing to break the monotony of the narrow band of flat, white waste within our vision, it was a joy tonight to catch a glimpse of Erebus. It emerged like a high turret out of the fog. The weather is mild, just a few degrees of frost.

20 November
Snow-storm the whole night, but despite this we have covered 20 km northwards. As I trudged along across this awesome desert of ice and snow, my thoughts have a life of their own. I think of Scott, I think of Amundsen. I have learned that something called friendship exists. I have come to know men willing to sacrifice themselves for their country

and for their convictions. Scott came to reach the Pole, and he did it. That he came as number two, that was fate.

21 November

At last a little sunshine, but not enough to dry out our sodden sleeping bags and clothes. The fog has rolled in over us again. Our mules hobble their way towards the end. 'Rani' will only eat biscuits; 'Abdullah' touches nothing, but just stands and stares forlornly ahead. The other three are off their food too. The only titbit they care for is rope, and this has endangered the whole load. [If they would have eaten (their rations) they would have been a huge success. . . . On the whole the mules failed to adapt themselves to this life, and as such must be considered to be a failure for Antarctic work – A CG]. Atkinson and Demetri failed to find Oates but nevertheless built a cairn surmounted by a cross.[11]

22 November

Splendid weather. The dogs leave us tomorrow for a direct trek to Cape Evans. We shall wait at the *Discovery* hut, and thence make an expedition up the coast for the relief of Campbell. The temperature is high, and we have the feeling of summer.

23 November

Bivouacked near 'Demetri Depot'. Thick mist tonight; we could hardly see more than a mule-length ahead. It's snowing and looks like storm. We are nearing 'Corner Camp' and can hardly wait.

24 November

For once in a way I shall be able to see this place in sunshine. It's about time. The dogs left today. They seemed to know they were making for home, that it was farewell to the Barrier, the world's coldest and most awful place.

25 November

Wind and drift a bit this afternoon, but it was fine when we struck camp. We crossed the stretch indented by crevasses, and 'Begum' managed to fall into one. She hung there in her sealskin harness and, sensible animal that she is, kept quiet while we hauled her up. [Two dog teams, with Cherry-Garrard, Demetri and myself, having pushed ahead of the mules, reached Hut Point – ELA].

11 *See* 15 November.

26 November

At 'Safety Camp' tonight. Since 'lunch' at midnight, Wright, Nelson, and I have hauled 'Abdullah's' sledge. The animal was exhausted and simply couldn't get on at all. Two years ago today we sailed south from New Zealand. This will probably be my last night on the Barrier, at any rate for some years.[12]

27 November

(*Hut Point, midnight*) At long last there's something cheerful to record. Campbell is here in the hut, and all his men are in fine shape at Cape Evans. [We saw men coming towards us and recognized all but one. Suddenly Williamson, who had pushed on ahead with his wonderful 'Gulab' shouted, 'It's Lieutenant Campbell!' A thunderous hurrah greeted this happy news, and we hurried to cover the last lap in towards land. We grasped the hand of the chief of the northern party to assure ourselves it was no ghost we had seen. Campbell it was, and bouncing with health too – TG]. They spent nine months in an ice cave where they could hardly sit upright. But nothing much had befallen them. During the winter it looked as though Browning would perish, but now he is all right. Atkinson and Campbell go over to Cape Evans tonight. As senior man, Campbell is now Commanding Officer.

(*Midday*) There hasn't been much sleep. There's a lot of smoke in the hut, and I feel as though I have caught a bad cold. The last night on the Barrier was incredibly warm. The sun roasted the tent so much that in the end I had to rip off every stitch of clothing and roll in the snow. Tomorrow we make for home at Cape Evans.

28 November

[*Cape Evans*] Once more in the lee of the walls of our good old hut.[13] Campbell's party looks splendid, so plump and well. Archer has fed them up with milk and honey. Dr Levick is the spit image of Henry VIII. Apparently they looked dreadful when they stumbled into the hut [on 7 November]. Campbell says our depots certainly saved the situation for them. Browning would clearly have succumbed had they not come upon fresh provisions. During the winter sojourn in the cave they had run out of tobacco and had tried to make tea leaves from seaweed. They lived exclusively on seal and penguin meat. They had an average of 1.3 matches a day to last them, and therefore kept alight a seal-oil lamp, which stank and smoked detestably. The cold was not bad; on

12 Gran considered returning with his own expedition at some future time. *See also* 14 November.

13 The surviving members of the expedition were now all at Cape Evans.

the contrary, they had sometimes to get the temperature down to prevent the snow melting. Here at Cape Evans it's full summer. Plenty of animal and bird life, and to the north the breakers of McMurdo Sound. Priestley, Deb, and I are soon to climb Mount Erebus.

29 November

Campbell and I went on a long trip today. We naturally had a great deal to tell each other. For the rest I've spent the day preparing for the Erebus venture.

30 November

We had to shoot 'Abdullah' and 'Begum' today. Poor animals, they were worn out and too far gone to recover. The weather has been foul.

1 December

Taylor's birthday today. I hope he'll be back in his dear Australia to celebrate. The weather has been perfect with a warm north wind. Masses of pack ice have entered the bay; we've seen some huge floes and massive pressure ridges. Deb, Priestley, Abbott, Hooper, [Dickason] and I set out for Erebus tomorrow. Atkinson, Cherry, and Archer leave for Cape Royds the same day.

The ascent of the volcano Erebus

2 December
[A party of six left Cape Evans. . . . with the main object of surveying the old crater (of Erebus), and if time permitted making an ascent to the rim of the present active crater – REP].

The first day has brought us only a 1,000 feet up, but our hopes are high for tomorrow and after. It was hot dragging the sledge over the Barne Glacier. Roasting sun and no wind. Priestley and Deb have gone down to Cape Royds. Williamson found some sea-bird's eggs this morning at Cape Evans – they're pretty early.

3 December
We haven't moved today because Deb found he had left some important things at Cape Evans. Priestley went down to Shackleton's hut and brought back some eggs with him – four per man. They tasted simply delicious, though I fear there was a chick in one of mine. Eggs seem to hatch like lightning in this part of the world.

4 December
Four thousand feet up. Heavy hauling and much sweat. The whole morning we climbed in thick fog, but by midday we had worked through it into brilliant sunshine. A sea of fog now lies below us.

5 December
Snow set in during the night, and we must stay quietly where we are. Priestley has been telling us about his time at Cape Adare.[1] I now understand that the northern coast is quite unsuitable for voyages of discovery. Carsten Borchgrevink[2] must have had appalling difficulties to contend with.

1 With the northern party.
2 On the *Southern Cross* expedition, 1898–1900.

6 December

The snowy weather continues; our tent is literally sinking into the masses of snow. The wind has backed a little, so perhaps we can hope for better weather.

7 December

This morning the weather cleared and we got under way. At midday we bivouacked near a nunatak,[3] which we conquered without much effort during the afternoon. This feature is a volcanic protrusion of Erebus itself. The old crater of Erebus is now only 4–5 km away. It looks beautiful – jagged and wild, jutting out over the slopes. We are separated from Erebus itself by a glacier. The slopes hereabouts are broken up by crevasses, but so far none of us has had the pleasure of making their deeper acquaintance. We are now at 6,000 ft.

8 December

We have reached 8,000 ft, and the old crater lies behind us. The glacier lying along the base is heavily seracced and full of precipices and crevasses. We have ascended into a veritable Alpine landscape. From this point we have a wonderful view over the mountains in the west, and we have seen a series of hitherto undiscovered tops west of Mount Tryggve Gran. We are really conscious of climbing now – the least effort takes our breath away. The air pressure is 21.5 in, much lower than at such heights in our [Norwegian] latitudes. The temperature is falling; in the night it was below –20 °C.

9 December

The day has passed in typical mountaineering routine. We have ferried our gear to higher ground, and have now camped at 9,000 ft. Tomorrow we shall begin the final ascent. Cold tonight, –25 °C as soon as the sun went down.

10 December

Good work. We are now at 11,000 feet and are camped in the so-called second crater. Deb and Dickason stayed behind at the 9,000-ft camp. [We were camped in the position from which I had decided to make the final ascent. After discussion with Debenham, I selected Gran, Abbott, and Hooper to accompany me to the top, leaving Debenham, who had slight mountain sickness, to continue his survey, and Dickason, who was feeling the height more than the other two men (ratings), to help him – REP].

Our bivouac site is excellent and relatively protected by a wild, jagged

3 Hoopers Shoulder.

crater wall. Towards the south the summit looms above us, and stormy clouds chase over the peak itself. Enormous clouds of smoke billow out of the volcano, and swirl about over our heads. There's a strong stench of sulphur, and the snow is tinted with green. We have six days' provisions, and so should with a bit of luck manage to reach the top.[4]

11 December

A long, cold night in the sleeping bag. It is worn out, and I can see through it in several places. Strong wind and pretty hefty drift. Now and again a violent cannonade from the volcano, like muffled thunder. Went out on a little trip after lunch to stretch my legs. What a barren, empty scene – just sulphur, ice and lava. The cold bites hard. We can't go fast enough at this altitude to keep warm. It looks like good weather. The summit is in sight and masses of smoke pour from it. Now 25 °C of frost.

12 December

We sit at the primus and wait for food. It's cold, some 30 degrees below [zero] and we are all shivering, our teeth chattering. The weather has suddenly turned perfect. Erebus is sparkling clear and alluring.

(*5 a.m.*) Am standing on the summit of Erebus! No living soul has climbed higher than us in the polar land. But this is no time to write. Hurrah! 13,000 feet up. Back to the tent. We're too exhausted to think. I feel awful and sick. Was nearly killed. Erebus played its tricks.

(*Evening, 9,000 ft Camp*) Arrived here in a miserable state. I must have been poisoned by the gases. Have borrowed Deb's sleeping bag.

13 December

After a fairly good night I'm much better today. Deb hardly got a wink in my sleeping bag. He just lay there, teeth chattering. It's clear my sleeping bag is finished. We have descended 4,000 feet. The weather is clear but blustery. It's frightful to be sick in this land. The temperature has risen considerably.

14 December

We are in storm and thick snow, a real blizzard. But we've been pretty lucky up to now, so we can't grumble. The overall result of our Erebus trip must be considered satisfactory, I must say. We have made a good collection of geological specimens; we have uncovered new areas and have had a marvellous opportunity of studying the volcanic activity. True, it's been a rough trip but, now that we're homeward bound

4 The sledge was used to a height of over 9,500 feet.

towards comfort and safety, the memory of the hardship fades to leave the adventure bright and clear.

The day before yesterday[5] I was too ill to record the story of our attack on the summit, and I will now make good the omission. It was about 2 a.m. when I turned out to see what the weather had to offer. It was bitterly cold, but calm and clear as a bell. I could not see the sun because of the vast billows of smoke the volcano was discharging. Before me lay a desolate landscape – just ice and volcanic ash. I was irresistibly reminded of the story of the first men on the moon. We made a warm breakfast, and then set off for the top. Our climbing speed was slow, because in the thin air we soon became breathless amd our hearts thumped noisily. By 5 a.m. we had entered thick sulphurous smoke, and a moment later we stood on the rim of the crater. Huge masses of smoke rose up and drifted away to the northwest. We had reached the summit from the southeast, and now and then the smoke swirled down and troubled us. The lip of the crater was uneven, and there were great stones everywhere. I climbed to the highest point and built a cairn. [. . . for the record I had prepared, I endeavoured with the help of Abbott and Hooper to light the hypsometer; but the breeze was too stiff – REP]. The volcanic rocks are incredibly light. I found I could lift some which were bigger than myself.

It was cold at the summit – over 30° of frost, and windy. [Gran and I . . . took a series of photographs on the rim of the crater, but we were unable to see more than a few feet down because of the steam and sulphur vapour – REP]. Hooper got frost-bite in one foot, and was immediately sent back down with Abbott for company. Priestley and I, however, took a new and longer route. We followed the outer edge of the smoke down the volcano's northern side, and eventually came upon some bell-shaped chunks of ice. They turned out to be hollow, and steam rose from inside them. I believe they act as a sort of valve for the volcanic activity. At this point Priestley found he had left a roll of exposed films at the summit. [. . . I discovered to my annoyance that instead of the record we had left a tin of exposed films at the summit – REP]. They constituted vital data, so I set off back up again. The wind had dropped considerably, and the smoke from the crater was less violent. When I reached the summit again, there was practically no sign of activity from the volcano and I therefore decided to have a closer look round. I climbed for a time in and about the blocks of lava and the ice bells, sketched the crater opening, and noted points of interest.

It was a wonderful sight. The Ross Sea lay open as far as the eye could see – not a trace of pack ice. To the west lay the mountains of Victoria

5 i.e. 12 December.

Land and, behind them, a shining plateau. About 15° northwest of Mount Gran I thought I could make out a mountain range. A multitude of peaks and pinnacles reared up above the ice plateau in the west. To be really useful here you'd need a theodolite and a sunny day. Suddenly I heard a gurgling sound and, before I had time to think, the ground beneath me began to tremble. From the crater up rushed a gigantic cloud of smoke. There was a clap of thunder, and the next second I was enveloped in blackness. Close by I spotted a patch of snow; I plunged into it and buried my head to save myself from choking. I lay there a time, and round about me fell lumps of what looked like tar. They were steaming hot and burned holes in my clothes. This awe-inspiring display lasted a couple of minutes more, then it began to clear, and I jumped up and began my descent as fast as my legs would go. I had just emerged from the smoke when Priestley came to meet me. He had witnessed these happenings from below, and really thought my days were numbered. [. . . he strolled out of the steam cloud all serene and looking none the worse for his adventure. He had had a unique opportunity of observing an eruption of Erebus. . . . Gran was fortunate in not experiencing any worse effect of the eruption than a slight sickness during the next few days, which we both attributed to the sulphur vapour – REP]. Together we made for our camp. We were both played out, and there was a moment when I thought we would never make it. At the end we were almost crawling.

Continuing drift and a hard blow. A couple of good days with sunshine at the hut at Cape Royds would work wonders.

15 December

We are in the Shackleton hut and it feels just as though we had jumped from winter to summer. Campbell, Atkinson, Wright, Cherry, Archer and Williamson are all here. Thousands of penguins are swarming round the hut.

16 December

Snow and wind. If the weather improves we shall move to Cape Evans tomorrow.

17 December

Snow-storm all last night and today. High seas in McMurdo Sound. It is cold in the hut.

Cape Evans and relief

18 December
We're back at Cape Evans. A rather strenuous trip and exciting too. The snow on the glacier[1] was deep and hid the crevasses. Dickason and I fell through one crack together, and lay dangling for a time at the end of our lines between two blue walls of ice. At Cape Evans everything is fine. Dr Levick is fatter than ever.

19 December
Glorious weather; we've spent the day sunning ourselves on the stable roof. Terrible dog fight this afternoon; we had to shoot one of the brutes.

20 December
Summer and sunshine. We're thoroughly enjoying the life. Nothing to think about, nothing to do – we just lie and plan the future. *Terra Nova* can't be so far away.

21 December
Went out on the glacier with Priestley this morning. A ski trip to the summit of Erebus would be a rewarding undertaking. Rivulets are beginning to run near the hut. The sun is strong. I lay half naked this afternoon sunning myself on the stable roof.

22 December
Midsummer day and the sun will begin its retreat to the north. It's really great to think we shall soon begin our journey back to warmer climes. Hope I'll be in Norway by midsummer night.[2]

1 Barne Glacier.
2 For the Feast of St Hans on 23 June.

23 December
For lack of anything better to do, we've been swapping our secret sporting ambitions. Nelson wants to buy a trawler and make a pleasure cruise around the world. Campbell and Atkinson have their eye on polar bear hunting in the Arctic Ocean. For myself, I plan an ascent of Mount Cook in New Zealand. It's a wonderful time of year here in the south. Tonight the sea is mirror calm. The pack ice is glittering, and the polar landscape is bathed in pure sunshine.

24 December
Christmas Eve, our thoughts fly far away. I shall whatever happens celebrate by eating tinned ptarmigan, of which there is plenty in Shackleton's hut.

25 December
I've spent a good deal of Christmas Day up on The Ramp. I devised a ski jump, and then proceeded to practice my jumps. We celebrated Christmas modestly tonight; our provisions would not really stretch to a luxury meal.

26 December
A day of sport. I continued with my ski-jumping this morning, and in the afternoon took a little swim in McMurdo Sound. I was standing down on the icefoot watching the penguins playing in the water. The sun was out and it was quite warm. I plucked up courage and dived in. I won't say the water was exactly warm, but perhaps it could have been worse.

27 December
My bathe yesterday chilled me. Despite the lovely sunshine I still haven't got the warmth back in me. Foolhardiness in these parts certainly does not pay. Indeed it is usually trifles that lead to disaster; our expedition has proved this time and again.

28 December
Terra Nova must have been underway a fortnight now, and if she does not run into heavy pack we'll see her soon.[3] For a change, the weather has been unpleasant today.

3 The ship had left Lyttelton, New Zealand, on 14 December under the command of Commander E.R.G.R.Evans, fully recovered from scurvy and specially promoted for Antarctic service.

29 December
In fine weather this life is tolerable, but in bad weather time drags. We've nothing left to do. Everything is packed and ready for shipment at a moment's notice. But it won't be long now.

30 December
Snow-storm with wind gusting to hurricane force. Every time it clears for a few moments out comes the telescope. Won't *Terra Nova* ever come?

31 December
The last day of this strange year has come. I hope 1913 will bring me some of the luck lacking in 1912. Tonight two years have passed since the polar land mass came into sight for the first time. It was just such a night as this when storm-driven clouds lifted now and again to uncover the might of the wild mountains.

1 January 1913
We have celebrated New Year for the third time in this desolation of ice. Let's hope it will be the last for this expedition. One more year here in the south would bring the most serious consequences. I am personally in good shape, but the same cannot be said for several of the others.

2 January
Thick fog banks have rolled in off the sea all day, and we cannot make out even the nearest objects. Let's hope *Terra Nova* will be lying in the bay when the fog lifts.

3 January
This morning the fog had disappeared, and it was like a fine summer day in Norway. Not a breath of wind, not a cloud in the sky. The pack ice lay in a glittering shimmer like quick silver. Hundreds of penguins sat on the floes enjoying the sunshine. Animal life is intense at the moment. In 'Gull Inlet'[4] there are thousands of sea birds, and out in McMurdo Sound we regularly see schools of whale.

4 January
Snow-storm from morn to night. I have been checking the provisions, and it is clear we have an abundance of essentials for at least a year. That at any rate is good to know.

4 A cove near Cape Evans.

5 January
I had a secret conviction that the 5th would bring the ship, but the day has gone and our faces have fallen. But we are not suffering any privation.

6 January
The penguins have given us a little show. We have a boat down by the icefoot. It is half-sunk, and the penguins have been using it as a swimming pool quite involuntarily. As the birds came hunting under the water, they saw the white shadow of the bottom of the boat and mistook it for an icefloe. They hopped upwards out of the water like lightning, and ended between the thwarts with noisy cries and shrieks. At one time a score of them were in the 'pool'. Despite terrific exertions they couldn't get out, because the water in the boat wasn't deep enough for them to get up enough speed to carry them over the side. Finally, frustrated and angry, the birds went for each other and a violent fight ensued. We had to intervene to keep the peace, and release them.

7 January
Great excitement in the hut this morning. Williamson saw a ship behind Cape Barne. We all rushed out to the point at Cape Evans, but there was nothing to be seen. I wonder how many ships we shall see before she really comes.

8 January
The ice is beginning to disappear even between the islands. The temperature is high and steady. The air temperature varies between two and five degrees [C] of frost and the sea is several degrees over zero.

9 January
'Ohole', one of the dogs, came back to the hut flecked with red. He was injured, and tonight I saw him hunting seal by himself on the ice. He is a nice animal but quite wild.

10 January
Out with 'Lappa' this morning; it was almost impossible to hold him. We've played a ball game called rounders tonight. Weather fine all day.

11 January
Strong north wind all day, and this evening the bay is full of drift-ice. Went up to the high ground this morning with 'Kumogay', and had a good view over McMurdo Sound. There was a lot of ice but nothing that would prevent a ship getting through. I fell while playing the ball

game tonight, and twisted my back so badly that I can hardly move.

12 January
Spent the day in my bunk, for my back is still too stiff for me to move. Masses of pack ice in the bay. Biting wind, horrid weather.

13 January
I must have twisted my back worse than I realized. When I went outdoors for a breath of air today, everything went black. I had to keep to my bunk for the rest of the day.

14 January
Still very stiff, but a bit better. Keeping to my bed.

15 January
Either the ship has encountered much pack ice, or else she started from New Zealand later than usual. Snow-storm in the night and today. My back is better, and I shall get up tomorrow.

16 January
Soon this day will have ended and still no ship. We have gradually begun to discuss the possibility of wintering here again, and shall soon begin to prepare for such an eventuality. But it's still a bit too soon to settle for the worst. Tonight we shot a sea leopard that came in on a floe. Weather fine.

17 January
The anniversary of Scott reaching the Pole. On 17 January last year *Terra Nova* arrived at Cape Evans.

Nothing happened today. I can't believe anything has befallen the ship. Had she gone down on the homeward voyage, they would surely have sent another vessel to our rescue. Tomorrow we start slaughtering seals for the winter. [We were to go on rations; to cook with (seal) oil, for nearly all the coal was gone – A CG].

18 January
Terra Nova in sight! Hurrah! Hurrah! Great jubilation. Hurrah!

(*Evening*) We are saved. It was a piece of luck, for we had this morning begun to prepare for another winter here. Teddy Evans is on board. All's well at home.

Terra Nova had a frightful return voyage to New Zealand last year. The coal supplies were minimal, and they had to make sail the whole time. Huge, stormy seas met them from the first moment. They arrived in New Zealand on 1 April. They had departed southwards again on 14 December. Sea and head winds had delayed them, but worst was the pack that stretched from north to south in a band 450 sea miles wide. It took the ship 18 days to break through this belt.

There was great delight in our party when the ship came in sight. When *Terra Nova* was close under Cape Evans, Teddy Evans shouted through the loud hailer: 'Is all well at Cape Evans?' One minute's silence. Campbell: 'The [southern] party reached the Pole on 17 January. But perished on the way back.' Complete silence on board and ashore. Teddy: 'Let go anchor.'

The world news is that the Serbs, Bulgars, and Montenegrans have thrashed the Turks. But it is late, and I must get my head down in my good old bunk for the last time.

19 January

(*On board*) Our next stay at Cape Evans lies in the future. The hut is closed, the mules have been shot, and the dogs brought on board. We're worn out for we've been on the go 36 hours. We bade farewell to our winter quarters at 6 p.m. and steamed up to Cape Royds where we collected the geological specimens from the Erebus excursion. We're rolling in the swell out in McMurdo Sound. Tonight we shall go about, so as to land a party as far south as possible. They will erect a cross at the top of Observation Hill in memory of our dead comrades.[5]

The gramophone is playing a wonderful tune – 'Eternal Waltz'. How I long to dance, dance, dance again after all these years. This waltz is the first breath of real life. Goodness, how good life seems tonight.

20 January

My 25th[6] birthday today, and Teddy Evans has ordained a celebration. Taylor hasn't forgotten his companions; he's sent us each a book. Good for him. The party for Observation Hill left this morning.

21 January

We are on our way to Granite Harbour. The cross-bearers returned today, having completed their sad task. It's a magnificent site for the monument. This evening, while we lay anchored to the ice, an iceberg drifted down towards us and, as we had no steam up, we had to set sail in great haste. Wonderful night with a slight southerly breeze. We got steam up during the night.

5 The cross, made of jarrah wood by the ship's carpenter, was nine feet high and inscribed to the five members of the polar party.

6 In fact his 24th. *See* 20 January 1912, footnote 33.

22 January
The vessel is anchored to the ice about two kilometres north of Cape Roberts. I shall accompany a party of six skiers to fetch our specimens from Cape Geology.

23 January
After a very successful ski trip we're back on board again and the ship has laid course for Evans Cove. My party consisted of Crean, Abbott, Keohane, Dickason and Hooper. As soon as the ship tied up, we jumped ashore and set off for the Bluff.[7] The going was superb, and we covered a good ten kilometres in the first hour. Suddenly we caught sight of some dark shapes which turned out to be male seals, and before many minutes we came upon an open channel 100 yards broad. There was only one thing to do and that was to try out Campbell's patent boat. It is constructed as follows: a specially treated canvas is rigged to cover the sledge; then tent poles set in a V-shape are laid athwart, the front being secured in a sleeping bag and the rear to the instrument box. The poles are then lashed tight to the covered sledge and this produces about a 2-ft freeboard. It only took ten minutes to rig up and launch the 'boat'. It floated like a duck; its builder Abbott was the first to try it. We gave him a ski for an oar, and when he had crossed we hauled it back with a line. Thus we managed to cross the gap in a relatively short time. This 'boat' was a splendid idea.

Two hours later we bivouacked beneath Discovery Bluff. Before us lay open water; it was that lead again, and I decided to find out if it wasn't possible to work the sledge along the side of the bluff. After a short rest we started the attempt. It was an exciting half-hour with moments that reminded me of Alpine climbs. The way to Cape Geology now stretched clear ahead; the surface was outstanding, and before long we were at our goal. We loaded 300 kg of rocks and fossils on the sledge and set off for home. When we came to the lead at the bluff, I saw some large floes drifting in fast. Two of them jammed together and before you could say 'knife' the lead was bridged over. We were over in a flash. The lads were delighted. A little later I set course for land; in two hours we were alongside. The new course had put us on the far side of the openings in the ice. Luck is everything here in the south.

24 January
Terra Nova has driven slowly forwards through massive pack. It's a big question whether we shall manage to get into Evans Cove.

7 Discovery Bluff.

25 January
Open water and just four hours' sailing from Evans Cove. The weather is perfect.

26 January
We reached Campbell's winter camp site at 4 a.m. What a splendid man he is to have led his companions through the fire so magnificently! We're on the way home again. What a wonderful thought! Through a bit of pack and then northwards bound.

27 January
Head wind but open water. We're steering due north. Teddy Evans has announced to all hands that by pre-arrangement with Scott he has assumed overall command of the expedition. Driving snow. We now stand watches. Rennick and I share the night watch. He is the nicest chap in the world; he got engaged last winter. Many will follow his example.

28 January
Just like a foggy day in the Channel. The sea is running quite high, and most of the land party are seasick. The rigging is coated white with ice and rime, and the sails so stiff they are almost impossible to manage. Nelson is on the sick list; his feet are frightfully swollen. I think it's very fortunate we didn't have to face another winter. It's tremendously exciting to be on the bridge. Icebergs loom up out of the murk without warning, and many times we've had to spin the wheel hard a-starboard to avoid collision.

29 January
A pity there are so many drifting bergs. We had a storm of wind from the south today and could have made a great pace, had we been able to hoist sail. But in such thick weather we just have to be careful. The ship looks extraordinary – she is completely iced up.

30 January
Last night was horrible. The rolling was so bad you could hardly lie in your bunk. The dogs were extremely disturbed and frightened by the pitching, and my dear 'Lappa' tried to jump overboard several times. But we're pushing on and in a few hours cross the Antarctic Circle. We have passed many icebergs. It's beginning to get darker.

31 January
If this [progress] holds, we'll be there in a week. We're steering as westerly a course as possible to get New Zealand abeam. Passed the

Balleny Islands in the night. Still a lot of bergs about. Almost dark tonight.

1 February

The number of bergs has risen sharply. This morning we sailed along one which was 40 km long. There must be a change in the current to cause all these ice giants to collect.

2 February

Poor visibility all day and difficult to navigate. At 11.30 a.m. we entered a swarm of bergs. For a time we were completely surrounded, and we only just managed to escape being crushed. I had just relieved Rennick when the look-out shouted, 'Ice ahead', and before I could say anything we appeared to have entered an enormous dock. In my distress I bellowed for Teddy Evans and rang down 'Full astern'. It was an exciting moment. Teddy arrived on the bridge, and I must say I was enormously impressed by the way he reacted. His orders flowed as though we were going through a daily drill, though he knew perfectly well he held the fate of 50 men in his hands. We crept along the walls of the 'dock' to find a way out. Luck was with us and we found the right passage at the last moment. We dubbed it 'Hell's Gate', because we've seen no ice at all since.

3 February

Northwards under full sail. With a bit of luck we should reach Lyttelton on Monday.

(*Midnight*) The fair wind has dropped; it's dangerous to make predictions. Pouring rain, our first rainy weather for several years. I remember promising myself down in the *Discovery* hut that I'd really enjoy my first day of rain. I would lie on my back and let it stream over me. Well, now it's raining, and I'm not keeping my promise.

4 February

Strong north wind all day and we're making only eastwards. The wind is slackening; perhaps we'll get a change. Heavy seas and decks awash.

5 February

Hurricane-force storm the whole night and today. We're just being driven before the storm. The poor dogs are utterly miserable. Teddy, Bruce, Nelson, and I have passed the time playing cards.

6 February

I don't think many slept last night. Just after midnight the hurricane was so strong you couldn't stand on deck. The sea got up awfully, and the ship was tossed about like a cork. Things worked loose and below decks it was chaotic. From midday the weather improved, and the wind backed more to the west.

7 February
Fine weather today but head wind. We've been sunning ourselves on deck. At last it's beginning to get warm and nice.

8 February
Wind northwest and we're making seven knots. We can't grumble while this lasts.

9 February
At breakfast New Zealand hove in sight, and we've steamed along the coast all day. We can really smell land tonight. How wonderful it is to see green fields.

10 February
We landed Pennell and Atkinson at Oamaru tonight. They will send a telegram to Central News. We are steaming up the coast. The whole crew are preparing the ship for port.

11 February
We've been waiting near the coast all night and today. Our contract with Central News requires us to reach harbour not before tomorrow. We were hailed by a small coastal vessel this evening. They seemed to know our news already. 'Sad news about Captain Scott', shouted the skipper. Yes, he was right.

A wonderful night with millions of stars, just such a night as we could have wished for to say goodbye to good old *Terra Nova*.

12 February
[At dawn . . . with white ensign at half-mast, we crept through Lyttelton Heads – A CG]. Back to civilization again. How wonderful it all seems. They came to meet us this morning; they came aboard and they gave us papers. In huge type it read: CAPTAIN SCOTT DEAD.

Yes, Scott is dead, the adventure is at an end, and the future lies ahead.

Retrospect

by **Basil Greenhill** and **Geoffrey Hattersley Smith**

In October 1974, Major Tryggve Gran made a visit to England which his daughter Mrs Ellen McGhie believes was the high point of the latter part of his life. He gave three lectures on Scott's Last Expedition, each lasting more than two hours on successive days, at the Royal Geographical Society, the Scott Polar Research Institute and Eton College. These lectures were *tours de force* by any standards; for a man of 85 they were astonishing performances.

At the beginning of the visit, on 23 October, a reception for Major Gran in the boardroom of the National Maritime Museum, Greenwich, gave us an opportunity to talk with him informally and mainly about the expedition. We are thus able to amplify the reflections contained in his diary. We have included between square brackets points relevant to our conversations but not mentioned.

Major Gran recalled his first meeting with Captain Scott in Norway [in March 1910] and the invitation to join the expedition as ski expert. He said that, if Amundsen had announced his South Polar plans six months earlier, he would not have accepted the invitation as he had no wish to compete against his countryman. In discussing the disaster that overtook the Polar Party, he pointed to two main causes: first, the decision to take five men to the South Pole instead of four and, secondly, the failure to provide any adequate arrangement for the party to be met on their return journey.

Scott's decision to take five men involved considerable added discomfort to the party, inasmuch as the tent, like all the others on the expedition, was organized and fitted around four occupants, with the tent drills designed to be carried out by four men. The extra man in the tent could well have been disruptive of sleep [and certainly extra time was needed for cooking. Moreover, the rations of food and oil cached for the Last Support Party and the Polar Party were made up in four-man units, so that there was some inevitable wastage and disproportion during redistribution].

The decision on a 5-man party can be traced back to a circumstance prior to the start of the polar journey. When the famous sequences of camp drill were taken near Cape Evans by Ponting for his documentary film, Scott selected Wilson, Lieutenant Evans and Bowers to be his fellow actors. From that moment onwards everybody assumed that Bowers would be in the Polar Party and that Scott had already made up his mind. This assumption was made particularly by Bowers. It was always thought that Wilson and PO Evans would go with Scott to the Pole but there was doubt about the fourth member of the party. In fact, it was Scott's intention that Wilson, Oates and PO Evans should accompany him to the Pole, while Lieut. Evans, Bowers, and POs Lashly and Crean would return as the Last Support Party. The inclusion of Oates in the Polar Party stemmed from Scott's sense of obligation to him for his financial support [and also no doubt for his sterling work with the ponies]. Bowers, however, was very distressed at his omission from the party and made this distress apparent to Scott, who in turn was distressed at Bowers' reaction. Despite their differences in background, he held Bowers in very high regard for his efficiency. He was the perfect merchant ship's mate, and in the organization of stores, the loading and discharge of *Terra Nova*, and the preparation of stores for sledge parties, of which he was in charge, nothing was ever forgotten or mislaid. Scott would say to him, 'Birdie, is there not a single thing forgotten?' and Bowers would reply, 'Nothing at all, Sir'; and this was always so. [It is our view that Huntford[1] put his finger on the overriding reasons for Bowers' last-minute inclusion in the Polar Party, namely, his expertise as a navigator and, to a lesser extent, his understanding of the complicated arrangement of supply depots along the route. These reasons appear to have escaped Major Gran and the other survivors of the expedition. On the other hand, because of a painting by Wilson of five men pulling a sledge (reproduced in black and white in the *South Polar Times*), it was suggested by Debenham that, even before he left Cape Evans, Scott may have discussed with Wilson the possibility of taking a five-man party to the Pole.][2]

For the final stage of the polar journey Bowers was without skis. This was because Scott had re-organized his party [on 3 January] having already told the original support party of four to depot their skis [on 31 December]. Although immensely tough physically, Bowers had very short legs and his great strength was somewhat undermined by the necessity to take more paces on foot than his four companions on skis, in order to keep up in the traces. When the party arrived at the

1 Huntford, R. 1979. Scott and Amundsen. London, Hodder and Stoughton.
2 *See also* the diary entry for 13 February 1911.

South Pole and found themselves forestalled by Amundsen, the effect was worst on PO Evans. The reason for this was that Scott had, if anything, over-emphasized the importance of priority at the Pole, thus encouraging the inference that non-priority would mean failure and financial disaster. Evans, a simple man, and perhaps more affected by dietary deficiency than the others who were physically smaller, thought that the consequences of being forestalled would be no special promotion for him and no monetary reward. These thoughts led in part to his rapid deterioration and to consequent delays on the return journey. An additional 230 yards made good per day would have brought the party to 'One Ton Depot' in time at least to survive [actually 280 yards from 4 January to 19 March, at the 'Last Camp']. Major Gran felt that the extra performance could have been achieved but for the apparently marginal factors induced by the 5-man tent and disappointment at the Pole. [He made no reference to the possible or probable incidence of scurvy.]

On the second main cause for the loss of the Polar Party, Major Gran said that, if the party had been met by a dog team at the foot of Beardmore Glacier, all would have been well. The failure to make adequate arrangements by Scott himself probably stemmed from the fact that Shackleton had worked without a relief party in 1908–09 and had come within 97 miles of the Pole. Scott considered himself a better man than Shackleton. In Scott's absence the decision on a relief party devolved on Lieutenant Evans, as Second-in-Command, and his character played a crucial role in events. Major Gran remembered Evans as an intensely ambitious officer; he courted popularity and was hail-fellow-well-met with all members of the expedition, characteristics from which Scott shied away. Before the start of the polar journey, Evans had already over-taxed himself on the spring depot journey to 'Corner Camp', when he tried to match himself with an expert skier (Gran) in temperatures down to –63 °F. He was exhausted and frostbitten when he returned to Cape Evans [on 15 September 1911]. On the polar journey, following the failure of the last motor sledge, he had loaded an excessive amount of stores on his own party's sledge and in the end again exhausted himself. It was only through the heroic efforts of Lashly and Crean that he survived the return journey, in charge of the Last Support Party, to reach Hut Point. (Major Gran remarked in passing that the motor sledges were not regarded as a failure on the expedition but, on the contrary, as a considerable success. It was amazing that one of them reached as far as it did. Nobody expected the sledges to do better, except Day, the mechanic, who saw himself riding to the Pole on one of them.)

After his return to Hut Point [on 22 February 1912], Evans had expressed himself as completely confident of the safe return of Scott and his party. Indeed, when his support party was returning slowly because of his own collapse, Crean was continually looking back, expecting to see Scott's party catching them up. On the other hand, Major Gran said that he himself and others stressed to Evans the fact that no party on a major Antarctic journey up to that time had returned except by the skin of its teeth; they referred to the southern journeys of Scott's 1901–4 and Shackleton's 1907–09 expeditions, and of course to Evans' own journey. Gran [who had returned to Cape Evans from the western journey on 25 February] wanted to deploy the strongest possible party up to the foot of Beardmore Glacier to assist Scott's return; he said that he and Wright were good navigators. Nevertheless, Evans would not authorize a full-scale relief party; he had no written instructions from Scott, who had left such matters to his discretion. In fact he tried to persuade Gran to return with him in *Terra Nova*, in which Meares (the dog expert), Simpson (the physicist) and others were also sailing that season. [It was on 29 February[3] that Gran saw Evans, in his cabin aboard *Terra Nova*, for the first time since the latter's return from the south, and recorded 'it became clear to me that the prospects of our five-man polar party were not so bright as most of the members of the expedition imagined' (TG). *Terra Nova* sailed from McMurdo Sound on 4 March.]

Major Gran referred to Cherry-Garrard's relief journey south along the line of depots with Demetri and a dog team. [They left Hut Point on 26 February and returned on 16 March]. The crucial factors on this journey were that Cherry Garrard could not navigate and, moreover, had very poor eyesight [compounded by 'misting up' of spectacles and snow goggles]. After lying blizzard-bound at 'One Ton Depot' for four days, during which the dogs ran wild, this party quite rightly under the circumstances returned. ['One Ton Depot' was significantly at about the last point on the polar route from which it was possible to 'raise' the land to the north, and so navigate visually in clear weather.] If they had continued with exact navigation, they would have saved the Polar Party. There were those at Cape Evans perfectly capable of the type of navigation needed, but they were not sent out. In the last resort, therefore, a measure of responsibility for the disaster rested on Lieutenant Evans.

[In assessing Major Gran's stricture on Lieutenant Evans' dispositions at this most critical stage of the expedition, three important points should be kept in mind; first, Evans was a very sick man, barely convalescent from being near death with scurvy; secondly, he was mindful of Captain Scott's expressed wishes that the continuity of the scientific programme at Cape Evans should not be broken; thirdly, a cooling of

[3] *See also* the diary entry for this date.

relations between Evans and Gran in later years needs to be weighed against the latter's criticism. Scott's expressed wishes were the reason why Wright, although a navigator, felt it his duty to remain at Cape Evans in charge of the scientific programme, following the departure of Simpson, rather than take Cherry-Garrard's place on the relief journey. A letter from Wright to his father, dated at Cape Evans on 2 March 1912, makes this point very clearly. From this letter and from his diary, it hardly appears that Wright shared Gran's belief in the need for a full-scale relief effort.[4] Following the return of the expedition to England, the question of the lack of a full-scale relief effort was indeed raised, notably by Dr T.V.Hodgson, biologist on the *Discovery* expedition, but we have only Major Gran's assertion that such a proposition was actually discussed at Cape Evans at the critical time.]

Major Gran spoke with warm feeling of Cherry-Garrard, referring to his shyness, his diffidence with women, and his reluctance to kill which had led to him being an ambulance driver in the First World War. The title of his famous book was not chosen by Cherry-Garrard himself but by his publishers. The winter journey was not 'the worst journey,' because those on it survived, and Cherry-Garrard was much too modest to have thought of using a superlative in this way. The polar journey was much worse.

On his flying experiences Major Gran had time only to recall with pleasure playing a small part in teaching Prince Albert (later King George VI) to fly [in 1919] and to mention that, years later at a family tea, the then Princess Elizabeth had sat on his knee.

We have recorded accurately our conversations with Major Gran from notes made shortly after the reception at Greenwich, and we have indicated the content of our own interpolations into what he actually said. We were left with an impression of his vigour and the clarity of his memory. He has written that he envied Captain Scott because he died having done something great. To us he referred to Scott as the finest type of officer – who would have gone far in the First World War and risen to flag rank, and withal a family man in the best sense, who was solicitous of his men. Certain it is that none on the expedition was more true to the memory of his leader than Major Tryggve Gran.

[4] We are much indebted to Miss P. F. Wright, Sir Charles Wright's daughter, for allowing us to refer to these documents.

Place names

The New Zealand Antarctic Place Names Committee is the responsible authority for names in the Ross Sea Dependency, which includes the area of Scott's last expedition. Place names take time to become stabilized. It is, therefore, not surprising that a number of names in the diary differ from those now officially approved for the various features, or that Tryggve Gran was sometimes inconsistent in his use of names. The following is a list of such approved names together with the variant forms or synonyms as used in the diary. Approved forms have frequently been given in footnotes where needed for clarity in the text.

Approved name	**Variant form or synonym**
Bay of Whales	*Whale Bay*
Bowers Piedmont Glacier	*Butter Point Glacier*
Devil's Punchbowl	*Devil's Punch Bowl*
Dominion Range	*Dominion Mountains*
Edward VII Peninsula	*Edward VII Land* or *King Edward's Land*
Erebus Glacier Tongue	*Glacier Tongue*
Flatiron	*The Iron*
Gondola Ridge	*Gondola Island*
Granite Harbour	*Granite Firth* or *Granite Fjord*
Gran, Mount	*Black-cap* or *Mount Black Cape* or *Mount Tryggve Gran*
Hjorth Hill	*Hjort's Mountain*
Kar Plateau	*Kar Cliffs*
Mackay Glacier Tongue	*Glacier Tongue*
Melbourne, Mount	*Mount Melba*
Minna Bluff	*Bluff Mountain*
North Bay	*Cape Evans Bay* or *Hut Bay*
Observation Hill	*Observation Point*
Razorback Islands (comprising Big Razorback Island and Little Razorback Island)	*Razorback*

Redcliff Nunatak	*Redcliff Nunakol*
Ross Ice Shelf	*The Barrier* or *The Great Ice Barrier* or *Ross Barrier*
Royal Society Range	*Society Mountains*
Ski Slope	*Ski Hill*
Suess, Mount	*Mount Gondola*
Turks Head Bay	*Tryggve Bay*
Turtle Rock	*Little Turtle Back* or *Turtleback* or *Turtle Island*
Wilson Piedmont Glacier	*Wilson Piedmont*
Windvane Hill	*Vane Hill* or *Windmill Heights*

It has not been possible to name on the maps every feature mentioned in the diary, but the locations of minor un-named features should be evident from the text.

Following the work of Scott's last expedition and in addition to *Mount Gran*, the name *Tryggve Point* (for a feature close northwest of Turks Head) commemorated the diarist. A third eponym, *Gran Glacier*, was later applied to a glacier flowing south into Mackay Glacier, west of Mount Gran, following the work of a New Zealand survey party on the Trans-Antarctic Expedition in November 1957.

Biographical notes

Antarctic service is referred to the ships of the following expeditions: National Antarctic Expedition 1901–04, in SY *Discovery* (Cdr R. F. Scott MVO, RN); British Antarctic Expedition, 1907–09, in RY *Nimrod* (Lieut. E.H.Shackleton MVO, RNR); British National Antarctic Expedition 1910–13, in RY *Terra Nova* (Capt.R.F.Scott CVO, RN); British Imperial Trans-Antarctic Expedition 1914–16, in SY *Endurance* (Sir Ernest Shackleton CVO).

Those listed below received either the Polar Medal in silver with clasp 'Antarctic 1910–13' or, in the case of holders of the silver medal, the clasp only. From the *Discovery* expedition Scott, Wilson, Lashly, (PO) Evans, Crean and Williamson already held the medal in silver with clasp 'Antarctic 1902–04'; (Cdr) Evans, on the other hand, held the medal in bronze (no clasp) and so received a second medal, in silver. From the *Nimrod* expedition Day and Priestley already held the medal in silver with clasp 'Antarctic 1907–09'. For the *Endurance* expedition Crean subsequently received the silver clasp 'Antarctic 1914–16'.

George Percy Abbott (1880–19 ?)
Petty Officer RN, with *Terra Nova* northern shore party, 1910–13; served World War I with RN, 1914–18 (invalided).

Walter William Archer (18 ?–1944)
Chief Steward RN (retired); cook in *Terra Nova,* 1910–12, and with Cape Evans shore party, 1912–13; served World War I with RN, 1914–18.

Edward Leicester Atkinson (1882–1929)
Surgeon RN, 1908; medical officer and parasitologist with *Terra Nova* shore party at Cape Evans, 1910–13 (in command, March-October 1912); served World War I with RN and RND, 1914–18 (Surgeon Commander DSO,AM, despatches); Surgeon Captain (retired), 1928.

Henry Robertson Bowers (1883–1912)
Lieutenant RIM, 1908; ship's officer and member of *Terra Nova* shore

party at Cape Evans, 1910–12; died on the return journey from the South Pole on or about 29 March 1912.

Frank Vernon Browning (1882–19 ?)
Petty Officer RN, with *Terra Nova* northern shore party, 1910–13; served World War I with RN, 1914–18 (Chief Petty Officer).

Wilfrid Montagu Bruce (1874–1953)
Lieutenant RNR, and ship's officer in *Terra Nova*, 1910–13; Commander RNR, 1913; served World War I with RNR, 1914–18 (Captain CBE,RD).

Victor Lindsay Arbuthnot Campbell (1875–1956)
Lieutenant RN, 1898; retired 1902; Lieutenant RN (emergency list), 1910; ship's officer in *Terra Nova*, and in command of northern shore party 1910–12, and at Cape Evans 1912–13; Commander (active list) 1913; served World War I with RN and RND, 1914–18 (Captain DSO and bar, OBE, despatches); retired 1922.

Apsley George Benet Cherry-Garrard (1886–1959)
Assistant zoologist with *Terra Nova* shore party at Cape Evans, 1910–13; served World War I in command of a squadron of armoured cars, 1914–16 (Lieutenant Commander RNVR, invalided).

Thomas C. Clissold (1886–1963)
Cook RN (retired); cook with *Terra Nova* shore party at Cape Evans 1910–12 (invalided); served World War I, with RN, 1914–18.

Thomas Crean (1876–1938)
Able Seaman RN, in Discovery 1901–04; Petty Officer with *Terra Nova* shore party at Cape Evans, 1910–13 (AM 'for gallantry' in saving the life of Lieutenant Evans returning from the polar plateau, 1912); Second Officer in *Endurance*, 1914–16; served World War I with RN, 1916–18.

Bernard C.Day (1884–1952)
Motor mechanic with *Nimrod* shore party at Cape Royds, 1907–09; with *Terra Nova* shore party at Cape Evans 1910–12.

Frank Debenham (1883–1965)
Australian geologist with *Terra Nova* shore party at Cape Evans, 1910–13; served World War I with OBLI, 1914–19 (Major OBE, wounded); Founder Director, Scott Polar Research Institute, Cambridge 1925–46; Professor of Geography, Cambridge University 1930–49.

Harry Dickason (1885–1943)
Able Seaman RN, with *Terra Nova* northern shore party, 1910–13; served World War I with RN, 1914–18 (Petty Officer).

Francis Randall Hugo Drake (18 ?–1936)
Assistant Paymaster RN, 1899; Expedition Secretary and meteorologist in *Terra Nova*, 1910–13; Staff Paymaster 1913; served World War I

with RN, 1914–18 (Paymaster Commander); Paymaster Captain (retired), 1928.

Edgar Evans (1876–1912)
Petty Officer RN, in *Discovery*, 1901–04; with *Terra Nova* shore party at Cape Evans, 1910–12; died on the return journey from the South Pole, 17 February 1912.

Edward Ratcliffe Garth Russell Evans [1st Baron Mountevans of Chelsea] (1881–1957)
Lieutenant RN, 1902; Second Officer in relief ship SY *Morning* on the *Discovery* expedition, 1902–04; Second-in-command of *Terra Nova* and of shore party at Cape Evans, 1910–12 (invalided); Commander, 1912; in command of *Terra Nova* and relief of the expedition, 1912–13 (CB); served World War I with RN, 1914–18 (Captain DSO, despatches twice); Rear-Admiral commanding Royal Australian Navy, 1929–31; Vice-Admiral and Commander-in-Chief, Africa Station, 1933–35 (KCB); visited Bouvetøya in HMS *Milford* in 1934 but was unable to land; Admiral and Commander-in-Chief, The Nore, 1935–39; London Regional Commissioner for Civil Defence, 1939–45; created Baron, 1945.

Robert Forde (1877–1959)
Petty Officer RN with *Terra Nova* shore party at Cape Evans, 1910–12 (invalided); served World War I with RN, 1914–18.

Demetri Gerof [correctly Dmitriy Girev] (1888?–1932)
Russian dog driver with *Terra Nova* shore party at Cape Evans, 1910–13.

Tryggve Gran (1889–1980)
Sub-Lieutenant RNorwNR; ski expert with *Terra Nova* shore party at Cape Evans, 1910–13; qualified as pilot in 1914 and made first flight across the North Sea, 30 July 1914; served World War I with RFC and RAF, 1914–19 (Lieutenant Colonel MC, wounded); Major RAF, 1919–21; transferred to RNorwAF; Major (retired), 1935.

Frederick J.Hooper (1891–1955)
Steward RN (retired); cook with *Terra Nova* shore party at Cape Evans, 1910–13; served World War I with RN, 1914–18 (Petty Officer).

Patrick Keohane (1879–1950)
Petty Officer RN, with *Terra Nova* shore party at Cape Evans, 1910–13; served World War I with RN, 1914–18.

William Lashly (1868–1940)
Leading Stoker RN, in *Discovery*, 1901–04; Chief Stoker with *Terra Nova* shore party at Cape Evans, 1910–13 (AM 'for gallantry' in saving the life of Lieutenant Evans returning from the polar plateau, 1912); served World War I with RN, 1914–18.

George Murray Levick (1877–1956)
Surgeon RN, 1902; medical officer and zoologist with *Terra Nova* northern shore party, 1910–13; served World War I, 1914–16; Surgeon Commander (retired), 1916; founded British Schools Exploring Society, 1932; recalled for service in World War II, 1939–42.

Dennis G.Lillie (1884–1963)
Research Officer, Marine Laboratory, Plymouth; marine biologist in *Terra Nova*, 1910–13.

Cecil Henry Meares (1877–1937)
Siberian and far eastern traveller; served South African War with Scottish Horse, 1900–02; in charge of dogs with *Terra Nova* shore party at Cape Evans, 1910–12; served World War I with RFC and RAF, 1914–18 (Lieutenant Colonel); retired, 1920.

Edward W.Nelson (1883–1923)
Research Officer, Marine Laboratory, Plymouth; marine biologist with *Terra Nova* shore party at Cape Evans, 1910–13; war service, 1914–18; Scientific Superintendent, Scottish Fishery Board, 1921–23.

Lawrence Edward Grace Oates (1880–1912)
Lieutenant, 6th Inniskilling Dragoons, 1901; served South African War, 1901–02 (despatches, wounded); Captain, 1906; in charge of ponies with *Terra Nova* shore party at Cape Evans, 1910–12; died on the return journey from the South Pole on or about 16 March 1912.

Anton Omel'Chenko (1883–1932)
Russian groom with *Terra Nova* shore party at Cape Evans, 1910–12.

Harry Lewin Lee Pennell (1882–1916)
Lieutenant RN, 1903; ship's officer in *Terra Nova*, 1910–13 (Commanding Officer, 1911–12); Commander, 1913; served World War I with RN, 1914–16; lost in HMS *Queen Mary* at the battle of Jutland, 31 May 1916.

Herbert George Ponting (1870–1935)
Photographer with *Terra Nova* shore party at Cape Evans, 1910–12.

[*Sir*] **Raymond Edward Priestley** (1886–1974)
Assistant geologist with *Nimrod* shore party at Cape Royds, 1907–09; geologist with *Terra Nova* northern shore party, 1910–13; served World War I with RE, 1914–18 (Major MC, despatches); Vice-Chancellor, Melbourne University, 1935–38; Principal and Vice-Chancellor, University of Birmingham, 1938–52; Kt, 1949; Acting Director, Falkland Islands Dependencies Scientific Bureau, 1955–59; President, British Association for the Advancement of Science, 1956; with RY *Britannia* to the Antarctic Peninsula, 1956–57, and US

Operation 'Deepfreeze' to McMurdo Sound, 1958–59; President, Royal Geographical Society, 1961–63.

Henry Edward de Parny Rennick (1881–1914)
Lieutenant RN, 1903; ship's officer in *Terra Nova* 1910–12 (Second-in-command, 1911–12); Lieutenant Commander, 1911; lost in HMS *Hogue*, North Sea, 22 September 1914.

Robert Falcon Scott (1868–1912)
Commander RN, 1900; MVO, 1901; commanded the *Discovery* expedition, 1901–04 (CVO); Captain 1904; commanded the *Terra Nova* expedition and the shore party at Cape Evans, 1910–12; died on the return journey from the South Pole on or about 29 March 1912.

[*Sir*] **George Clarke Simpson** (1878–1965)
Meteorologist, Indian Meteorological Department, 1906–20; seconded as meteorologist with *Terra Nova* shore party at Cape Evans, 1910–12; FRS, 1915; CBE, 1919; Director, UK Meteorological Office, 1920–38; KCB, 1935; President, Royal Meteorological Society, 1940–42.

Thomas Griffith Taylor (1880–1963)
Australian senior geologist with *Terra Nova* shore party at Cape Evans, 1910–12; Professor of Geography, University of Chicago, 1929–35, and University of Toronto, 1935–51.

Thomas S. Williamson (1877–1940)
Able Seaman RN, in *Discovery*, 1901–04; Petty Officer, in *Terra Nova*, 1910–12, and with *Terra Nova* shore party at Cape Evans, 1912–13; served World War I with RN, 1914–18 (wounded).

Edward Adrian Wilson (1872–1912)
Medical officer, zoologist and artist in *Discovery*, 1901–04; Chief of Scientific Staff, zoologist and artist with *Terra Nova* shore party at Cape Evans, 1910–12; died on the return journey from the South Pole on or about 29 March 1912.

[*Sir*] **Charles Seymour Wright** (1887–1975)
Canadian physicist with *Terra Nova* shore party at Cape Evans, 1910–13; served World War I with RE, 1914–18 (Major OBE, MC, despatches); Director of Scientific Research, Admiralty, 1934–46 (KCB); Chief of Royal Naval Scientific Service, 1946–47; Director, Marine Physical Laboratory, Scripps Institute of Oceanography, La Jolla, Cal., 1951–55; physicist with US Antarctic Research Program, 'Byrd Station', 1960 and 1965.

References

[A CG] Cherry-Garrard, A. 1951. *The worst journey in the world.* One-volume library edition with some corrections and a postscript. London, Chatto and Windus.

[ERGRE] Evans, E.R.G.R. 1921. *South with Scott.* London, W.Collins Sons and Co. Ltd.

[TG] Gran, Tryggve. 1974. *Fra tjuagutt til sydpolarfarer* [From kid to south polar explorer]. Oslo, Ernst G.Mortensens Forlag.

[RFS] [ELA] [REP] Huxley, L. (Ed.). 1913. *Scott's Last Expedition.* Vol. I.
The journals of Capt. R.F.Scott, RN, CVO; Vol. II, p. 298–349.
The last year at Cape Evans. By Surgeon E.L.Atkinson, RN; p. 350–58.
The ascent of Erebus. By R.E.Priestley. London, Smith, Elder and Co.

[TGT] Taylor, T.Griffith. 1916. *With Scott: the silver lining.* London, Smith, Elder and Co.

Index

Footnotes (n) are shown with the page number

Numbers in italics refer to plates

Abbott, PO G. P. 172n, 222, 224, 226, 234
'Abdullah' (mule) 212, 220, 222
Adare, Cape 22–23, 37, 63, 172, 223
Adélie Land (Terre Adélie) 37
Admiralty Mountains 39
Alcock, Sir W. J. 20
Alexandra, Queen 17, 139n
Amundsen, G. 12
Amundsen, L. 14
Amundsen, Capt. R. 10, 12–13, 56, 57n, 64, 72n, 83, 89, 97, 110, 114, 117, 138–39, 172, 175, 179, 181, 186
telegram to Scott 14, 63, 68, 84
and Scott 14–17
lands at Bay of Whales 15, 62
letter to King Haakon VII 18, 219
depot journey 56n
chances of success 82, 118, 128
Gran's dream 153
reaches South Pole 216, 239
Andes 96
Antarctic Circle 32–33, 235
Antarctic Continent 96, 179
Anton *see* Omel'chenko, A.
Archer, Chief Steward W. W. 175, 178–79, 181, 185, 199, 203, 206–07, 221–22, 227
'Archibald' (temperature station) 107n
Armitage, Cape 52, 65, 124, 127, 137, 139
Arrival Bay 98
Arrival Heights 98
Atkinson Surgeon E. L. 16, 23–24, 47n, 67–68, 71, 75–76, 84, 171, 175–76, 237, *15*
indisposed 49, 50, 52
as parasitologist 80, 88
at Cape Evans 84–139, 195–210, 222–33
as footballer 87–88, 91
lectures 93, 118
lost in blizzard and frost-bitten 106–08
at Hut Point 178–95
and expedition plans 202, 209
on search journey 212–21
Aurora *see* Southern Lights
Backdoor Bay 112
Balleny Islands 236
Barne, Cape 120, 152, 231
Barne Glacier 44–45, 88, 90, 96, 119, 121, 170, 206–07, 223, 228n
Barrier, The *see* Ross Ice Shelf
Baumann, Capt. V. 9
Beardmore Glacier 18, 23, 83, 89n, 96n, 172, 175, 177, 181, 203n, 209–10, 215–17, 240–41
Beaufort Island 152, 161
Beauman, Wing Cdr E. B. 19
'Begum' (mule) 212, 220, 222
Bergen (Norway) 9, 155
Bernacchi, Cape 144n, 168–69
Big Dipper 126
Big Razorback Island *see* Razorback Islands
Billiards 186, 195–97, 203
Bird, Cape 166
'Birdie' *see* Bowers, Lieut. H. R.
Bjaaland, O. 64n, 82
Black-cap *see* Gran, Mount
Black Cape, Mount *see* Gran, Mount
Blériot, L. 19
'Blossom' (pony) 57, 61, 63
'Blucher' (pony) 56, 61–63
Blue Glacier 171
'Bluff Camp' *see* Minna Bluff
'Bluff Depot' *see* Minna Bluff
Bluff Mountain *see* Minna Bluff
Bluff, The *see* Discovery Bluff
Bolinder Company 11
'Bones' (pony) 109–10
Borchgrevink, C. E. 10–11, 56n, 172, 223
Bowers, Lieut. H. R. 16, 22, 34, 47n, 50, 53–54, 57–59, 175, 239
in charge of stores 48, 239
at *Discovery* hut 68–76
at Cape Evans 80–105, 114–27, 132–38
quarters 80
visits Hut Point 83–84
suffers frost-bite 93n
lectures 94
leaves for Cape Crozier 105
on western journey 127, 132

leaves for South Pole 138
on polar journey 239
death 23–34, 216–17
Bowers Piedmont Glacier 171n
Brown, Sir A. Whitten- 20
Browning, PO F. V. 172n, 221
Bruce, Lieut. W. M. 43, 236
Buc (France) 19
Butter Point 140, 143, 170, 190n, 192
Butter Point Glacier *see* Bowers Piedmont Glacier

Campbell, Lieut. V. L. A. 12, 22–24, 36, 43–45, 49, 63, 82, 172–74, 177–80, 188, 190, 192, 202, 218, 220, 234–35
at Hut Point 221
at Cape Evans 222–33
Canopus 126
Cape Evans Bay *see* North Bay
Cape Town 13, 22
Cardiff 13
Caruso, E. 46
Castle Rock 65, 67, 69, 74, 76–77, 98, 186, 189, 194, 206
Central News (agency) 237
Chalmers, Port (New Zealand) 29
Champagne 103, 133
'Cherry' *see* Cherry-Garrard, A. G. B.
Cherry-Garrard, A. G. B. 22–23, 30–31, 38, 47n, 68, 71, 75–76, 171n, 175, 222, 227, *15*
on depot journey 49–65
at Cape Evans 80–105, 114–38, 195–232
and stone hut 89
edits 'South Polar Times' 103, 115
leaves for Cape Crozier 105
leaves on polar journey 138
leaves for 'One Ton Depot' 177
at Hut Point 187–95
lectures 199
on search journey 212–21
Chess 108, 110, 122
'Chinaman' (pony) 138
Christmas 38, 156, 229
tree 104
'Christopher' (pony) 138
Christchurch (New Zealand) 14–15
'Cigan' (dog) 180
'Clarence' (temperature station) 107n
Clissold, T. C. 79, 92, 109–10, 116, 134–35, 139–41, 175, 178, 180
Clothing 47, 54, 74, 108, 135
see also finnesko
Cloudmaker, The 209–10
Coal *see* geology
Coats Land 172
Colbeck, Cape 22, 62
'Cook' (dog) 95
Cook, Mount (New Zealand) 15, 19, 229
'Corner Camp' 16, 62–63, 65, 71, 114, 122, 125–26, 135, 172, 175, 178, 180, 187, 209–11, 214, 220
Crater Hill 52, 67
Crean PO T. 18, 23, 47n, 52, 64–65, 68, 71, 75–76, 83n, 84n, 87–88, 139, 178–79, 181, 185, 234, 239–41, *17*
reaches Hut Point from polar plateau 175
at Cape Evans 197–211
on search journey 212–21
Crevasses 133, 156, 162, 168–69, 220
Crow's-nest 31, 174
Crozier, Cape 22, 37, 40, 62, 101–02, 108n, 114, 210
Cruden Bay (Scotland) 19
'Cryst' (dog) 190
Cuff Cape 154

Dailey Islands 70
Dark room 80
Day, B. C. 30n, 38, 80, 83, 84n, 90, 97, 102, 106, 110–13, 115, 118, 122, 135–37, 175, 180
leaves with ship 178
Debenham, F. 30n, 38, 70n, 72, 76, 239, 5, *11*, *22*
as cook 74, 99, 144, 163
at Cape Evans 80–97, 101–41, 175–88, 202–22
quarters 80–81, 85–86
at *Discovery* hut 98–100
as geologist 110, 158, 160
lectures 122
knee injury 136, 141, 146, 204
on western journey 143–71
birthday 156
as cartographer 157
aboard *Terra Nova* 171–74
on Mount Erebus 222–25
Demetri *see* Gerof, D.
'Demetri Depot' 213, 220
Devils Punchbowl 155
Dickason, AB H. 172n, 122, 224, 234, *21*, *22*
Discovery Bluff 147–48, 152, 161, 234
***Discovery* expedition** 22n, 71n, 162, 182, 241–42
***Discovery* hut** *see* Hut Point
Discovery, Mount 206
***Discovery*, SY** 50
Dogs 35, 47, 82, 89, 91, 95–97, 99, 109, 112, 175n, 177, 183, 241
loss at sea 30
and penguins 39, 41, 140
landed 41
on depot journey 49–65
Amundsen's 62, 114, 117–18
Dominion Mountains *see* Dominion Range
Dominion Range 96n
Dominoes 109–10, 112, 119
Drake, Paymaster F. R. M. 43
'Dreadnought' (knoll) 95n, 206
Dunedin (New Zealand) 29
Dunlop Island 145n, 169

Eastern party *see* northern party

Edward VII Land *see* Edward VII Peninsula
Edward VII Peninsula 22n, 37n, 49, 63, 96–97, 172
Electrical instruments 80
Elizabeth II, Queen 242
Emperor penguins *see* penguins
England, Mount 148–49
Erebus Bay 176, 189
Erebus Glacier Tongue 41, 48–49, 52, 63, 77, 98, 122n, 133, , 179, 181, 187, 189, 194
Erebus, Mount 18, 22, 40n, 41, 43–45, 52, 56, 68, 81, 83, 92, 103, 106, 113, 115, 117, 120, 126, 140–41, 149, 179, 190, 205, 211, 219, 233, *18, 19, 20*
ascent 24, 222–27
Eton College 238
Evans, Cape 15–16, 18, 22, 24, 40–41, 49, 51n, 68, 76, 78, 85, 88, 98–100, 113, 124, 126, 153, 164, 170–74, 177–80, 183, 185–86, 192, 194, 221, 228, 231, 239–42, *23*
building of hut 42
description of hut 79–81, *4*
hut routine 88, 110, 203–04
members of party at hut *2*
Evans Cove 23, 153, 163, 167, 172–74, 181, 235
Evans, Mount *see* Marston, Mount
Evans, Lieut. E. R. G. R. (later Adm. Lord Mountevans) 12–13, 16, 19, 23, 34–35, 47n, 54, 57, 61, 63, 65, 177, 181, 200, 229n, 233, 235–36, 239
at *Discovery* hut 67–76
at Cape Evans 79–123, 128–37
quarters 80
as surveyor 82
on spring journey 124–27
on polar journey 137, 172n
returns to Hut Point with scurvy 175
in command of *Terra Nova* on final voyage 229n, 233–37
Gran's comments on 239–42
Evans PO E. 18, 70n, 75–76, 87–88, 92, 105n, 111, 116, 127, 139, 164, 175
on polar journey 239–40
death 23, 216–17

Fefor (Norway) 11, 22
Ferrar Glacier 144, 170
Ferrar Valley *see* Ferrar Glacier
Festningsplass (Oslo) 10
Filchner, Dr W. 172n
Finnesko 47n, 58, 70, 105, 111, 121, 176, 218
Finse (Norway) 35, 104
Fire 199–200, 208
First View Point 146n
Fish (and fishing) 48, 76, 88, 158
Flatiron, The 154n, 156, 160
'Fodder Camp' 65, 67, 69
'Fodder Depot' *see* 'Fodder Camp'
Food 70, 73, 103, 110, 113, 127, 153, 156, 161, 207–08
see also pemmican
see also seals
see also sledge rations
Football 86–87, 90–92, 136, 231
Forde PO R. 47n, 54, 57, 68, 71, 75–76, 84n, 90, 122, 131, 136, 140, 175n, 5, *9*
on spring journey 124–27
on western journey 143–71
snow-blind 169
aboard *Terra Nova* 171–74
leaves with ship 178
Fossils *see* geology
Fram (polar ship) 9, 14, 19, 22, 57n, 63, 173, *1*
'Framheim' 57n, 82, 83n, 96
Frederikshald *see* Halden
Frost-bite 93, 106–08, 122, 124, 127, 132, 157, 215–16
Funchal (Madeira) 13
Fundy, Bay of (Newfoundland) 20

Galdhopiggen (Norway) 169
Gap, The 52, 65, 67, 71, 185
Geology 93, 122, 155, 225, 235
coal 160
fossils 98n, 158
mapping 121
minerals 154
Geology, Cape 148–49, 151, 155, 160, 163, 235
George V, King 81
George VI, King 242
Germany 60, 162, 193
Gerof, D. 23, 82–83, 84n, 87, 90, 121, 134–35, 175, 177, 187–91, 195n, 199–201, 210–13, 218, 220–21, 241
Girev, D. *see* Gerof, D.
Gjertsen, Lieut. H. F. 82n
Gjoa (polar ship) 11
Glacier Tongue *see* Erebus Glacier Tongue
Gneiss Point 145, 169
'Go cart' 92–93
Gomphiocephalus hodgsonii *see* springtail
Gondola (Island) *see* Gondola Ridge
Gondola, Mount *see* Suess, Mount
Gondola Ridge 158n, 160n
Graham Land 96
Graham, P. 19
Gramophone 79, 84, 100, 103, 109
Granite Firth (**Fjord**) *see* Granite Harbour
Granite Harbour 23, 136, 146, 150n, 154, 159, 163, *7*
hut 148–49, 151, 233, *8*
Granite House (**Hut**) *see* Granite Harbour
Gran, Lieut. T. *5, 12, 15, 16, 17*
life 9–20
as diarist 9, 88, 93, 110, 115
Antarctic ambitions 9–11, 18–19, 198
and Shackleton 10
as skier and ski instructor 11, 15, 18, 33, 35, 64, 69, 85, 89, 118, 133
invited by Scott 12, 22, 238

relations with Scott 13–18, 110–11, 121
on Ilha da Trindade 13
and Amundsen 14–15, 238
in *Terra Nova* 29–40, 171–74, 233–37
as fortune teller 38
and motor sledge 41
to go on depot journey 44, 47n
skis to Cape Royds 44–45, 112, 116, 207–08
birthday 47, 164, 233
skis for filming 47
on depot journey 49–65
skis with pony 50–51
skis back with mail 52
returns for snow-shoes 53
and dogs 58, 176, 178, 183–84
opinion of Oates 60
injures knee 60–61
assesses Amundsen's chances 63, 83, 172
at *Discovery* hut 66–78, 98–100, 189–93
suffers from cramp 16, 70–71
and Wilson 72
as cook 74, 124, 150, 155–56, 166
returns to Cape Evans 76–78
at Cape Evans 79–97, 101–23, 128–42, 175–88, 194–211, 228–33
description of base hut 79–81
quarters 80–81, 84–86
as surveyor 82
physical measurements 85n, 102, 119, 186
hut routine 88, 110, 203–04
as world traveller 90, 164
his English 94
as *racounteur* 109, 134
to go with western party 110
on spring journey 124–27
assesses Scott's arrangements 128, 136, 171–72, 177, 238–42
poem for 'South Polar Times' 129
carries flag to Hut Point 17, 138–39
on western journey 143–71
and seeds 149, 152, 160–61, 163
falls through sea ice 151
as doctor 154, 157
writes play 164
poem from Taylor 164–65
to take charge of stores and meteorology 192
lectures 196, 198, 201–02
as clown 203
on search journey 212–21
on finding of polar party 215–17
on Mount Erebus 222–27
climbs Mount Cook 19
flies North Sea 19, *24*
with RFC and RAF 19–20, 242
with RNorwAF 20
opinion of Lieut. Evans 239–42
opinion of Cherry-Garrard 241–42
Gran, Mount 157, 169, 224, 227, *6*
Great (Ice) Barrier *see* Ross Ice Shelf
Grimstad (Norway) 20
'Gulab' (mule) 206, 212–14
'Gull Inlet' 230
Gulls (and eggs) 152–56, 162–64, 211, 223
'Guts' (pony) 49, 57
Haakon VII, King 10, 12, 18, 97n, 219
Hagen and Company 11, 176
Halden (Norway) 10
Heiberg, S. 155
Hjort Hill 169
Hjort's Mountain *see* Hjort Hill
Hodgson, Dr T. V. 242
Holmenkollen (Norway) 64, 201
Hooper, F. J. 83n, 84n, 88, 110, 121, 136, 179–80, 184–85, 199, 201, 222, 224, 226, 234
on search journey 212–21
Hoopers Shoulder 224n
Horn, Cape 31
Horses *see* ponies
Huntford, R. 17n, 239
Hut
stone 89, 101
see also Evans, Cape
see also Granite Harbour
see also Hut Point
see also Royds, Cape
Hut Bay 70
see North Bay
Hut Point 15–18, 41, 49, 70, 76, 79, 83, 105, 121, 137, 167, 175–82, 190, 210
Discovery hut 46, 50, 52, 63–77, 84, 98–100, 124–27, 134–35, 170, 179, 212, 220, *3*
Hut Point Peninsula 189
Hutton Cliffs 186, 189

Ibsen, H. 111, 203
Icebergs 32, 45, 78, 97, 120, 134, 145–46, 170, 235–36
Ice caves 86
Igloo 101, 112, 115–16, 118–19
Inaccessible Island 86, 96, 117–18, 130, 206
***Invincible*, HMS** 13, 20
Iron, The *see* Flatiron, The
Italia (airship) 20

Jaeren (Norway) 19
'Jehu' (pony) 138n
'Jimmy Pigg' (pony) 50, 56, 62–63, 67
Johansen, F. H. 82–83
'Jonah Medal' 42, 196–98
Jotunheim (Norway) 39, 143, 201
Joyce, E. 51n
'Julick' (dog) 112, 120

Kar Cliffs *see* Kar Plateau
Kar Plateau 153
Keohane, PO P. 24, 47n, 54, 57, 67–68, 72–76, 84n, 90, 138, 171n, 175, 178, 187–92, 234
at Cape Evans 194–211
on search journey 212–21
Kerr, Adm. M. 13, 20

'Khan Sahib' (mule) 204, 212–13, 217
King Edward VII Land *see* Edward VII Peninsula
King Edward's Land *see* Edward VII Peninsula
King George V Land 172n
Knutsen, Lieut. Col. W. 19
Kristiania *see* Oslo
Kukri Hills 170
'Kumogay' (dog) 190, 210, 231

'Lady' (dog) 117
'Lall' *see* 'Lall-Khan'
'Lall-Khan' (mule) 184, 196–200, 204, 207–17
Lamps
acetylene 69, 72
blubber 72
'luxury' 72
Langlauf 64, 184, 207
'Lappa' (dog) 190, 212, 231, 235
Lashly, CPO W. 23, 83n, 84n, 107, 136, 178–81, 239–40
reaches Hut Point from polar plateau 175
at Cape Evans 197–211
on search journey 212–21
'Last Camp' 216–17, 240
Leads *see* pack ice
Levick, Surgeon G. M. 44–45, 172n, 221, 228
Little Razorback (Island) *see* Razorback Islands
Little Turtle Back *see* Turtle Rock
London, Port of 12, 22, 95
'Lower Glacier Depot' 217
Lyttelton (New Zealand) 15, 237

Mackay Glacier 148, 153, 156, 162, 169
Mackay Glacier Tongue 146n, 149, 153, 162
McMurdo Sound 22, 37, 40–41, 55, 68, 98, 119, 141, 149, 159, 161, 166–69, 176, 179, 183–85, 222, 227–31, 233, 241
Madeira 13–14, 22, 104
Magnetic instruments 80
'Marie' *see* Nelson, E. W.
Marston, Mount 149
Maud, Queen
sledge flag 11–12, 156
Mawson, Sir D. 19, 172
Meares, C. H. 45, 47n, 80, 84n, 127–28, 134–35, 138–39, 175–77, 182, 241
on depot journey 51–65
at *Discovery* hut 67–75
at Cape Evans 90–121
lectures 120
leaves for Hut Point 121
leaves with ship 178
Melba, Dame N. 46, 79
Melba, Mount *see* Melbourne, Mount
Melbourne (Australia) 13–15
Melbourne, Mount 173
Meteorology 115
balloon apparatus 78, 117, 120, 141, *13*
meteorological instruments 80
meteorological observations 110, 114, 119, 196–97
Midwinter day 103, 202–03, *15*
Milne, C. 19
Minna Bluff 56n, 57, 191, 215
'Bluff Depot' journey 51n
Moss 152
Motor sledges 44, 89, 102, 115, 118, 135–37, 172, 180, 240
trials 11
sledge lost in landing 41–42
'Mukaka' (dog) 99n, 100
Mules 172, 176, 233, *14*
on search journey 201–22

Nansen, Dr F. 11–12, 22
Nansen, Mount 173
Napoleon 122
National Maritime Museum 238
Nelson, E. W. 41, 44, 229, 236, *15*, *17*
at Cape Evans 80–96, 101–119, 136–40, 175–88, 194–207
starts with western party 143–44
birthday 201
as skier 207
on search journey 212–21
New Glacier 148, 156
New Harbour 144, 170n
New Year 39, 158, 230
New Zealand 14–15, 173, 232–33, 235, 237
Nichols, Dr R. L. 136n
***Nimrod* expedition** 160n
camp site found 51n
depot found 143n
'Nobby' (pony) 57, 59n
Nobile, Col. U. 20
'Noogis' (dog) 195, 201
North Bay 48n, 107n, 119, 175, 179n, 185–86, 196, 198, 201, 205, 207
Northern party 37n
North Pole 12–13, 20
North Sea
flight 20, *24*
Norwegian-French Arctic Expedition 19
Norwegian Geographical Society 10
Norwegian National anthem 86n, 91n, 92
Norwegian Naval Cadet College 9
Norwegian Technical Museum 19
Nunatak (crag surrounded by ice) 157n

Oamaru (New Zealand) 237
Oates, Capt. L. E. G. 18, 34, 47n, 175, 181, 239
on depot journey 51–65
at *Discovery* hut 67–76
at Cape Evans 84–97, 101–23, 128–38
quarters 80
and ponies 81, 88, 110

lectures 91–92, 116
leaves for South Pole 138
death 23, 217–18, 220
Observation Hill 52n, 74, 126, 233n
Observation Point *see* Observation Hill
'Ohole' (dog) 231
Omel'chenko, A. 81, 140, 143–44, 175, 178, 180
'One Ton Camp' *see* 'One Ton Depot'
'One Ton Depot' 18, 22–24, 59, 175, 180, 215–16, 218, 240–41
Oslo 10, 21n, 31

Pack ice 32, 36–39, 161–62, 166, 168
ice floe 33, 170
lead 32, 34–35, 37, 234
pancake ice 40n, 173
Paraffin
leakage 215
Parasitology 80
Peary, Cdr R. E. 10, 12
'Peary' (dog) 95
Pemmican 54n, 74n, 150, 155, 161, 164, 170
Penguins 33–34, 36–39, 41, 209, 229, 231
emperor 22, 101, 114, 208, *14*
Pennell, Lieut. H. L. L. 37, 43, 136, 149, 166, 168, 174, 180, 237
Pianola 81, 110
Ping-pong 91
Poker (game) 106
Polar party 175, 177, 216–17
causes of loss 238–40
Ponies 30, 39, 47, 109
landed 41
on depot journey 49–65
snow-shoes 51
'night' travel 53
adrift on pack ice and loss 65, 67–68
stable 81, 176
on polar journey 138–39, 172
'Ponko', 'Ponters' *see* Ponting, H. G.
Ponting, H. G. 36, 46, 134, 172, 180, 198, 239
and killer whales 42
films skiing 47
at Cape Evans 79–97, 102–23
dark room 80, 110
lectures 83, 89, 94, 104, 115, 118–19, 123
films polar party 138–40
leaves with ship 178
Pram Point 65, 68, 71–72, 74–75
Priestley, R. E. (later Sir Raymond) 30n, 38, 43–45, 172n, 228, *21*, *22*
on Mount Erebus 222–27
Primus *see* stoves
Ptarmigan (tinned) 37, 87, 113, 229
'Punch' (pony) 57
Punta Arenas (Chile) 14
'Pyaree' (mule) 212

Queen Mary Land 172n

'Rabchick' (dog) 195
Ramp, The 92, 95, 107, 110, 120, 229
'Rani' (mule) 212, 220
Razorback *see* Razorback Islands
Razorback Islands 76–77, 98, 118, 132, 137–39, 181, 185, 193
Redcliff Nunakol *see* Redcliff Nunatak
Redcliff Nunatak 157n
Rennick, Lieut. H. E. de P. 82, 235
Retreat, Point 151
Roberts, Cape 146, 153, 159–63, 171
depot 168, 234
Robertson Bay 63
Ross Ice Shelf 15, 22, 24, 40, 50–51, 64–65, 71, 82, 97, 124–26, 129, 212
Ross Island 22, 84, 149, 152, 161
Ross Sea 14, 39–40, 43n, 126, 140, 147, 161–62, 226
Royal Geographical Society 238
Royal Society Range 40n
Royal Yacht Squadron 29
Royds, Cape 10, 40, 92–93, 100–01, 112, 116, 118, 136, 152, 222–23, 227, 233
Shackleton's hut 41, 45, 87n, 113, 207–08, 223, 227, *21*, *22*

Sabine, Mount 39
'Safety Camp' 51, 62–65, 67, 71, 124–25, 127, 139, 221
'Sahib' *see* 'Khan Sahib'
Sails, Bay of 145n
St Hans, Feast of 228n
'Salt Lake' 189n
Sallying 47n, 174
Sastrugi (snow ridges) 105, 126, 144, 146
Scientific instruments
see electrical instruments
see magnetic instruments
see meteorology
Scott, Capt. R. F. 33, 37, 45, 57, 62, 158, 181, 185–86, 200, 202, 232, 235, 237
and motor sledges 11, 42–43
and skis 11–12, 34–35, 175
and Gran 12, 15–18, 22, 51, 58, 110, 238
and Amundsen 14, 63, 68, 84
and *Terra Nova* 38
lands at Cape Evans 41, 44, 46
plans for depot journey 44, 47n
on depot journey 49–65
and ponies 51, 58–59, 65
camp routine 54
and five-man polar party 57, 177, 238–39
at *Discovery* hut 66–78
returns to Cape Evans 76–78
at Cape Evans 79–127, 132–138
quarters 80
visits Hut Point 83–84
outlines plans 88–89
as world traveller 90
birthday 96–97
lectures 97

at midwinter dinner 103
on western journey 127, 132
leaves for South Pole 138
on polar journey 171–72, 175, 177, 238–42
death 23–24, 216–18
Scott, Mrs R. F. 11
Scott Island 34
Scott Polar Research Institute 218n, 238
Sea kale 149, 152n, 155, 160–61, 163
Sea leopard *see* seals
Seals 34, 36, 38, 147, 150–51, 170, 181, 211
as food 68–69, 121, 148, 155, 221
killing 68, 71–72, 75, 138, 149, 152, 154, 163, 182, 191, 200
sea leopard 232
Shackleton, Sir E. 10, 19, 40–41, 45–46, 50–51, 66, 89, 93, 113, 143, 181, 240
Shirase, Lieut. C. 172n
Signals 179–80, 182, 192
bonfire 107, 162, 195
flare 99, 108
rocket 79, 107–08
Simonstown (South Africa) 13
Simpson, G. C. (later Sir George) 78, 80, 88–89, 95, 105, 110n, 119–20, 127, 136–37, 141, 175–76, 180, 241
lectures 115
leaves with ship 178
Skåluran (shipbuilder) 11
Ski Hill *see* Ski Slope
Skis (and skiing) 11–12, 34–37, 44–45, 47, 53, 109, 177, 184, 207, 234
bindings 47, 94, 102, 111, 122
boots 105, 121
waxes 46, 128
jumping 85–86, 121–22
with dogs 117
on polar journey 175–76, 239
Scott's 218
Ski Slope 69, 71, 190
Skua Lake 101
Skuary, The *see* Evans, Cape
Sledge flags 11–12, 156, 164
Sledge rations 54, 118, 166, 170, 205, 238
Shackleton's found 51
see also pemmican
see also food
Sledge, man-hauling 46, 77, 98, 116, 150, 184, 214n
under sail 145
as boat 234

Sleeping bags 76–77, 114, 121, 125, 127, 150
Oates' 218
'Snatcher' (pony) 116
Snow-blindness 42, 49, 157, 169
Snow-shoes 184
ponies' 51, 53, 116
Society Mountains *see* Royal Society Range
South America 96
South Bay 102, 104, 106, 107n, 110–11, 115, 118–19, 177, 181, 184n, 185, 189, 201, 207
Southern Cross 126
***Southern Cross* expedition** 11, 56n, 172n, 233n
Southern Lights (*aurora australis*) 74–75, 83, 86–87, 90–92, 95–96 106, 110, 114, 120, 126
South Polar Times 103–04, 115–16, 123, 129, 195, 203, 239
South Pole 13–14, 50n, 56, 57n, 59, 82–83, 89, 96, 128, 153, 175, 179, 216, 239
Sperm Bluff 159
Sponges 48
Springtail 154n
Stable *see* ponies
'Stareek' (dog) 180, 210
Störmer, Prof. C. 92
Stoves
at Cape Evans 81, 109
blubber 68–69, 72, 102, 148, 163, 166, 191
primus 54, 147, 166, 170, 200, 208
Strand Moraines, The 171n
Stromboli (Italy) 101
Suess, Mount 159n, 160n
Svalbard 20
Sverdrup, Capt. O. 9–10

Tangholmen's Light (play) 164
Taylor, T. G. 9, 15, 23, 45, 70n, 76, 5, *10*
at Cape Evans 80–97, 101–23, 128–42
quarters 80–81, 85–86
lectures 119
poem to Gran 130, 164–65
as field leader 140
on western journey 143–71
as cook, 147, 166
birthday 148
poisoned finger 154–55, 157
aboard *Terra Nova* 171–74
leaves with ship 178
Teddy Evans, Cape *see* Evans, Cape
Telephone 137, 179, 183
Tent Island 98, 107, 115, 118, 127, 130–32
Tents 114, 124, 128, 131–32, *7, 18*
Terra Nova, RY 96, 112, 136, 149, 153, 176–77, 180–82, 185, 202, 228–30, 241, *1, 23*
specifications 22n
in Port of London 12
sails from London 13
on passage south from New Zealand 15, 29–40
in storm 29–31
as ice ship 38
reaches Cape Evans 41
at Erebus Glacier Tongue 49
at Bay of Whales 63
and relief of western party 159, 161n, 162–67, 169, 171, 175, 178
sails north 179
relieves expedition 232–37
Terror, Mount 40, 52, 56
Tetrazzini, Mme L. 46
Thorne and Company 113
Tide crack 111
Toboggan 117

'Trigger' *see* Gran, Lieut. T.
Triumviraten (novel) 13
Trindade, Ilha da 13n
Trinidad Island *see* Trindade, Ilha da
Tryggve Bay *see* Turks Head Bay
Tryggve Gran, Mount *see* Gran, Mount
Turks Head 93, 133, 183
Turks Head Bay 132
Turtleback *see* Turtle Rock
Turtle Island *see* Turtle Rock
Turtle Rock 122, 134–35, 194

'Ubduggery', 'Ubdugs' 81
Ulrikken (Norway) 113
'Uncle Bill' (pony) 57
'Uncle Bill' *see* Wilson, Dr E. A.
Union Jack 17, 138

'Vaida' (dog) 190
Vane Hill *see* Windvane Hill
Venus 11, 113
Verdens Gang (newspaper) 10
Verne, Jules 80, 141, 148
Victoria Land 40, 226
Vince, AB G. T. 71n

'Weary Willie' *see* 'Willy'
Weddell Sea 14, 57n, 179
West Antarctica 14
Western Mountains 49, 55, 68, 84, 104, 112, 117–18, 140, 206
Western party 43n, 70, 93, 110, 136, 143–71
Whale Bay *see* Whales, Bay of
Whales 36
fin 31
killer 42
Whales, Bay of 11, 22, 62–63, 96, *1*
Whewell, Mount 39
White Island 55, 65, 126, 183
Williamson, PO T. S. 42, 189, 227, 231, *17, 21, 22*
at Cape Evans 175–88, 202–06
on search journey 212–21
'Willy' (pony) 49–51, 57–62, 64
Wilson, Dr E. A. 16,22, 33, 47n, 175, 239
and skiing 34
on depot journey 51–65
at *Discovery* hut 66–76
at Cape Evans 84–105, 114–23, 128–38
quarters 80
lectures 87, 90
leaves for Cape Crozier 105
on Amundsen 118
leaves for South Pole 138
death 23–24, 216–17
Wilson Piedmont (Glacier) 147, 169
Windmill Heights *see* Windvane Hill
Windvane Hill 81, 119, 179n, 183–84, 186, 192, 195–97, 199, 202, 204
Wordie, Sir J. M. 19
Worsley Cdr F. A. 19
Wright, C. S. (later Sir Charles) 15, 19, 30n, 38, 45, 172n, 227, 241–42, *16*
at Hut Point 70n, 75–76, 189–93
at Cape Evans 80–92, 105–17, 139, 175, 179, 184, 188, 194–206
leads search journey 212–21
Wright, Miss P. F. 242n

Printed in the UK for HMSO
Dd 718110 c.50 4/84

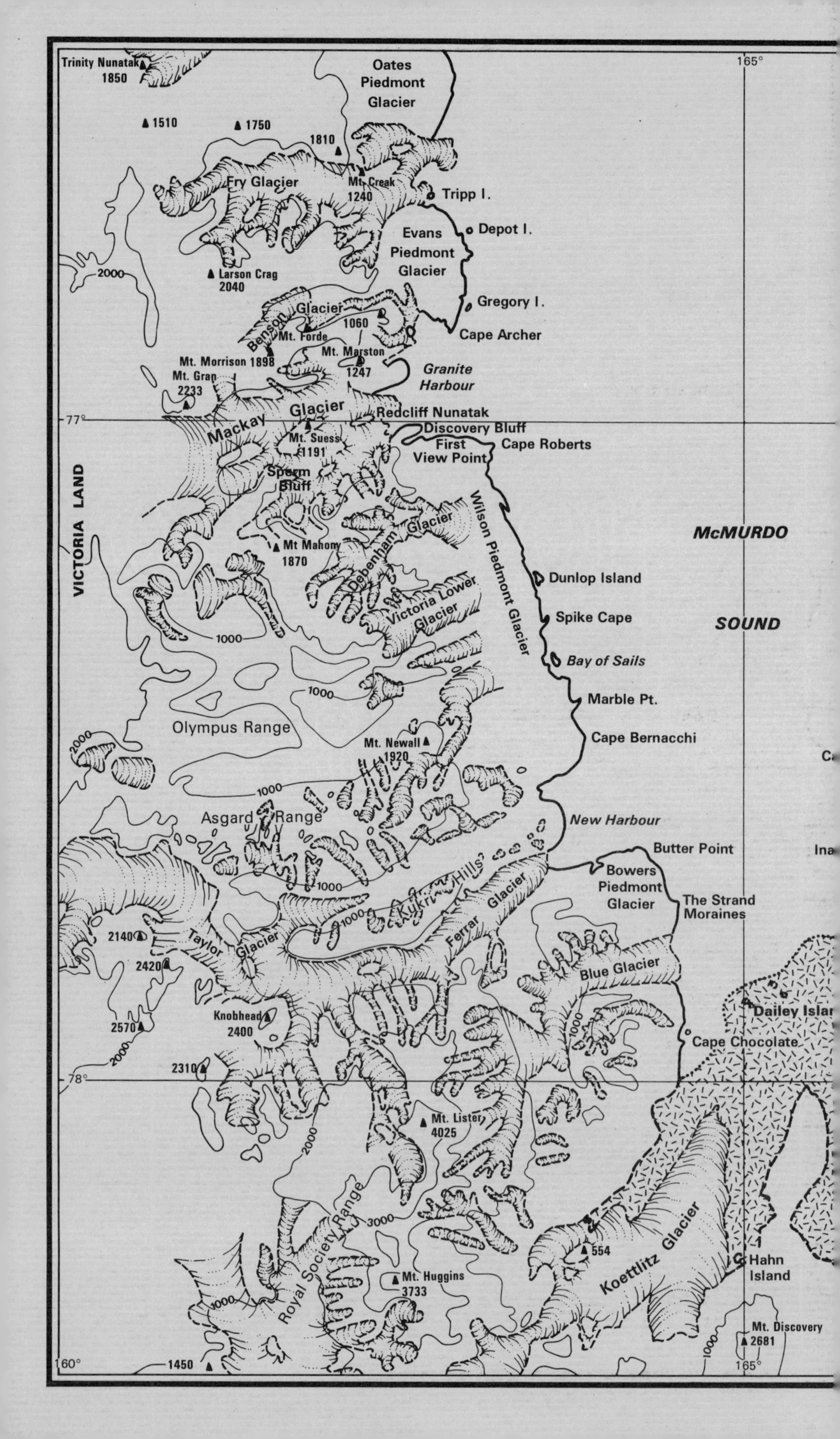
Trinity Nunatak
1850
1510
1750
Oates
Piedmont
Glacier
1810
Fry Glacier
Mt. Creak
1240
Tripp I.
Depot I.
Evans
Piedmont
Glacier
2000
Larson Crag
2040
Benson Glacier
Mt. Forde
1060
Gregory I.
Cape Archer
Mt. Morrison 1898
Mt. Marston
1247
Granite
Harbour
Mt. Gran
2233
Mackay Glacier
Redcliff Nunatak
Mt. Suess
1191
Discovery Bluff
First
View Point
Cape Roberts
Sperm
Bluff
VICTORIA LAND
Debenham Glacier
Wilson Piedmont Glacier
Mt Mahony
1870
McMURDO
SOUND
Dunlop Island
Spike Cape
Victoria Lower
Glacier
1000
Bay of Sails
Marble Pt.
Olympus Range
Mt. Newall
1920
Cape Bernacchi
Asgard Range
New Harbour
Butter Point
Bowers
Piedmont
Glacier
Kukri Hills
Ferrar Glacier
The Strand
Moraines
Taylor Glacier
2140
2420
Blue Glacier
Dailey Islan
Knobhead
2400
2570
Cape Chocolate
2310
Mt. Lister
4025
3000
Royal Society Range
554
Koettlitz Glacier
Hahn
Island
Mt. Huggins
3733
Mt. Discovery
2681
1450
160°
165°
77°
78°
Ina
C